As for Me and My House

As for Me and My House

Keys to a Flourishing Family and a Fulfilled Ministry

Daryl J. Potts

WIPF & STOCK · Eugene, Oregon

AS FOR ME AND MY HOUSE
Keys to a Flourishing Family and a Fulfilled Ministry

Copyright © 2020 Daryl J. Potts. All rights reserved. Except for brief quotations in critical publications or reviews, no part of this book may be reproduced in any manner without prior written permission from the publisher. Write: Permissions, Wipf and Stock Publishers, 199 W. 8th Ave., Suite 3, Eugene, OR 97401.

Wipf & Stock
An Imprint of Wipf and Stock Publishers
199 W. 8th Ave., Suite 3
Eugene, OR 97401

www.wipfandstock.com

PAPERBACK ISBN: 978-1-7252-6632-2
HARDCOVER ISBN: 978-1-7252-6633-9
EBOOK ISBN: 978-1-7252-6634-6

Manufactured in the U.S.A.   JUNE 29, 2020

Dedication

To my wife, Elaine, and my children, Matthew & Kate, Hannah & Jonathan, and Kayla, also to our wonderful grandchildren, Malachi, Lydia, Olive and Jonty. The love, joy and fulfillment you generate in our family and ministry cannot be quantified on this side of heaven. This book is dedicated to you.

Table of Contents

List of Figures x
Foreword xi
Preface xiv
Acknowledgments xv

INTRODUCTION xvi
Context of This Study
    Foundations for This Study
    Triple "A" Model
    Theological Reflections on the Family

PART 1—ASPIRATION
Chapter 1—From Conversion to the Cause of Christ 3
    Conversion
    Commitment
    Call
    College

Chapter 2—High Ideals and Hard Realities 15
    Spiritually Focused Ideals
    Family Focused Ideals
    Obsessive Aspirations

PART 2—AWARENESS
Chapter 3—The Blessings of the Ministry/Family Journey Ministry 41
    Significant Blessings
    Spiritual Blessings

Chapter 4—Ministry-Related Burdens 58

Chapter 5— Family-Related Burdens 78

Chapter 6—The Ministry Couple 94
    The Minister's Marriage
    The Minister's Spouse
    The Minister's Husband
    Ministry-Imposed Challenges

Chapter 7—The Minister's Children 110
    A Surprising Discovery
    An Inspiring Spiritual Focus
    Ministry-Imposed Difficulties

PART 3—ATTENTION

Chapter 8—Things that Work along the Ministry/Family Journey 123
    Giving Attention to the Minister's Marriage
    Giving Attention to the Minister's Family
    Giving Attention to the Spiritual Well-being of the Family

Chapter 9—Reflective Evaluation, Insightful Decisions, and Proactive Protection 142
    Reflective Evaluation
    Insightful Decisions
    Proactive Protection

Chapter 10—Stable Support Structures & Sustaining Resources 159
    Stable Support Structures
    The Tyranny of No Support
    The Value of a Mentor
    The Value of Structured, Ministry-Related Support
    The Value of the Unofficial Support from Family and Friends
    The Value of Placing some Support Structures around Your Children
    Sustaining Resources
    Spiritual Resources
    Relational Resources

Chapter 11—Recommendations for the Ministry/Family Journey 175
    Family-Focused Recommendations
    Protection-Focused Recommendations
    Ministry-Focused Recommendations
    Spiritually Focused Recommendations

CONCLUSION 201
The Triple "A" Model

Bibliography 211

List of Figures

Figure 0:1	The Triple "A" Model of Ministry Function and Family Fulfillment
Figure 1:1	The Emerging Pattern from Conversion to Credentialed Ministry
Figure 1.2	Conversion to Credentialed Ministry to Expanding Calling, Commitment, . . .
Figure 2:1	The Hierarchy of Priorities Approach to the Ministry/Family Journey
Figure 2:2	The Complementary Approach to the Ministry/Family Journey
Figure 12:2	The Triple "A" Model of Ministry Function and Family Fulfillment

Foreword

I'm a pastor's kid. I'm a husband, a father, and a grandfather. I pastor a church and lead a movement. The subject of family is of immense importance to me—it's our first church. More importantly, family is of utmost importance to God—he created family before he created the church.

Over four decades of Christian leadership, I have had plenty of interaction with mums and dads and sons and daughters in church life. Some have inspired me. Others, however, have left me saddened as I have witnessed the toll that leadership has taken on individuals and family units. It is my great desire to see the families of pastors flourish as they fulfill the call of God on their lives, which is why I'm happy to endorse *As for Me and My House*, by my friend, Daryl Potts.

Ministry families are exposed to both blessings and burdens; the blessings are amazing, yet the burdens can often be difficult, and if not attended to, can be damaging to the family. Having witnessed the effects of many challenges upon many ministry homes, I believe this book will help pastors, spouses, elders, board members, and churches become more aware of the realities ministry families experience. My prayer is that due attention will be given to the pastor's family so they can enjoy flourishing family and fulfilled ministry lives.

I have known Daryl for over 30 years, during which time he has been a pastor and leader within the Australian Christian Churches (formerly Assemblies of God in Australia). Daryl's ministry has been fruitful, and his family has flourished, with each of his three children serving the Lord. Daryl's PhD research, together with his ministry and family experience, will encourage and inspire you to lift your family and ministry to new levels of health and wholeness.

Pastor Wayne Alcorn
President
Australian Christian Churches

Preface

THIS BOOK HAS BEEN written out of my PhD dissertation of focused research regarding ministry and family life. Having been a pastor for over thirty years, as well as being a husband of a very special wife and father of three wonderful children, I have always had a great desire to see my family flourish as I have engaged in my ministry call. The problem has been the great dearth of genuinely researched literature available to advise and equip pastors and their families throughout my time in ministry. Apart from a few studies from the likes of Norman W. H. Blaikie, *The Plight of the Australian Clergy* (1979), David and Vera Mace, *What's Happening to Clergy Marriages?* (1983), and Cameron Lee and Jack Balswick's *Life in a Glass House* (1989), there has been limited empirical research to inform ministers and their spouses regarding the ministry/family journey.

When faced with the question regarding my own dissertation, my decision for a research topic rested on my two greatest passions: family and ministry. Therefore, with the guidance of my supervisors, and the willingness of many pastors and spouses to become vulnerable and to be interviewed so as to share the deeper stories of both the blessings and burdens of their ministry/family lives, I have been able to complete my research and write this book. I trust that my findings and formula will be both informative and inspirational to those who have responded to the call of God and engaged in his ministry while also partnering and parenting within a family setting. I pray God's grace will equip you to enjoy a flourishing family and a fruitful ministry and as you fulfill his divine call.

Acknowledgments

I COULD NOT HAVE completed a book of this magnitude without the wonderful support of incredible people. I am grateful to so many people who have journeyed with me in recent years to advise, support, and encourage me along the journey. Firstly, I would like to honor my wife, Elaine, and three children, Matthew, Hannah, and Kayla, for their love, support, and patience as I have journeyed as a pastor, husband, and father, often stumbling along, trying to maintain some balance between my responsibilities as a husband, father, and pastor.

Secondly, I would like to honor the credentialed ministers and spouses interviewed for this research, who have voluntarily opened their hearts and lives and shared the joys and challenges of their ministry/family journey. Though it has not always been easy, your vulnerability has allowed this research to be developed with insight and authenticity that will assist current and future ministers and their spouses to engage in their ministry calling and enjoy fulfilled family lives.

My appreciation also goes to those that have offered support and advice in intellectual and technical areas: Rev. Professor Denise Austin (my primary supervisor), Dr. Juhani Tuovinen (my associate supervisor), Rev. Professor Stephen Fogarty (President of Alphacrucis College), and Rev. Dr. Stuart Devenish (Tabor College, Adelaide). Your wisdom and knowledge have been invaluable in bringing this research to completion. Much appreciation also goes to my colleague and friend, Rev. Dr. Kevin Hovey, for his encouragement along the way.

I also owe a great deal to those within the Australian Christian Churches movement, particularly the National Executive and Pastor Sean Stanton (National Secretary), who gave permission to conduct my research with credentialed ministers and spouses within the movement.

Introduction

THE TITLE OF THIS book comes from Joshua 24:15: "As for me and my house, we will serve the Lord." We have a plaque at our home that declares this passion of our heart, so that not only would we as a husband and wife serve the Lord, but also that our children and future generations would know and serve the Lord. At the time of writing this book, our eldest grandson Malachi is about to be baptized in water and I will have the honor of preaching at the church that my daughter and son-in-law are involved in on this very special occasion.

Joshua 24:15 has been the desire and declaration of ministry couples for centuries. Yet the heartache of many ministers and their spouses is the realization that even though they have ministered to many and have been instruments to strengthen people's spiritual lives, the spiritual well-being of their own immediate family is not always where they would like it to be. Many sadly observe members of their own family who no longer attend church, having turned away from the faith of their ministry-engaged parents. For many ministers and spouses, both those presently in ministry and those starting out, there is a great desire to find keys to prevent their family members from falling away from the faith. The heart of every pastoral couple is to function in their ministry and at the same time see their family flourish in this present world and in the kingdom of God.

In the light of the dearth of research regarding the ministry/family journey, this book investigates how ministers and their spouses perceive that their involvement in ministry affects their family lives. It further explores the components that contribute toward the spiritual well-being of their family, while fulfilling the unique responsibilities associated with the ministry vocation.

My Triple "A" Model of Ministry Function and Family Fulfillment asserts that credentialed ministers and their spouses will more likely experience satisfaction in regard to the spiritual well-being of their family as they function in their ministry calling if they: enter the ministry with a measured Aspiration; have a resolute Awareness of the advantages and adversities associated with the ministry/family journey; and give continual Attention to their family by responding intentionally, spiritually, and protectively, while drawing upon sustaining resources and establishing reliable support structures. This book details the key elements of the Triple "A" Model and provides a way for pastors to move forward with confidence in their quest to engage meaningfully in their ministry and enjoy a flourishing family life.

Passions and Perplexities of Ministry Life

The ministry/family journey at times encounters perplexing dynamics that are often unique to the vocation of ministry alone. In general, Christian ministers have two great passions in their lives: the first relates to their roles and responsibilities as spouses and parents of the families they love and care for; the second relates to what they perceive as the divine call of God upon their lives and the responsibilities of pastoring and leading their church or ministry. One of the most difficult challenges ministers face is balancing time and attention given to these two passions. There are times when this challenge is more difficult than it seems, and the consequences can affect clergy families significantly.

An example of the extreme tension that can arise in a minister's home was reported in *Christian Century* in 2007.[1] The report described the story of a pastor in Tennessee who was shot dead by his wife after a build-up of stress in the family had erupted into an argument with her pastor/husband regarding finances. Tony Rankin, a pastoral and family counsellor in Tennessee, described the desperate situation, "Besides someone who has been killed, you've got a pastor's wife who is obviously in excruciating mental distress, and you've got children as well. All those things make it really sad."[2] Rankin states it is possible that pastoral spouses endure many pressures unknown to parishioners, and that—at the time of being interviewed—he deals with more than two dozen instances of silently suffering spouses each month.[3]

1. "Slain Pastor's Wife Convicted," 14.
2. "Slain Pastor's Wife Convicted," 14.
3. "Slain Pastor's Wife Convicted," 14.

Although the above is an extreme case, my research reveals that there are significant stress factors upon the spouses and children of those who are involved in Christian ministry, often felt at extreme levels, which are unique to those in Christian ministry. There are very few occupations where the spotlight shines upon the spouse and children of the professional (perhaps except for politicians and celebrities) as it does upon the minister's family. Many expectations placed upon the Christian minister, their spouse, and children often tend to be unrealistic and unfair. There is often an expectation placed on the minister's spouse and children to be just as equipped as their ministry spouse/parent. The weight of these expectations is therefore carried by ministers and their families, and can often cause great heartache. The need to address these issues is critical.

Foundational Context—Family Stress Theory

In consideration of the more scholarly aspects of my research, I offer a brief description of the process by which my research was conducted in order to lay a foundation and understanding of the context in which it was established. It was important to place this research within a theoretical framework that will make sense of the social world of the families investigated, and at the same time allow for more appropriate, empirically based recommendations for future families, therapists, counsellors, educators and researchers.

The approach taken in my research is based on ideas emanating from family stress theory. Cynthia Bennet states that "Family stress theory is a developmental theory emerging from family science which explores how families' adapt and even grow and thrive when faced with situational stressors or transitional events, while other families seem to deteriorate and disintegrate under similar circumstances."[4] There was considerable focus on family crisis and family well-being in the United States throughout the twentieth century. This focus began in the 1920s with graduate students from the University of Chicago researching family stress and coping strategies.

These research endeavors continued over the ensuing decades, with models such as Hamilton McCubbin and Joan Patterson's Double ABC–X Model of Family Adjustment and Adaptation (1982, 1983). This model was based on their longitudinal study of families to explain and predict

---

4. Beckett, *Family Theory*, 1.

how families recover from crisis and why some are better able to adapt than others.[5] Their Double ABCX Theory revealed three stages of family stress and coping: precrisis, crisis, and postcrisis. This was particularly relevant to my research regarding ministry families due to the longitudinal stresses and demands that are regularly experienced by families who are engaged in ministry. The ministry/family journey is not a short-term career but rather a lifelong calling. Further investigations regarding the underlying dynamics within families have been undertaken throughout the twenty-first century by researchers like Froma Walsh, who formulated a process model of family resilience that highlighted family qualities that may reduce stress and vulnerability during crisis situations.[6]

To fully appreciate my findings, it is important to understand the design and methodological basis for this research. I selected Australian Christian Churches (formerly the Assemblies of God in Australia) ministers and spouses for investigation as this movement has not been examined in respect to the impact that being involved in ministry has on the life of the minister's family. The research consisted of an investigation via the process of conducting semistructured interviews with ACC-credentialed ministers and their spouses.

Regarding the research methodology, I employed a critical realist epistemology which informed an interpretivist theoretical perspective. The interpretivist theoretical perspective then informed a grounded theory methodology, which then informed the methods of semistructured interviews which were employed to gather the data. These semistructured interviews were then analyzed according to the grounded theory process of open-coding, axial-coding and selective-coding to ground the theory based on the data that had been obtained. Following analysis of the responses of the participants engaged in this research project, I sought to develop findings that will contribute to knowledge about pastoral practice to enhance the experience of pastoral families. As the data from the research was analyzed, I developed the Triple "A" Model of Ministry Function and Family Fulfillment. Using the data gathered, the Triple "A" Model is illustrated in the following diagram:

---

5. Weber, *Individual and Family Stress*, 82.
6. Greeff and Van Der Walt, "Resilience in Families," 348.

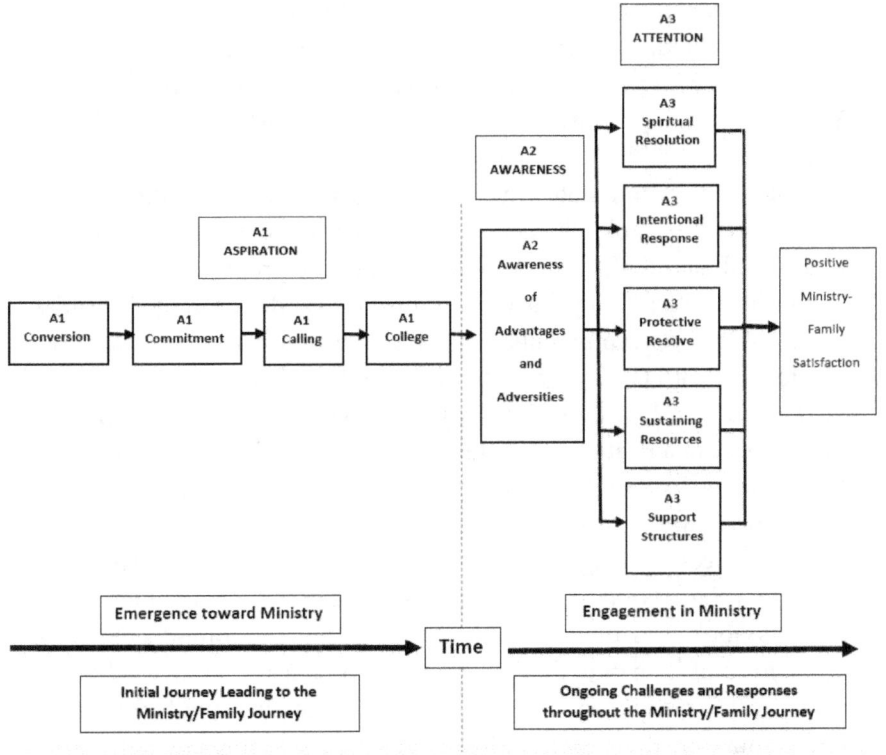

Figure 0:1 The Triple "A" Model of Ministry Function and Family Fulfillment

The Triple "A" Model of Ministry Function and Family Fulfillment demonstrates that ministers and their spouses who: enter the ministry with a measured (A)spiration; have a resolute (A)wareness of the advantages and adversities associated with the ministry/family journey; and give continual (A)ttention to their family by responding intentionally, spiritually and protectively, while drawing upon sustaining resources and establishing reliable support structures, will more likely experience satisfaction in regard to the spiritual well-being of their family as they function in their ministry calling.

Theological Reflections on the Family

The foundation of the ministry couple's calling is established on a strong commitment to the Bible. In this light, a book regarding the ministry/family journey calls for a biblical-theological reflection of the family, where the center of the covenant activity of God is acknowledged. As previously stated, "As for me and my house we will serve the Lord" is a verse from which the title of this book emanates, and also a motivational Scripture for many ministers and spouses who desire to see their children continue in the faith they proclaim.

Stephen Barton states that "when taken as a whole, the Bible is for Christians a book which reveals the true nature of human identity under God, an identity which is explored in the predominantly social-economic-political-religious idiom of marriage and the family."[7] Healthy relationships between parents and children further strengthens a closer relationship with God.[8] In fact, those who follow God are called his *children* (John 1:12; Eph 3:14). Stanley Grenz notes that humans are created in the image of a relational Trinitarian God of love.[9] In light of this, Gary Deddo holds that family relationships "are analogous in human form" to the divine Trinity.[10]

When considering the social theology of the family, Roy Anderson states that the "World of creation upholds the basic humanity of family, and it is God's work of covenant love that outlines the contours of family as the form of humanity that reflects his own image and likeness."[11] This covenant of freedom in love secures, yet also releases the family to be both unique in themselves individually and also complete collectively within the covenant of love.

Arnold Wolf states: "The consequence of divinity is family . . . We should not be surprised that the God of the Bible who has no family considers every family a Holy Family."[12] Wolf further states: "God does not extricate us from the human predicament of family, but He implicates Himself in every human predicament, not least in the tensions and anxieties of the home. When God says that creation is good, He means all creation and especially the particular creativeness of the family."[13]

Much of Christ's instruction concerning the family is simply a restatement of the creation ordinances (Matt 5:27–32). Thatcher suggests

---

7. Barton, *Family in Theological Perspective*, 6.
8. Deddo, *Karl Barth's Theology of Relations*, 36.
9. Grenz, *Social God*, 175.
10. Deddo, *Karl Barth's Theology of Relations*, 36.
11. Anderson and Guernsey, *On Being Family*, vii.
12. Wolf, "Toward a Theology of Family," 281.
13. Wolf, "Toward a Theology of Family," 282.

that Jesus emphasized the value of children within the kingdom and society as a whole (Matt 19:13–15).[14] The apostles emphasized the concept of the family in their preaching (Eph 5:22; 1 Cor 7:1–28; 11:3; Eph 6:1–4; Col 3:18; 1 Tim 5:8; 1 Pe 3:7), highlighting the importance of closeness, openness, sacrifice, and relationship. The fact that the first churches were in private homes, and that the initial converts were usually family groups, gave a specific appeal to the family image of Christianity (Acts 16:31). The common term for "house" was a term that was often used in both the Old Testament and the New Testament for the idea of "family" as we observe in Joshua 24:15. Belonging is one of the greatest advantages of family life, having the assurance that you are accepted even when you make mistakes. Such acceptance assures the family member of their place in their home, in spite of differences of opinion and differences in behavior and vocation.

The Scriptures emphasize that believers are empowered by the Holy Spirit to empower others such as those within their family. Social researcher Mark McCrindle posed the question regarding how people have been influenced regarding their perceptions and opinions of Christians and Christianity. The response he received was that 67 percent of Christians stated that their parents and family had influenced their perceptions regarding Christians and Christianity. McCrindle's findings encourage us to follow the biblical mandate in Proverbs 22:6 to "train up our children in the way that they should go so that when they are old, they will not depart from it." Such empowering allows each member of the family to grow and reach their full potential as they are encouraged and empowered by their parents and siblings. This empowering also has ramifications for ministers and their families. Qualifications for becoming a church leader appear to include a healthy and balanced family life (Titus 1:6; 1 Tim 3:4).[15]

Thatcher points out that God continually displays his heart for the generations of the future (Deut 6:6–7; Ps 112:1–2; 145:4). This desire to connect future generations of the family with an intrinsic relationship with their creator was clearly emphasized in Deuteronomy 6:4–9, known as the "Shema" amongst modern Jews. The New Testament further describes the empowerment of the Holy Spirit, stating: "the promise is to you, to your children, and to those far off" (Acts 2:39b). Ephesians 6:4

---

14. Thatcher, *Theology and Families*, 57.
15. Feddes, "Caring for God's Household," 290.

instructs fathers to bring their children up with the discipline and instruction that comes from the Lord, again displaying an aspiration for generational transformation. The New Testament also gives us some examples of how the faith of a parent was passed down to the next generation, such as Philip's daughters (Acts 21:9) and Timothy's grandmother Lois and mother Eunice (2 Tim 1:5).

By way of contrast, the Old Testament demonstrates the dangerous ramifications of ministers who display poor parenting. The high priest of Israel, Aaron, compromises God's standard of worship (Exod 32:1–6) and his sons Nadab and Abihu later followed the same example (Lev 10:1–3) and experienced God's wrath. Another poor example is the high priest Eli's lack of parenting abilities by not disciplining his sons Hophni and Phinehas, who treated their spiritual responsibilities as a career that would benefit themselves, rather than as a call that was for the benefit of others (1 Sam 2:22–25).

Hezekiah, the king of Israel, is another poor example of a leader and father who was not concerned for the generations that followed, as we see in 2 Kings 20:16–19. Here the prophet Isaiah prophesied that the descendants of Hezekiah would be taken into captivity to the palace of Babylon due to Hezekiah's pride and boasting of his own achievements. Hezekiah's response is found in 2 Kings 20:19: "The word of the Lord you have spoken is good," Hezekiah replied. For he thought, "Will there not be peace and security in my lifetime?" Hezekiah's lack of responsibility for the generations that were to follow him is obvious, as his only concern was for his own comfort and security during his lifetime.

The following chapter, 2 Kings 21:1–18, describes Hezekiah's son Manasseh. Verse 6 describes Manasseh's lack of love for his own son: "He sacrificed his own son in the fire, practiced divination, sought omens, and consulted mediums and spiritists" (2 Kings 21:6). Verse 11 describes the prophet's description of Manasseh's reign: "Manasseh king of Judah has committed these detestable sins. He has done more evil than the Amorites who preceded him and has led Judah into sin with his idols" (2 Kings 21:11). Hezekiah's lack of heart for future generations quickly transferred to his son Manasseh, only Manasseh took it to another level by sacrificing his son in the fire. This is not the heart that Christians and ministers are to have for the future generations of their children and grandchildren. Christian parents and ministry parents have a responsibility for the generations that follow, to pass on their faith by word and example from a heart of love.

Throughout the interviews regarding the ministry/family journey, many participants stated that their greatest desire was for the spiritual well-being of their children. Many expressed that as they were engaged in the work of the ministry, their greatest concern was that their children would also embrace the faith of their credentialed parent(s) and follow God's will and purpose for their own lives. Both the Old Testament and New Testament affirm God's transformational strategy for future generations. The Triple "A" Model of Ministry Function and Family Fulfillment presents a model that will assist ministers and their spouses to engage in their ministry function and at the same time safeguard their family's spiritual well-being.

This book will assert that ministers and their spouses will more likely experience satisfaction in regard to the spiritual well-being of their family as they function in their ministry calling if they adopt the Triple "A" Model of Ministry Function and Family Fulfillment I have developed and presented as a result of my research. Part 1 of this book will focus on the first "A" of the Triple "A" Model, i.e. Aspiration. Part 2 will focus on the second "A," which is Awareness, and part 3 will focus on the third "A," which is Attention.

Part 1: Aspiration

THE FIRST ELEMENT OF the Triple "A" Model of Ministry Function and Family Fulfillment is Aspiration. The importance of having a measured aspiration regarding ministry and family engagement is critical for the goal of ensuring a satisfying ministry/family outcome. High aspirations are important for ministers and their spouses, as it keeps them motivated to reach the unchurched, and see the church grow and achieve its God-given purpose on the earth. However, these aspirations need to be fulfilled while maintaining proper consideration of the minister's family. Those that surge forward toward their aspirations and goals without a consideration and awareness of the well-being of their family will be in danger of sacrificing a healthy connection and communication with their family, which might result in family members resenting and rejecting God and his church.

This first section of this book will explore and inform pastors and their spouses regarding the value of having a measured aspiration toward their ministry that will result in a balanced focus concerning both ministry and their family. The first chapter of this section will discuss the participant's experiences regarding their call to ministry. Chapter 2 will explore and discuss the aspirational ideals that ministers and their spouses revealed throughout the interviews in which they participated as part of my research.

Chapter 1

From Conversion to the Cause of Christ

The Wonder of God's Emerging Call

MANY OF THE PASTORS and spouses that participated in my research regarding ministry and family identified a time in their life where they sensed God calling them into ministry. Such a perception of the call of God stimulates a unique inner motivation amongst those who are involved in Christian ministry compared to those who are involved in other vocations. H. Richard Niebuhr explains it as "that inner persuasion or experience whereby a person feels himself directly summoned or invited by God to take up the work of the ministry."[1] Many people speak about a specific moment when this "call-experience" took place. For the person who responds to such a perceived call, they often think there is now no other vocational option for their life. They have a unique commitment to what they believe is the divine call to serve God and his people, rather than choosing a career that is suitable to their own ambitions.

As I analyzed the participants' responses, it became evident that each minister's journey commenced quite some time before they were ordained into the ministry. Four progressive stages were revealed throughout my research as part of the minister and spouse's journey toward their ordination. These stages are: conversion, where participants spoke about their initial salvation encounter; commitment, where participants spoke about their desire to serve God in their local church; calling, where participants spoke about their calling to the vocation of ministry; and

---

1. Niebuhr, *Purpose of the Church*, 64.

college, where participants spoke about going to a Bible college or ministry-training institution to be further equipped for their ministry calling. A concept defined as "an emerging call" was identified as a pattern in the data as participants reflected on their journeys toward their ministry appointment. To illustrate this pattern, I developed the following diagram:

Figure 1:1 The Emerging Pattern from Conversion to Credentialed Ministry

J. Robert Clinton sought to understand the stages of the minister's journey in his book, *The Making of a Leader*, where he presents what he terms "The Upward Development Pattern" that describes the spiral of growth in being and doing. He states that in each *being* cycle there is an increased depth of experiencing and knowing God; and in each *doing* cycle there is increased depth of effective service for God. The final result of the upward development pattern is a fusion of being and doing.[2] As the following process portrays:

1. Being—conversion or sense of awareness of salvation
2. Doing—leadership commitment
3. Being—inner-life growth
4. Doing—development and use of ministry skills
5. Being—ministry philosophy becomes life-based (John 15:5 reality)
6. Union life—being and doing fused[3]

Clinton's Upward Development Pattern has similar characteristics to Figure 2:1, which was developed from the empirical data of my semi-structured interviews. The first four stages of conversion, commitment, calling, and college that precede credentialed ministry from my research have some similarities to Clinton's pattern.

2. Clinton, *Making of a Leader*, 156.
3. Clinton, *Making of a Leader*, 156.

Clinton's work confirms the presence of progressive patterns from conversion toward ministry function such as that which emerged within the data of my study, even though their patterns are slightly different. The journey along this progressive pattern needs to be travelled with a realistic expectation of ministry, rather than being idealistically distorted as ministers and their spouses move towards fulfilling the call of God on their lives. Understanding the progressive processes that unfold throughout the early seasons of a minister's journey is vitally important in establishing ways to improve outcomes for ministry function and family fulfillment.

Many ministers and their spouses who enter ministry too quickly after their initial salvation, and with unrealistic and idealistic aspirations, can often find they struggle to function well in their ministry life and to find fulfillment in their family life. The apostle Paul was very clear regarding not promoting a new convert too quickly (1 Tim 3:6) as he realized that doing such was not sustainable for ministers to go the distance. Paul himself underwent a lengthy preparation period in his own life and ministry before he was released to become the great apostle we now know and revere.

Throughout many years of being a Christian and a minister, I have also witnessed several potential ministers who have had wonderful conversions. These passionate and enthusiastic new Christians have subsequently been treated as trophy converts by their pastors and thrust into the limelight of ministry far too soon, only to experience the pain and perplexity that can come when dealing with the human aspects of ministry. Such disappointing experiences within the ministry has resulted in some becoming discouraged and disillusioned with the ministry, the church, and even with God. Had they been afforded the opportunity to develop their understanding of what commitment to the local church really means, and to experience the confirmation of the call of God and ministry preparation in a credible training college, many might have gone the distance. Many of those that entered the ministry before they were properly equipped might still be in ministry today had they been adequately prepared with measured aspirations.

I have also noted others who have experienced a wonderful conversion and have been committed to serving in their church over an extended time and have sensed the call of God into full-time ministry, and yet have not engaged in any formal study at a credible ministry institution. Unfortunately, those who have been thrust into a ministry role without adequate ministry preparation have found themselves floundering through difficult times and often give up on their ministry dream, feeling inadequate for the task of leading the church. The importance of not trying to take shortcuts by avoiding the difficult steps of the process from conversion to credentialed ministry has been evident in many who have become discouraged, disappointed, and disillusioned in their ministry journey. These potential ministers that had once sensed the call of God upon their lives to full-time ministry, but weren't fully prepared with measured aspirations toward their ministry destination, are now left wondering what went wrong.

One male minister described his journey as follows: "I was a bit of a wild character when I came to the Lord, and I grew very quickly in God, and before long I was a deacon and then an elder. Then we went to a country town and pioneered a church." This particular minister and his wife wanted to participate in my research as they wanted to tell their unhappy story regarding their son to help future ministry couples avoid making the same mistakes. Their son, now in his forties, wants nothing to do with God, the church, or his parents, as he said he was robbed of his father when he needed him the most throughout his teenage years. Their story began as a very excited and enthusiastic couple of young Christians who were converted when their son was just eight years old. Their love for Jesus and their passion to serve him meant they just couldn't do enough for God.

Their church responded by quickly promoting them into leadership and ultimately sending them out into ministry before they even had a chance to learn about the realities of church life and what commitment to a local church really meant. Note, they also had no actual ministry training at a credible Bible college or ministry-training institution. Therefore, their desire to be in ministry and their desire to grow the church overshadowed their responsibilities toward their son, who felt neglected and felt very much left to his own devices. This wasn't so much a deliberate neglect of their son; it was more a case of unrealistic aspirations that resulted in a lack of awareness of their son's needs and therefore a lack of attention toward their son to alleviate the challenges he was facing. We will be further commenting on the need for awareness and attention throughout this book.

Had this young Christian couple been delayed from ministry for a time and allowed to develop measured aspirations toward their ministry call, and perhaps been mentored and prepared regarding the burdens that accompany the blessings of being in ministry, their son might still be in the kingdom of God and their relationship with him might be rich and rewarding. The value of undergoing healthy preparation toward ministry life through being committed to a local church, where they receive coaching and a confirmation of God's call to ministry and then prepare themselves by enrolling in a credible ministry-training institution, cannot be overestimated.

Conversion

Conversion appeared to be the catalyst for many of the respondents' initial call into ministry. The following are some of the initial stories that were told by the participants that were interviewed for this research:

A female minister, when referring to her conversion and immediate sense of call, explained: "I was saved when I was fifteen, going on sixteen, and had a very dramatic conversion. I was the first Christian in my family. I probably had a very strong sense of the call of God on my life from the moment I was saved."

A male minister, explaining the beginning of his ministry/family journey, emphasized his conversion, commitment, and call in the following statement: "I was saved in 1979 and married in 1981. We went to a Church of Christ for two years. I went to an interdenominational Bible college for two years, and we had our first child while we were at Bible college. It wasn't necessarily a good experience, as it was a high-pressure situation with a lot of demands and very little in the way of resources."

Another pastor also explained his conversion, commitment, and call: "I got saved in March 1984 at a church in a country town, and the church really grew quickly, and from that moment I went through all sorts of ministry life, from being a musician in the church to being on the door, to running the youth, to my first opportunity to preach, and then I got a probationary minister's credential."

The above ministers, along with many others throughout my research interviews, emphasized the importance their conversion had in their lives and the significance their conversion had upon their ongoing sense of commitment to God and his church. This then led to their eventual sense of call and ministry development. The key motivator of maintaining their first love, rather than forgetting about that first encounter with Jesus as is so clearly expressed in Revelation 2:4, is significant to ministry sustainability amid fulfilling the many responsibilities and demands that engagement in the ministry entails. A significant comment in this regard comes from the wife of a pastor when advising those who are just starting out in ministry: "Try to keep your heart fresh, because when you begin you're all fired up, but if you're not careful, that fire will die out and you lose sight of what you began to do." Whatever you do, don't forget the wonder of your conversion experience, don't lose your first love.

Commitment to the Local Church

Further analysis of the stories of participants as they spoke about their ministry/family journey revealed that their commitment to their local church and their calling into ministry were the two most important stages of their journey into ordained ministry. It is important that ministry candidates experience the realities of church life prior to engaging in the vocation of ministry. Those who have demonstrated a commitment to their local church over a sustained period as part of their aspiring ministry journey are often more likely to enter their ministry journey with realistic expectations. It was revealed in the interviews that it is throughout this commitment process that the ministry candidates encountered a divine call to ministry. A female minister, whose husband was also a minister, spoke about their transition from their commitment to their church into their calling into ministry: "It is hard to say when you have started ministry, because there was not a beginning and ending thing. It was seamless, as we were serving in the church for many years before going into full-time paid ministry." Their call was confirmed as they engaged with the church via the various ministry experiences that such a commitment entails.

The Strength of the Call to Ministry

One of the key stages of the ministry journey has been the emphasis on calling that was expressed by the ministers and their spouses as they discussed their ministry journey. When work is viewed as an extension of a person's faith it is likely to be perceived as a calling.[4] Katherine Brookes, when describing the difference between a job, a career, and a calling, states: "Individuals with a calling orientation are more likely to find their

---

4. Davidson, "Religion and the Meaning of Work," 135–47.

work meaningful and will modify their duties and develop relationships to make it more so. They are found to be more satisfied in general with their work and their lives."[5]

Grant Bickerton states that "religious workers are a unique occupational cohort whose experience of work appears to include both high levels of stress and high levels of satisfaction."[6] Often these experiences are determined by the minister's understanding and commitment regarding their calling. To many involved in full-time Christian ministry, their primary motivation to begin such a vocation has much to do with a perceived inner call rather than pursuing a preferred career. Bickerton states:

> People who perceive work to be a calling report greater work, health, and life satisfaction, increased work hope, intrinsic work motivation, career decision self-efficacy, lower absenteeism and improved occupational commitment, more problem-focused coping, work engagement, and less stress, depression, and conflict between work and nonwork spheres of life.[7]

The value of pastors reminding themselves of the time that they experienced their calling into ministry cannot be overemphasized regarding their ministry/family well-being. Pentecostals often trace their heritage back to the Wesleyan Holiness movement and the great words of John Wesley, "I look upon the world as my parish."[8] Research suggests that callings are associated with identity formation, leadership gifting, and self-legitimization.[9] It is claimed that work takes on new meaning and transcendent significance when it is seen as a calling, a sacred duty, a service opportunity, or a way to serve God for a higher purpose.[10] When it comes to the association of calling in regard to Christian ministry, Ronald Hagerman states that "calling is an assignment prescribed by God with a sense of accountability to work for purposes other than one's own."[11]

---

5. Brooks, "Job, Career, Calling," para. 5.
6. Bickerton, *Spiritual Resources*, 30.
7. Bickerton, *Spiritual Resources*, 39.
8. Kim, *Reconciling Mission*, x.
9. Grey, "Divine Calling, Organizational Voice," 51.
10. Christopherson, "Calling and Career," 219.
11. Hagerman, "Occupational Stress and Clergy Support," 76.

Research published in the *Journal of Career Assessment* by Anna Praskova et al., in 2015, regarding calling and careers of emerging adults, discovered moderate negative associations with career indecision, demonstrating that individuals with higher career calling also reported being less indecisive in regards to career choice.[12] This study further showed significant positive correlations with life satisfaction, demonstrating that when young adults have a stronger career calling, they also report higher levels of life satisfaction.[13] The factors given by those scholars, make it legitimate to assume this would be true, possibly even to a greater degree, in the ministry vocation.

Pastors who embrace the joy of their calling and celebrate the fruitful results of their call will continue to dedicate themselves to fulfill the demands their call requires. When work itself is seen as serving God or fulfilling divine purposes, work-related strivings take on new significance and meaning, resulting in increased motivation, commitment, large investments of time and energy, and a greater likelihood of task accomplishment.[14] Pastors that become disillusioned with their ministry and sense of calling often become indecisive and disheartened regarding their future due to their sense of purpose being tested.

Unfortunately, there are many in pastoral leadership who have perceived a call from God but have not persevered in ministry due to the many pressures of ministry life. Quenton P. Kinnison states, "There seem to be few other professions where a person can be as highly trained as a pastoral leader and be so maligned by her or his clients for being so well trained."[15] This concept of the call of God that involves leading people that do not always want to respond to such leadership adds a further dimension to the pressures of the ministry vocation. Such tensions then have the potential to spill over into the family life of the minister. The call of God upon the minister is of vital importance when pastors seek to be ordained. Ordination and credentialing are not so much about giving a person a call of God for their ministry, but rather recognizing the divine call of God that already exists upon a particular minister.

When speaking about their ministry/family journey, the participants reflected upon their early Christian experience and the moments

---

12. Praskova, "Development and Initial Validation," 18.
13. Praskova, "Development and Initial Validation," 19.
14. Hagerman, "Occupational Stress and Clergy Support," 38.
15. Kinnison, *Transforming Pastoral Leadership*, 8.

when they felt that God had called them into full-time ministry. One pastor talked about discussing the call of God upon his life early in his relationship with the person who eventually became his wife: "We got together early in our Christian walk and that's when we started to talk about it, what my desires were, and my call was." His wife also commented separately, saying:

> Going to Bible college was a big deal. You know you have to leave your home and your family and sell up everything and go to Bible college and support yourself, so it wasn't a decision that we made lightly. We both felt that it was the right thing to do, that it was something that God was calling us to, and my husband felt that call before I did, and then I got on board with it too.

Another particularly reluctant pastor's spouse stated she never wanted to marry a pastor, yet acknowledged that God had called him into the ministry:

> It's interesting because the one job that I said that I would never do is to be a pastor's wife, because I felt that I fell so short of the mark in that regard. Having grown up in a main-line Church, I would hear many people criticizing the pastor's wife for many petty reasons, so I was fearful of the expectations that people place on the wife of a pastor. But when God calls you, you just must do it.

In the discussions regarding how their spouse handles the ministry/family journey, the concept of a calling arose again as the participants considered the strengths of their spouse regarding their successful navigation of their journey of ministry and family. The following are some comments that the male ministers made regarding the calling of God upon their wives:

- "She has always had a strong sense of a ministry call from a younger age for her own life. We have always ministered together, as I've often been involved in the worship area in most churches and she's got involved in more pastoral ministry."
- "My wife carries a call in her own life, rather than being the minister's help-meet."
- "My wife handles the ministry/family journey brilliantly, she is my secret weapon and my greatest strength . . . she always gets it, she is

with me, she helps me to balance the thing—we work as a team in our ministry and family life.

Participants in my research that stated they were satisfied with their ministry/family journey expressed the importance of God's call to ministry upon their spouses three times more often than those who stated they weren't satisfied with their ministry/family journey. Perhaps this understanding of the call to ministry and the commitment to such a call had an influence on the family of these participants that was a key to them experiencing a sense of satisfaction regarding their children's spiritual outlook. The importance of the spouse having a sense of call to the ministry would undoubtedly affect how the family perceives the ministry/family challenges they contend with from time to time. Provided there is a realistic aspiration regarding their ministry calling, understanding and valuing the call of God can lead to ministry/life fulfillment for the minister, their spouse, and their children.

College

The divine call that was revealed as a result of their commitment and service in their local church resulted in the participants enrolling in a ministry-training institution to further equip them for their ministry role. The majority of the participants indicated that they had trained for ministry at a Bible college or ministry training institute within their denomination, with only one participant, a female minister who was relatively new to ministry, declaring she had yet to enroll in a college for ministry training. One-third of the ministers had undergraduate degrees or postgraduate degrees. One-third had vocational education training qualifications, i.e., diplomas in ministry, and one-third had Certificate Four qualifications in ministry. Many were committed to life-long learning and intended to further their education and qualifications.

In regard to their ministry-training institutions, the highest number of participants indicated that they received their awards from their denomination's college. One of the benefits of being trained in a Bible college or ministry-training institution, apart from the obvious ministry education and training that is received, is the opportunity to form relationships with other ministers and spouses in the making. These relationships with other soon-to-be ministers and their families often develop into lifelong friendships and support networks.

H. B. London Jr. and Neil Wiseman, in a study of pastors, discovered that 90 percent of pastors feel they are inadequately trained to cope with ministry demands.[16] Such a statistic confirms the need for ministers to enter the ministry better prepared for the joys and challenges that ministry bestows upon a newly appointed pastor and his/her family. Added to this, with the higher emphasis within society regarding educational qualifications, it is important that pastors continue to improve their qualifications as they engage in their ministry vocation. This lifelong learning approach will help them improve their leadership and ministry practice, as well as position them for influence and credibility within the wider society.

The majority of those interviewed in my research who expressed that they were satisfied with their children's spiritual outlook and that all of their children regularly attended church noted the value of their Bible college experience. This confirms that a realistic aspirational process of preparation prior to ministry, one which includes ministry training, fares well for those who desire to engage in ministry and enjoy a flourishing family life that enhances the spiritual well-being of their family.

Chapter Summary

Many of the participants in my study began by talking about their conversion experiences. They also spoke about their commitment and service in their local church. The majority explained that as they were committed to serving God in their local church setting, they sensed a deeper call of God upon their lives to some area of vocational ministry. This sense of divine call resulted in them enrolling in ministry training college to further equip them for their ministry vocation. This process of the emerging call from conversion to fulfilling their call to ministry can be ever-expansive throughout the minister's journey, where an expanding layer of aspirational enlargement of the minister's influence can continue to take place along a similar process. The following diagram illustrates the expansive process that could continue throughout the life of a minister as he/she grows and develops further in regard to their influence and impact. Such growth in influence and impact would still need to take place with measured aspirations in order to ensure the continual well-being of the minister's family.

16. London and Wiseman, *Pastors at Greater Risk*, 20.

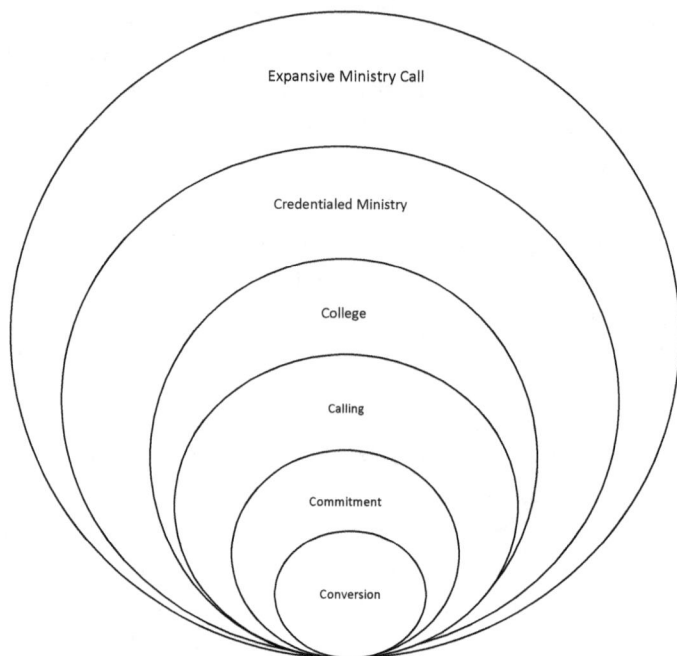

Figure 1.2 Conversion to Credentialed Ministry to Expanding Calling, Commitment, and Cause

The first feature of the Triple "A" Model of having a measured Aspiration is confirmed in this chapter. A measured aspiration that celebrates conversion and encourages commitment to their local church and training at a quality college or institution as they confirm their calling assists pastors and their families in their efforts to lead an enriched life. Such a measured aspiration is also perpetual as they continue to grow and develop and achieve greater impact and influence throughout their ministry/family journey. As their ministry grows, the minister must maintain a resolute awareness of how her/his expanding influence affects the family, and consequently maintain continued attention to their family along their ministry journey.

Chapter 2

High Ideals and Hard Realities

THROUGHOUT THE SEMISTRUCTURED INTERVIEWS, the question was posed to the participants as to what their ideal picture was regarding their ministry/family journey. The question was meant to evoke their big dreams, their Hollywood-inspired imaginations of what the perfect life of being engaged in ministry and enjoying a happy and healthy family life would look like. Participants discussed the picture that they would envision in an ideal ministry/family environment. These insights provided an indication of the aims and goals of the participants in relation to their aspirations for their ministry and family lives. Ministers and their spouses discussed their aspirational ideals in light of the realities of their present experiences. I have categorized their most frequent responses into Spiritually Focused Ideals and Family-Focused Ideals.

Spiritually Focused Ideals

The spiritual well-being of the family

One of the highest emphasized ideals was in regard to the spiritual well-being of the family. This ideal was expressed by comments such as the ideal of each family member identifying their own calling, the ideal of the parents facilitating their children's passions and callings, and the need to have strong peer groups for their teenagers to be encouraged spiritually. A female minister, whose husband is also a minister, stated her desire for her children's spiritual welfare: "As for my kids, I just want them, in an ideal setting to, first and foremost, have a very real relationship with God."

The Australian Christian Church's doctrinal statement affirms, "We believe that salvation is received through repentance toward God and faith in the Lord Jesus Christ . . . the believing sinner is regenerated, justified, and adopted into the family of God and becomes a new creation in Christ Jesus and heir of eternal life (Titus 2:11; 3:5–7; 1 Pet 1:23; 1 John 5:1).[1] Such a desire for the spiritual well-being of their children is grounded in their call to bring salvation to all people through the ministry in which they are called. Due to the relationship they have with their immediate family members, such an ideal is a high priority for ministers and spouses. For those ministers and their spouses whose children have drifted away from their faith, such a situation weighs heavy on their hearts.

As the theme regarding the spiritual well-being of the family emerged, another female minister voiced her ideal: "I guess my ideal picture is that my family would have a similar outlook to ourselves, that the church and ministry would inspire them to love the church and love God for themselves." A minister's spouse further stated: "Obviously my ideal picture would be to see our children grow up and to love God and to find a ministry of their own." Each of these comments have clearly articulated their ideal regarding the spiritual health and well-being of their family, particularly their children. They have declared their desire to see their immediate family embracing the faith of their ministry spouse/parents. Celebrating the conversion of many people in the church and community has great reward, however such celebrations can be dampened when members of their own family turn away from the Lord. In a further chapter that relates to what works along the ministry/family journey, we will explore some intentional actions that have assisted ministers and their spouses to enhance the spiritual well-being of the family while they have engaged in their ministries.

Doing ministry together with the whole family involved

Following the ideal of the spiritual well-being of the family, another frequently expressed ideal was being involved in ministry together with the whole family. This ideal was expressed with comments like: "My ideal picture would be that your kids are involved and love the journey," "I would see the ideal of them all serving in whatever their gifting and

---

1. *Doctrinal Basis of the Australian Christian Churches*, 4.8.

capacity is and I believe that one day that will be the case," and "All of our family having a relationship with Jesus and serving him in our own gifted way."

Each of these statements regarding the ideal of having the whole family involved in ministry is an admirable aspiration. However, if these idealistic aspirations are expressed as expectations upon the spouse or children of the minister, they have the potential to produce resentment and discouragement rather than excitement and inspiration in the hearts of the family members toward serving God as a family. Wisdom and discretion, accompanied by much prayer, are certainly valuable elements in each family situation. The future chapters in this book regarding things that work and things to avoid or do differently will be very helpful to achieve such aspirations.

An authentic example

The ideal of the family having an authentic example to model themselves on within the home was also significant. Many comments expressed that parents wanted to set an authentic example for their children to follow, such as: "Hopefully they would be able to see what dad and mum preached on Sunday was lived out throughout the week," and "I think the family would need to show a great sense of honesty and integrity, openness, forgiveness, and those sorts of things. Being willing to admit when you're wrong, being able to share your weaknesses and your strengths, and being open about who you are as a person, authentically." A female minister recommended the importance of staying authentic in the following statement:

> I would also tell them to stay authentic, because the thing that I experienced over many years was the disconnect between my real self and my public self, and that can lead to finding yourself in a place where you are no longer enjoying what you are doing because you're not being your real self and you're trying to perform rather than minister.

Some research was conducted on the importance of the home environment, particularly the influence of the parents, in influencing the later religious orientation (whether positively or negatively) of the minister's children. A study of adult pastors' children, conducted by Kimberley Strange and Lori Shepherd, revealed that if their parents had established a warm, loving, relationship with them, and had given them the freedom to be themselves and make choices, had made them feel important and spent time with them, had portrayed a genuine and consistent spiritual role model, and, finally, had maintained boundaries between church and home, they were more likely to be religiously committed.[2]

Comments regarding having an authentic example were made by the participants in my research who stated they were satisfied with their children's spiritual outlook, whereas no comments were made in this regard by participants who were not satisfied with their children's spiritual outlook. Participants recognized the value of the family being able to observe the authenticity of their ministry-engaged spouse/parent, displaying the reality of their faith when it wasn't being observed by the public eye. The conclusive evidence from both my own research and research conducted by others is that the ideal of having an authentic example in the home is very significant in regard to the spiritual well-being of the family.

Positive perception of the ministry/family journey

The importance of ministry families having a positive perception of ministry cannot be overestimated. The challenge that ministers and their spouses often face is when their family view the ministry or the church in a negative light and therefore become reluctant to attend church or follow the faith of the ministry spouse/parent. A female pastor explained the example that she and her husband set for their children: "Our ideal was to teach our family to look for the very best in people. . . . So being always very positive about the people in the church was our ideal and so I think that rubs off." Unfortunately, the author has seen the opposite of this take place in both pastors' and nonpastoral Christian homes. I have seen families exposed to and highlighting the negative issues of church life, and as a result some family members begin to resent the people of the church and eventually God himself rather than respect the church and honor God.

The ideal of ministry families having a positive perception of the ministry/family journey was further emphasized by a female minister whose husband was also a pastor, where she stated that she wanted to make church a positive experience in the lives of her family. Such an ideal

---

2. Strange and Sheppard, "Evaluations of Clergy Children," 53.

is one that pastors and spouses should not only dream about, but rather they should pray about and act upon by focusing on the good things that are happening and the good things God is doing. Leave the discussions of the not-so-good things to the privacy of your prayers or the privacy of those that have the ability and responsibility to implement the required change that is necessary. This is a key ingredient to achieving the ideal of a positive perception of the ministry/family journey.

Family-Focused Ideals

Adding to the spiritually focused ideals, the theme of the importance of the family became prominent in the respondents' ideals as the participants discussed their ministry/family journeys.

Quality time with the family

Time with the family is one of the greatest challenges ministers and their spouses have said they wrestle with. According to Morris and Blanton, clergy spouses expressed adequate time together as being an essential ingredient for healthy family functioning.[3] One pastor explained: "I think the ideal would be in the sense that the family would have good quality time together." Another minister also stated a similar desire to give more time to his family: "For me it's about being with the family as much as possible. Of course I've had times when I've been away and times when my church life has taken me away. But I'm always looking to be there, to be at the big things with my kids through the years, not miss the graduations, not miss the big concerts." The spouse of a minister lamented the times her family missed out:

> I think ideally it would have been better for my husband to be around more. When I say my husband was away, I mean he was away from the home, he would be at Bible college or he would be out at meetings, so immediately after he would get home from work, he would rush his dinner down and then he would have to go out, that's what I mean about him not being around.

During the discussion of the ideal picture of the ministry/family life, two female ministers suggested they would like a maid like an Alice

---

3. Morris and Blanton, "Influence of Work-Related Stressors," 194.

from *The Brady Bunch* who could do the washing, ironing, shopping, and cooking, so that when they arrived home after fulfilling their ministry responsibilities they could then spend more time with their family. Another pastor's wife stated she would like to "have one day a week when you spend time together and don't have to use that time to get the groceries, for example, and just relax and be together."

In Vivian Grice's research with pastors' children aged 18 to 35, almost all participants raised the issue of availability, either directly or indirectly, by commenting on the time cost of ministry, and parental absence from the family because of ministry work.[4] One solution suggested by a pastor was to make Saturday a family day: "The ideal would be to have the Saturday off with the family, so that you could spend some time with the family. Because if you've got children at school age they are at school on Monday when you take your day off, and your wife is at work on Monday . . . So, the ideal would be to have Saturday off completely with your family." David and Vera Mace, in their early well-researched book entitled *What's Happening to Clergy Marriages?*, note a similar dilemma for pastors in relation to clergy time perils: "As everyone knows, Sunday is the pastor's busy day; Saturday is often sermon preparation time; and most of the important church meetings, and many counselling sessions, are scheduled in the evenings."[5] These are the times when the family is mostly at home.

Time with the family needs to be prioritized and planned. The ideal of being able to spend more time with the family should not be considered optional for those who can spare a little time; this should be a necessity for those who desire to have a flourishing family life while engaged in their ministerial responsibilities. When the ideal of spending more time with the family becomes optional, the relationships within the family will not flourish but will rather become fragmented, and your ministry will lack lasting fulfillment.

Healthy family relationships

Research has revealed that spending more time with the family leads to healthy family relationships, however, there are also other elements that enrich a minister's family relationships. My research data confirmed the

---

4. Grice, "Pastor's Kids," 119.
5. Mace and Mace, *What's Happening to Clergy Marriages?*, 64.

desire in the hearts of participants to give attention to their marriage relationship. Jack and Judith Balswick suggest that, "from a biblical perspective, the ethic of family includes the mandate that each member is to be cared for, thus emphasizing the value of each family member and their entitlement for respect, consideration, sensitivity and understanding within the family relationship."[6] Having an understanding of each other's world and needs was described as an incredibly important component of a healthy relationship between a minister and spouse, as a pastor in my interviews explained: "Firstly you have to know who you are as a couple before you even think of your kids. It's very much understanding each other, because if you don't understand each other then you could be walking in a journey that's totally opposite to the way your partner is going."

Many of the ministers and their spouses mentioned the negative, stressor-related impacts that working in ministry had on their marriages. Understanding the stakes, the participants in my research provided some insightful reflections based on their own life experiences and observations. The value of giving attention to maintaining a healthy marriage relationship is of extreme importance for those engaged in ministry, as the foundation of a fulfilled family life is a fulfilled marriage relationship. A pastor stressed: "Our first priority was to build a healthy marriage and family and let the flow of ministry come out of this."

Author Stephen Barton states that married couples who raise their children in a loving home add great value to community well-being at large.[7] For over thirty years as a pastor, as I dedicated children to the Lord, I would say to the parents that the greatest thing they could do for their child was to love each other. The outcome of healthy relationships between the ministry parents results in healthy relationships between the parents and their children. This then results in already-close relationships with God being further strengthened.

As noted in Kimberley Strange and Lori Shepherd's research on adult pastors' children, it was revealed that if their parents had established a warm, loving, relationship with them, then they were more likely to be religiously committed.[8] My research confirmed that a key to having a satisfied outcome in regard to children's spiritual well-being was in

---

6. Balswick and Balswick, *Family*, 317.
7. Barton, *Life Together*, 8.
8. Strange and Sheppard, "Evaluations of Clergy Children," 53.

regard to the minister and spouse being intentional about investing into their relationships with each other and with their children. This investment further resulted in their children wanting to continue to follow the faith of their ministry-engaged parents. A male minister stressed the following to pastors:

> Don't think that you are indispensable, but understand that your family are indispensable, you can't afford to lose them. At some time, you may leave your church, and then you ask yourself what you have left. You've either got a great relationship with your wife and with your kids, or you had a great relationship with your church and may have lost your kids and your wife by living a life with a sense that you are indispensable to the church.

My research concluded that being intentional about healthy family relationships builds family unity and helps each member of the family know they are valued. The importance of having ideals for healthy family relationships in the midst of the blessings and the burdens that accompany the ministry/family journey cannot be over emphasized, as healthy relationships within the family precede healthy relationships with God and healthy ministries within and beyond his church.

Communication with the family

Many married couples in ministry find that daily relationship stress occurs due to a lack of communication as a result of being consumed with ministry responsibilities. This, in turn, leads to negative assumptions and misunderstandings and therefore further stress in their relationship. Many participants, when asked what they would do differently, said "I would communicate with the family better." This statement was an indication of the desire of ministers and their spouses to relieve some of their marital stress by communicating more effectively, thus enhancing their marriage relationships. This is also confirmed in some case studies undertaken by Thomas Ledermann et al., that revealed that "both relationship stress and marital communication in conflict situations have an effect on the quality of intimate relationships."[9] One pastor noted the importance of allowing his wife to communicate her struggles with being the wife of a pastor: "My wife has found herself battling with the

---

9. Ledermann et al., "Stress, Communication, and Marital Quality," 199.

pressures of being a pastor's wife, so communication is the whole key to get that balance and knowing what's right for your family."

Another pastor explained, "When things can't be done to the degree that some of the family members would like, we would talk about that and we would all understand the journey and sacrifice, and work together to bring balance to our family life." He continued, "So I think it would be a lot of good heart-to-heart conversations, pretty much asking the kids where they are at, how they're feeling, and what their journey is looking like and what's happening in their life as well." The ideal that many ministers and spouses described in regard to the ideal of communication with the whole family is a very significant goal leading to family health and well-being throughout the ministry/family journey.

Living in a sustainable ministry/family model

One of the ministry couples I interviewed, both of whom were engaged in ministry with different areas and ministry expressions, explained that they wanted to set a sustainable model for ministry, both for themselves and for their family. Both the husband and the wife explained they were children of pastors and that both of their fathers had experienced burnout in ministry. The husband explained: "Both my wife and I saw our fathers burnout in ministry, and in my father's situation it was a pretty ugly picture . . . and we also watched that in a different way with my wife's dad. So, from a very early stage in our marriage, we were very cautious in regard to the dangers of ministry." He continued, "We both said that we need to find a sustainable model of ministry because we don't want to end up in that same place."

There have been several studies recently on mental health support for clergy and the importance of making wise life choices for sustained harmony in the home.[10] Pastors who do not pay attention to having a sustainable model for their ministry/family lives will not only be candidates for burnout in their own lives, but their families will also miss out on the time and attention from their ministry spouse/parent they desperately need and deserve. Burnout is not only a danger to pastors, but also a potential danger to pastors' wives. Research has revealed that 45 percent of

---

10. Weaver, et al., "Mental Health Issues among Clergy," 395.

pastors' wives say the greatest danger to them and their family is physical, emotional, mental, and spiritual burnout.[11]

According to Roy Oswald, "burnout involves overuse of listening and caring capacities, dealing with too many needy people, and having too much responsibility. This results in physical and emotional exhaustion, cynicism, disillusionment, and self-depreciation."[12] In order for ministers and their families to flourish rather than falter, it is important that ministers and their families establish sustainable lifestyles as they fulfill the call of God for their lives.

Sustainable models that involve wise choices, balanced focus, and sustaining resources are key factors to prevent pastors, their spouses, and their families from burning out while engaged in the ministry call. The pastor that was interviewed and emphasized living in a sustainable model concluded, in regard to his ideal, as follows: "[A]n ideal picture of ministry and family life for me, is where something is sustainable, where we are actually enjoying it and where all the relationships are healthy." This is a healthy ideal and an essential aspiration for ministers and their spouses to aspire to.

Having right priorities for the family

A sustainable model would entail having right priorities for the family. This was another ideal that was expressed throughout the interviews. Amongst the many challenges ministers and their spouses are confronted with, another important challenge is that of balancing the priorities of time and attention that they give to their family and their ministry. Lee and Balswick claim, "The minister and his wife have many roles to fulfill. They must care for both their own family and the congregational family. Sometimes, in shuffling back and forth between roles, they may lose track of the boundaries between the families."[13]

A female pastor, whose husband was also a minister, emphasized how she applied her ideal of priorities for her marriage and family: "If there was any pressure put on me I would actually challenge it back, and I would push back toward our priorities of family and our priorities of marriage." Another minister's wife stated, regarding the wrestle she

---

11. Cordeiro, *Leading on Empty*, 32.
12. Oswald, *Clergy Self-Care*, 58.
13. Lee and Balswick, *Life in a Glasshouse*, 164.

would have in regard to prioritizing the family over ministry, "I think the issues were in regard to those priorities of what God expects and what do our children need... When saying 'no' to people, when it may have been the only time that they were available to meet up, but it actually clashed with something that the boys had on that was really important, it was just a bit of a struggle." This aspirational ideal of having right priorities for the family, as in many of the other ideals, needs to be at the forefront of the minds of ministers and their spouses, otherwise when priorities are skewed, both the family and the ministry will pay an enormous price.

The hierarchy of priorities (with God first, family second, and ministry third) compared to the complementary approach to their ministry/family life.

The ideal of having right priorities for the family, as explained above, extended to another level when the participants spoke about their ideals for their ministry/family journey. Several participants mentioned the importance of clarifying clear priorities in their ministry/family lives, such as God first, family second, and ministry third, which I defined as a "Hierarchy of Priorities." For many years this has seemed to be a formula that ministers have alluded to, some would suggest legalistically. However, their intentional desire to dedicate themselves to God, then their family, and then their ministry, with all other aspects of life such as health, recreation, and other endeavors following in priority, came from a sincere desire to please God and fulfill their family responsibilities. The following diagram illustrates this concept.

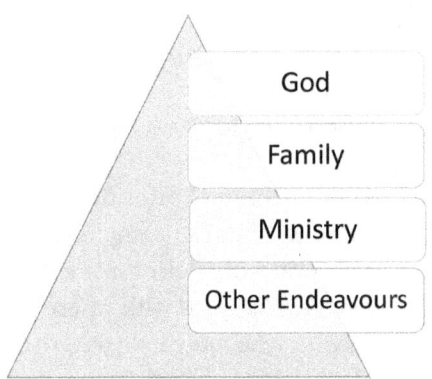

Figure 2:1—The Hierarchy of Priorities Approach to the Ministry/Family Journey

This ideal was mostly emphasized by the participants who expressed that they were satisfied with their children's spiritual outlook. Perhaps this is not so much the result of having the right formula or being legalistic, but rather having clear intentions regarding their focus on God and then their family before any other priorities, so that their family is not lost in the midst of their many other endeavors.

Another notion that was suggested was having a complementary approach to ministry and family rather than the approach as in the above hierarchy of priorities. This was advocated by several who stated that they weren't satisfied with their children's spiritual outlook. The complementary approach to the ministry/family journey emphasizes that everything complements everything else, rather than compartmentalizing priorities into different segments or levels of importance. This notion proposes that God is a part of every aspect of our lives, including family and ministry (which theologically is quite true). However, the difficulty with this approach is that the focus on God and family can be lost amid the many other demanding issues that life serves up to ministers if God and family are not a distinctive and intentional higher priority. An illustration of this notion is seen in the following diagram.

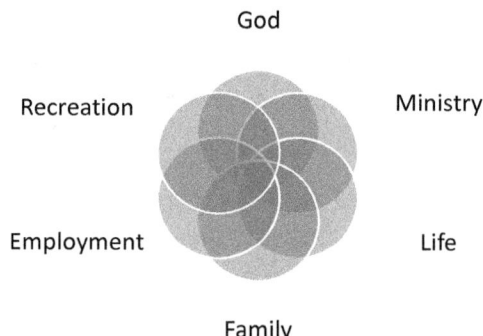

Figure 2:2—The Complementary Approach to the Ministry/Family Journey

The ideal of having intentional priorities for God, then the family, then the ministry, rather than the complementary approach of everything complimenting everything else, seemed to work for families who indicated they were very satisfied with where their children were at spiritually. One pastor's wife, who sadly indicated that her son had turned away from God, stated what her ideal would be now, in light of her own experiences: "Well God first, then family, then church. We did make a mistake and we put church first before family, and that came back to bite us as the years went on. Our son said to somebody else that we were not there for him, but we were there for everyone else, so we do regret that as we made a big mistake in neglecting him."

Having a balanced ministry/family life

Healthy family relationships, sustainable models, and having right priorities occur in partnership with having a balanced ministry/family life. A male pastor stated that his ideal for his family included well-adjusted family balance: "My ideal is that they would love God, and that they would grow up where we would fulfill our destiny, and they would fulfill their destiny through that journey. Having well-adjusted kids, well-adjusted family balance, not super spiritual." A female minister stated: "I would ensure that there was a good balance of family time and serving the people of the church and church activities." A male pastor stated, "My ideal would be a true balance, time-wise and priority-wise, between family and ministry." The wife of a male pastor lamented the lack of balance that her husband demonstrated in regard to their ministry/family journey: "Whatever was going on there at the church, that would always have to come before the family, so I think a balance there would have been good, I think a fair bit of pressure was on the family from that side of things." The ideal of having a balance between the responsibilities of the ministry and the joy of spending time with the family was consistent throughout the interviews.

Some helpful thoughts for ministers and spouses were expressed in regard to maintaining balance. A female pastor recommended her solution of being in the zone wherever you find yourself:

> The concept of being in the zone is a thing that has really helped me get more perspective in balance of family and ministry. The thinking is that when you are in the zone, you are in the zone.... It's very important that when the time is set aside to do what you're supposed to do in a ministry setting, that you do it well, that you do it with your whole heart, and you do it diligently, and you complete it. And when you are at home in that zone, as with my husband, it's very important that I do that well too.

A male pastor suggested the importance of scheduling time for family:

In the earlier years, when I was still single I was doing more than 12 hours a day in ministry and also working, but then when we got married and started having children, I concluded that we needed to work on how we could balance ministry and family, so we were able to work together on it and set a schedule where we could organize both our ministry and our family.

The ideal of having a balance in your ministry/family life was especially highlighted by those who stated they were satisfied with their children's spiritual outlook. Although balance is not always easy to quantify or embrace, it is certainly an ideal that should be in the uppermost focus in the minds and hearts of ministers and their spouses as they continue to fulfill their ministry and seek the spiritual well-being of their family.

Protection from negative church issues

Another ideal that was discussed was the ideal of the family being protected from the negative church issues that can often surface throughout a ministry journey. Although there are many positive experiences that occur throughout a minister's life, there can be some negative issues and frustrations that arise also. Issues with congregation members, leaders, board members, other pastors and the like can often frustrate ministers and their spouses, and at times these frustrations need to be voiced. A problem shared is a problem halved.

However, it is very important that these issues and frustrations are voiced in an appropriate setting and with an appropriate person that has the perspective and maturity to hear them. The spouse and children of ministers are not the most appropriate people for ministers to voice their frustrations and concerns. One pastor stated his ideal aspiration if he was given the chance to start over again: "I would keep my family close knit; I wouldn't allow them to know what the politics of the church were. I wouldn't let them know what was going on in the church, and I'd protect them a lot more. The kids don't need to know all that happens behind the scenes, they'd get upset with the church because the parents told them too much."

One male minister reflected on a conversation he had with a more mature minister in his early days: "A mature minister once said to me, don't share everything. Why burden your loved ones? You should be protecting them and not burden them with every silly thing and silly action that people in the ministry context might do. But I didn't listen to that, and we paid a price." This same minister, who endured some challenging times in the early years of his ministry, emphasized his desire to have been more sensitive in regard to what he shared with his wife:

> The lesson that I learned over 25 years ago was that I should have shielded my wife from the nastier, unattractive experiences that I had seen in the church context, and not share so much with her. I didn't know who else to share with, and so I shared some things with her. . . . So that was 25 years ago, and we have learned the lessons and we have not repeated them.

The ideal of the family being protected from the negative church issues that can often surface throughout a ministry journey needs to be a firm aspiration for every ministry couple and not just a passive option.

No expectations on the children

Another ideal that was emphasized was the ideal of having no expectations placed upon the children of the ministers. Many expectations that are placed upon the children of the minister, though not necessarily intentional, often seem to be unrealistic and unfair. In the professional world there are very few occupations where the spotlight shines upon the spouse and children of the professional (perhaps with the exception of politicians and celebrities, although these tend to be protected by their ability to isolate their families using their more abundant resources). Numerous children of ministers have experienced people placing expectations on them to be as knowledgeable as their ministry parent, or to conduct themselves as if they were ministers themselves. Such expectations create enormous burdens that are unique to ministry families alone. One spouse of a minister commented: "I have seen both here and overseas, pastors pushing their kids into things that they wanted them to do, but for the kids it wasn't really their thing, and I didn't want that for my kids. I definitely didn't want that for my kids."

A study regarding the effects that growing up in a minister's home has upon the religious commitment of the adult child found that the strongest negative stressor was "expectations" due to being the pastor's child.[14] A further study by Strange and Shepherd that evaluated children of clergy versus nonclergy children to ascertain whether a negative

---

14. Anderson, "Experience of Growing Up," 393.

stereotype actually exists, revealed that PKs (pastors' kids) are bombarded with stress and high expectations.[15] Though all children must learn to adapt to social expectations, the expectations placed on pastors' children may be more intensive than most.[16] In addition to an expectation of great piety, clergy children are also expected to attend every church function and to volunteer more readily than their peers.[17] Unrealistic expectations that are placed on family members of ministers was a common comment from those that stated they were not satisfied with their children's spiritual outlook. The wife of a pastor and the mother of a son that has turned away from the church and also his faith lamented the pressure of unrealistic expectations placed upon their child while he was quite young: "Our son had some major issues in that he had people putting expectations upon him to behave like a pastor's kid and didn't allow him just to be a normal child and grow up in the church. People would often put things upon him that were too much for him as a child."

A female minister stated her desire for her children's spiritual welfare as follows: "As for my kids, I'm protective of my kids because of the expectations that other people put upon them." Lee and Balswick revealed: "Positive and negative expectations alike can be experienced by the pastor's child as unrealistic or restrictive, with possible dangerous consequences for his or her emotional adjustment . . . Often it is simply assumed, for example, that the pastors' son will also be a pastor one day."[18] Such difficult expectations and experiences in church life can be due to the congregational members not being aware of the boundaries that are necessary in regard to the children of the minister.

This ideal that was emphasized, of having no expectations placed upon the children of the ministers, is an ideal that expresses the pastor and spouse's desire for their children to experience a normal upbringing. This ideal is a goal for their children to encounter Jesus for themselves without the pressures and potential hurts that can be imposed upon them due to the unrealistic expectations congregation members might place upon them. Such an ideal or aspiration also needs to be measured against the reality that expectations upon ministers' children will always be there to a certain extent; therefore it is the minister and spouse's responsibility

---

15. Strange and Sheppard, "Evaluations of Clergy Children," 53.
16. Lee and Balswick, *Life in a Glasshouse*, 163.
17. Lee and Balswick, *Life in a Glasshouse*, 91.
18. Lee and Balswick, *Life in a Glasshouse*, 173.

to prepare their children for such expectations, but to also be protective of their children to reduce the negative impact that such expectations may have on their children.

Having less burden on the pastor's wife

For many years there has been an expectation that although in most cases only the pastor is financially employed by the church, the wife of the pastor is also expected to fulfill certain responsibilities. Many have spoken about the church getting two for the price of one. This has often left the pastor's wife with pressures to fulfill pastoral duties, even if she has not been trained as her husband has been. Such expectations and pressures add to the burden of the pastor's wife, who may also be busy in her role as a wife to her husband and mother of her children, not to mention the fact that she may be employed in her own career.

There are some interesting differences in how the congregation responds to the wife of a male minister compared to the husband of a female minister. When the husband of a female minister supports his wife by attending midweek meetings such as small group meetings, prayer meetings, leader's meetings and the like, the church normally responds positively and often verbally, encouraging the husband for the way he supports his wife in her ministry. However, when the wife of a male pastor supports her husband by attending midweek meetings as described above, as well as usually leading the worship ministry, the women's ministry and children's ministry, the church in most cases never says a word. Their expectation is that "if she is a true pastor's wife, that is what she is expected to do, she's the pastor's wife, and that is her calling."

Throughout my interviews with ministers and their spouses, the ideal of having less burden on the pastor's wife surfaced several times. Following are some relevant comments that were discussed: "The ideal would probably be with my husband being in full-time ministry and with me only working in a very small portion so that there is less burden on myself as a pastor's wife, so that the kids are not left on the sidelines," and "I have always said that when the Lord sent them out 'two by two' I doubt that He meant a husband and wife." These comments reflect the ideal of having less burden on the pastor's wife, so that the wives of ministers can enjoy their lives as ministry spouses, rather than endure the ministry/family journey and feel obliged to carry the same load that her husband has been employed by the church to carry. This aspirational ideal should not just be considered as wishful thinking, but rather an ideal that pastors and churches should act upon to ensure that the wives of pastors carry the burden that Jesus promised in Matthew 11:30 when he proclaimed that "My yoke is easy, and my burden is light."

Encouragement and support from our Church and denominational leaders

Several pastors and spouses within my research interviews lamented the lack of support they desired from their church and denominational leaders in regard to their ministry and family. When speaking about their ideals, many commented on their desire for support within their ministry function so they could spend more time with their family. A female minister stated the following: "Well I guess for me, having support of a great eldership team and leadership around me, so that I would be able then to have time to myself, have time with my husband, and have time with my children that wasn't pressured and stressed." Another female minister who ministered alongside her husband, stated that she and her husband were in desperate need of support: "I'm actually living in a state of heightened anxiety at the moment and I think my husband is as well, but I don't know if he realizes that, because there's not much support for us at this time." A male minister, whose wife was also a minister, acknowledged some support from within his denomination, however he stressed that this support came at his initiative, rather than theirs: "I must acknowledge the wonderful support we did have from our denominational leaders at critical times of concern and need. However, due to the time constraints of the leader's structure and responsibilities, it often meant that their support always remained as a result of our initiative and never theirs." Morris and Blanton revealed that clergy and their spouses found it difficult to obtain relief from stress due to the absence of social support, with feelings of loneliness and isolation by clergy families being a common experience.[19] The ideal of receiving encouragement and support from church leaders and denominational leaders is not a negotiable ideal but rather a necessary structure for ministers and their spouses to have in place in order for their ministry to be fruitful and their family to flourish.

---

19. Morris and Blanton, "Influence of Work-Related Stressors," 189.

Having financial strength

A bivocational pastor stated: "In order to keep the balance between ministry and family the ideal is that you are paid full time so that you can give yourself fully to the ministry and also fully to your family." This ideal of having financial strength while fulfilling your ministry/family responsibilities was regularly stated as an ideal regarding ministry/family life. A husband of a female minister also stated his ideal regarding financial strength: "I guess in an ideal world we would both be financially independent enough to really serve the Lord in ways that we feel we are called to do." A pastor whose children were now adults lamented: "You've got to be careful from a resources point of view that you don't put your kids at a disadvantage, and that becomes a great challenge for the kids. Because I don't think the kids should be hurt or disadvantaged because of the ministry, and so that's an interesting kind of tension between the call and parenting and providing for your family."

In regard to ministry finances, Lee and Balswick state: "Quite simply, if they don't have enough money, their financial obligations become burdens and a certain source of family stress."[20] Financial strength was stated as both an ideal and an issue that the participants wrestled with in regard to their ministry/family journey. Further attention will be given to the challenge of limited finances in the chapter regarding difficulties that ministers and their families wrestle with.

Obsessive Aspirations

In her fascinating study of the needs of clergy families, Linda Mileman observes that, "demands of the ministry, unlike almost any other profession, impact the whole family. . . There can be great joy, a sense of fulfillment and purpose, and also loneliness, frustration, and pain."[21] Data from my research reveals that clergy have an ideal picture of what the ministry/family journey should look like, but this needs to be measured against realistic aspirations.

An analysis of the data regarding the ministry couple and how each spouse handles the ministry/family journey was undertaken. The data revealed that the male pastors can tend toward an obsessive aspiration,

---

20. Morris and Blanton, "Influence of Work-Related Stressors," 193.
21. Hileman, "Unique Needs of Protestant Clergy Families," 121.

underestimating the toll ministry takes and the price families often pay while trying to achieve a healthy ministry lifestyle. It can be seen that a strong ministry call can boost satisfaction, provided there is a positive awareness of the needs of the spouse and family and that they are responded to appropriately.

The research revealed the importance of the first feature of the "Triple A" Model regarding the recommendation that the ministry couple have a measured, realistic aspiration at the beginning and throughout their ministry/family journey. This includes a measured focus and balance of ministry responsibilities and family responsibilities, which is always necessary for those couples who desire to have a fruitful ministry and a flourishing family. Pastors often fall into the trap of competition in order to "climb the ecclesiastical ladder of success."[22] An obsessive ministry focus can cause ministers to lose sight of the thing that matters most in their lives—their family. Issues such as the toll ministry takes upon their spouse, the time demands of ministry, the potential of ministry/family imbalance, and the price that ministers and their families pay for the sake of ministry must be taken into consideration.

Within the twenty-first-century ministry world, it appears the danger of an obsessive focus on ministry is prevalent, particularly amongst male pastors, and such an obsession can take its toll on the minister's family. An analysis of the data reveals that the female spouses of the ministry couples often felt that their clergy husbands seemed to be consumed with ministry demands, which affected their family in a negative way. One spouse stated:

> I think my husband would say that he was too involved in his mind, mentally. That he didn't put enough attention on the special things that the children were involved in, in their early days. So, he didn't remember a lot of those events in the children's early days and therefore felt that he didn't put enough store or attention on those things, or value on those things that he should have. He was always thinking about the next thing, rather than living in the moments when the children were growing up.

Such an obsession is due to having an imbalanced aspirational focus regarding ministry and family. The first feature of the Triple "A" Model of Ministry Function and Family Fulfillment, having a measured aspiration regarding ministry, is critical in helping ministers keep their ministry focus in balance with their family responsibilities.

22. Hileman, "Unique Needs of Protestant Clergy Families," 129.

It was frequently discussed by the female spouses that ministry demands take their toll on the family. The male spouses also struggled with time limitations. The issue of their male spouse struggling with ministry/family balance was brought up many times. Anthony Pappas states the pastor's life is like a five-ring circus or a five-arena rodeo. These arenas are the intrapersonal, the interpersonal, the pastoral role image, the congregational, and the environmental.[23] The aspirational challenge of finding balance in the midst of these arenas requires effort and focus regarding ministry and family.

Further comments were expressed regarding the perspective that the male spouses and their families had paid a heavy price due to their involvement in the ministry. Research reveals that ministry couples often pay an unseen, unacknowledged, and unappreciated heavy price for dedicating their lives to ministry. One study found that pastors often feel owned by their congregation.[24] Many ministers fall into the trap of spending excessive amounts of time at the church.[25] A wife of a male pastor lamented "I think it's becoming really quite difficult in the amount of paperwork that he finds himself doing every day, so time is becoming less." As the female participants discussed the obsessive focus on ministry by their male spouses, the highest frequency of comments was in regard to their spouses' struggle with time limitations. This confirms the findings of Wayne Hill, et al., that time intrusions negatively affected the quality of life for clergy families.[26] The problem with these obsessions with ministry is that they can do irreparable damage to a minister's marriage and family. Some ministers exhibit an obsession for ministry as if they were still single, without responsibilities to their wife or family. Rosemary Radford Ruether states that the roots in regard to the depreciating of marriage and family are not just discovered in the twenty-first century, but such devaluing of marriage and family stem back to first-century society.[27] Despite the centrality of the family to ethnic identity and social maintenance, both the Greco-Roman and the Jewish worlds of the first century comprised movements and ideologies that were anti-family. In the Greco-Roman world, for example, there was a misogynist tradition that saw wives as so great a burden that men were better off not

23. Pappas, *Pastoral Stress*, 9.
24. Morris and Blanton, "Predictors of Family Functioning," 28.
25. Goetz, "Is the Pastor's Family Safe at Home?," 39.
26. Hill et al., "Understanding Boundary-Related Stress," 147.
27. Ruether, *Christianity and the Making of the Modern Family*, 21.

marrying at all. The philosophers of the first century also encouraged single life.[28] It seems there are times when some ministers are still in a first-century mindset, living with an obsession for ministry that devalues their marriages and families.

A comparison of the comments made regarding an obsessive focus on ministry revealed that overall the male participants were more obsessive regarding their ministry focus than were their female counterparts. Such an obsession would no doubt lead to marriage and family neglect, where the over-aspirational, ambitious minister becomes unaware of the issues his family encounters, which then means the minister cannot give the appropriate attention the family requires.

One particular spouse of a male minister who was obviously hurting and wanted to help others, when describing her ministry/family journey states, "Ahhh, it was hell on wheels. Some of it was great and some of it was 'get me out of here.'" Having unrealistic aspirations can sometimes be inspired by triumphalist expectations regarding ministry, which are then followed by the realities that the ministry/family journey presents. These realities can often be a shock, and in many cases, a disappointment in the lives of those that have not been prepared with a measured aspiration regarding ministry. Further introduction and preparation by mature ministers to the realities of ministry will result in the development and maturity of those that are new to ministry. Such development and maturity assist them to refocus their approach to ministry toward their family and the people that they minister to, rather than focusing on goals of achieving success for their own sense of achievement and reward.

Chapter Summary

Throughout this chapter regarding the aspirational ideals and realities of the ministry/family journey, we have explored the spiritual aspirations of ministers and their spouses, such as the spiritual well-being of the family, doing ministry together as a family, the importance of the family having the privilege of observing an authentic example in their ministry home, and the family having a positive perception of the ministry/family journey. Following the spiritual aspirations of ministers and their spouses, we then considered the aspirations that they discussed regarding their family. Ideals such as having quality time with the family, enjoying healthy

---

28. Ruether, *Christianity and the Making of the Modern Family*, 22.

family relationships, clear communication within the family, living in a sustainable ministry/family model, having right priorities for the family, being intentional regarding those priorities, having a balanced ministry/family life, protecting family members from negative church issues, having no expectations placed upon the children, having less burden on the pastor's wife, and having financial strength.

Added to this focus on spiritual and family aspirations were the realities and dangers of having unrealistic or obsessive aspirations. Examples of this obsessive focus on ministry as described by the spouses of ministers were: the toll that ministry takes upon their spouse and family; the time demands of ministry; ministry/family imbalance; and the price that ministers and their families pay for the sake of ministry. These obsessive aspirations were said to have had a grave impact upon the minister's spouse and family, and as such, the ministers needed to become more realistic and measured in order for their families to flourish as they engaged in the ministry vocation. Overall, the first feature of the Triple "A" Model of Ministry Function and Family Fulfillment that recommends having a measured aspiration regarding ministry is critical in helping ministers keep their ministry passion in balance with their family responsibilities.

Many ministers and their spouses enter ministry with high ideals regarding how they will fulfill their ministry roles alongside their family responsibilities. The difficulty arises when the realities of the ministry/family journey begin to unfold. The ideals of the pastors and their spouses often indicated areas of the ministry/family lives that they felt were lacking. Throughout this book several of these ideals will appear as issues they wrestled with, or things they would have improved should they have had the opportunity to begin their ministry lives over again.

Summary List of the Ideals of the Ministry/Family Journey

Spiritually Focused Ideals

The spiritual well-being of the family

Doing ministry together with the whole family involved

An authentic example

Positive perception of the ministry/family journey

Family-Focused Ideals

Quality time with the family

Healthy family relationships

Communication with the family

Living in a sustainable ministry/family model

Having right priorities for the family

The hierarchy of priorities (with God first, family second, and ministry third) compared to the complementary approach to their ministry/family life.

Having a balanced ministry/family life

Protection from negative church issues

No expectations on the children

Having less burden on the pastor's wife

Encouragement and support from our church and denominational leaders

Having financial strength

Personal Reflection

Consider some other ideals for your ministry/family journey.

Part 2: Awareness

The second element of the Triple "A" Model of Ministry Function and Family Fulfillment is Awareness. The importance of having a resolute awareness of both the advantages and the adversities the minister's family experience due to their ministry and family engagement is critical for the goal of ensuring a flourishing family amid the many responsibilities of ministry. This second part of this book will explore and inform pastors and their spouses of the value of having a resolute awareness regarding the blessings and the burdens their family experiences. The first chapter of this section (chapter 3) will highlight the blessings that being involved in ministry has upon the minister's family which the ministers and their spouses revealed throughout the semistructured interviews of my research. Chapters 4 and 5 will highlight many of the burdens the ministers and their spouses revealed. Chapter 6 will discuss the impact that being in ministry has upon the marriages and spouses of the ministers, and chapter 7 will explore and discuss the impact that being in ministry has upon the minister's children.

Chapter 3

The Blessings of the Ministry/Family Journey

HAVING CONSIDERED THE IMPORTANCE of the aspirational ideals that many pastors and their spouses highlighted, we will now take a look at the importance of being aware of the blessings that engagement in ministry has upon the family, both collectively and individually. The burdens are often the overriding experiences that are emphasized in the ministry/family journey, yet there are also many blessings or advantages that the ministry family experiences due to being in ministry.

Participants in my research discussed many of the positive experiences that were enjoyed by their family due to their journey in ministry. These experiences were many and varied and are a great resource for families to appreciate in the midst of the many challenges they face throughout their ministry/family journey. A way to address the underlying issues that consume the focus and time of ministers is to maintain a resolute awareness of the blessings that ministry families experience. An ability to focus on the blessings that involvement in ministry bestows upon the family will add to the goal of enjoying a positive family experience that increases the spiritual well-being of the family while engaging in ministry. Several categories were highlighted regarding the blessings that being in ministry releases upon the family. There were both significant natural blessings and spiritual blessings that the family experienced. In fact, the participants unknowingly emphasized ten significant natural blessings and ten spiritual blessings throughout the interviews. I will now focus on both clusters of these blessings accordingly.

Significant Blessings the Minister's Family Experienced

There were many significant blessings that the participants discussed when presented with this question: What were the blessings the family experienced as a result of being involved in the ministry/family journey? Following is an account of these many blessings as pastors and their spouses discussed the benefits that were enjoyed by their family due to their involvement in ministry.

The opportunities for travel and holidays

The advantages of being able to travel and have holidays in various places due to the opportunities that ministry affords was one of the main natural benefits expressed by the pastors and their spouses. Often families would travel to different places throughout their nation and other parts of the world as they attended ministry conferences or travelled to places where the spouse/parent ministered through their teaching or preaching gift.

Several comments from the interviews revealed the respondent's appreciation of this blessing. A pastor's wife stated, "I think our girls have lived a pretty good life, because of ministry. They have travelled around the world with us." A female pastor stated, "I think we've travelled as a culture in our family, so I think for our children travelling with us in ministry is their normal, it's positive, but it's a positive normal, and it is a blessing." A male pastor stated "Through the ministry we've been able to see the world for want of a better word, and show our kids the world, and I don't think that would have ever happened had we not been in ministry."

Mission trips were also considered as blessings for the family. One female pastor explained, "We have had the privilege of being able to involve our children in mission work in Indonesia, Malaysia, the Philippines, South Africa, and to let them have the privilege of experiencing the blessings of that." A male pastor whose wife was also credentialed, and who engaged in substantial missions endeavors, stated, "As a couple (and alone) we have travelled more than many of our nonministry peers. The sense together of feeling that we have made a difference in people's lives through ministry has been wonderful and very meaningful." Overall, the blessings of holidays and travel that ministry involvement affords to families is something that ministry families need to have a resolute awareness of, especially during those times when ministry seems to be difficult.

Relationships they formed in the church and through ministry connections

Another benefit of ministry as expressed in the interviews was the relationships that were formed in the church and through ministry connections. Lee and Balswick state that although there are hazards that may be unique to the clergy family, there are also unique advantages, such as meeting people from different cultures and backgrounds.[1] In one survey, for example, the minister's wife wrote the following: "We have had people in our home whom other children have never had the benefit of knowing: African pastors, foreign missionaries, evangelists, other preachers. Our kids have been able to talk to them, play games with them, and find out more about the world and what makes people tick."[2]

There were many comments expressed regarding the blessings of the relationships that family members developed due to their ministry experiences. A spouse of a female minister stated, "I guess the natural one for us in our outback town was getting involved with different people in the community, relationship building with people that you don't naturally have relationships with." A female minister explained, "There's the friendships that we've all developed which have been wonderful." Another female minister stated, "Well the first thing that comes to mind is the wealth of relationships . . . our family get to journey with people, they get richer relationships, they get to be part of people's lives being changed."

Another minister who ministers alongside her husband spoke about relationships that have been developed around the world, "The children have also developed great relationships with people around the world. They have had the opportunity to go and stay with people on their own, with people that they have met due to our ministry." Another pastor expressed his appreciation of the benefits of ministry, "Wow, that's headed for a long list of blessings: firstly, significant relationships with people who we got close to through ministry." These are just a few of the statements that were expressed in regard to the blessings of developing relationships that they formed in the church and through ministry connections.

---

1. Lee and Balswick, *Life in a Glasshouse*, 163.
2. Lee and Balswick, *Life in a Glasshouse*, 163.

Becoming closer as a family

Becoming closer as a family was highlighted as another benefit of being involved in ministry. There are times in ministry, due to relocation, when the family moves away from their extended family and friends. In the early days of such a move they realize the value of their immediate family due to having no one else, therefore they value each other quite considerably. Also, in times of ministry growth and progress, and sometimes stressful ministry moments, they draw closer by supporting each other.

A husband of a female minister spoke about how they had become closer due to their family moving to a country church, where his wife was the senior minister: "So our ministry has meant that we have become much closer with one another than we would have been otherwise. Because we've had to rely on one another more, we've had to rely on God a lot more for our provision and so on." Another minister expressed something similar, "The positive experiences and blessings of being involved in ministry that flowed over into family life have been things such as the opportunities to regroup and draw closer to each other even in stressful moments that we faced at church." A children's minister also emphasized the value of ministry bringing the family together, "Another positive was that we were all together doing the children's ministry when the children were younger." The ministry has the potential to cause the family to draw closer together as conveyed by the above comments, which can be a great blessing of being involved in the ministry vocation.

Social skills

Social skills were emphasised by participants as their family developed an ability to relate to people of all ages, nationalities, and backgrounds. A female pastor commented, "I think church kids have got an advantage socially. I think they really benefit because they know how to talk to all age groups." Another female pastor also emphasized, "I think one of the things that I think is fantastic is the skill to relate to people of all ages. Because of the church community they have had to mix with senior people, they had to mix with adults, they mix with teenagers, so they've had a great opportunity for social development, because of all the different ages, and the different demographics."

There is possibly no safer place for children and teenagers to meet people of a variety of ages, social statuses, cultural differences, and demographic variations than in the church. Pastors' families are more likely to be exposed to such social variations than any other families in society. This is largely due to their standing within the church and the congregation's inclination to want to meet the other members of the pastor's family. Thus, by plight, rather than by purpose, the family members of the pastor develop social skills in relation to how to communicate with and appreciate the social differences of many different kinds of people. These people skills also enhance their emotional intelligence, which can further enhance their callings or careers as they are employed as adults.

The provision of God

The provision of God regarding finances was another blessing that ministry families experienced. Such a blessing was highlighted in a way that the whole family recognized God as the provider of their needs, often described as "miraculous." One female pastor stated this as a very practical blessing, "I think some of the really practical stuff is some of the provision that our family has received over the years that they have been able to see." A male pastor also spoke about the family's appreciation of God's provision throughout his ministry, "The blessings have been that they have seen the provision of God in the hardest of times. Every one of them know from the blessing that they have seen that our sufficiency is not from the government, it's not from other people, even though God has used many other people to bless us."

A pastor's wife also stated the blessings of finances upon their ministry family, "We have also been blessed financially by the grace of God even though we have never been paid a lot for ministry. Yet God has provided all of our needs in so many ways and beyond our needs." This blessing of God's material provision as a result of their ministry involvement instills faith in the hearts of the ministers and their family, that God will supply all of their needs according to his riches in glory as Philippians 4:19 declares.

Opportunities that came their way

Frequently, due to the family of the minister being more publicly visible to the congregation than other families, and probably being around the church more frequently than other families, opportunities to serve in the church or use their musical or vocal skills arise. One male pastor expressed his appreciation of this blessing, "Ministry has provided opportunities for us to release the gifts and talents that God has put in our lives, to serve him and give back to the body, and I don't think there's any greater satisfaction than that." A female pastor was also very grateful for this, "I appreciate the blessing that my kids experienced through growing up in children's church, and then also going into youth, then being able to sing in the choir and play drums." This benefit of opportunities that came their way also applied to opportunities to meet the guest speakers and go to dinners with those that were guests of the church. This was another positive benefit that being involved in ministry created for the family.

Enjoying some of the benefits of being a pastor's kid

Enjoying some of the benefits of being a "pastor's kid" (PK) was also emphasized. One pastor commented that "We have tried to help our kids enjoy and see some of the benefits of being a pastor's kid." He continued, "For our kids, it's often those simple things like being able to meet the preacher or being able to go somewhere where the other kids can't. . . . we've always painted those as being the blessing of God upon our family because of ministry."

Another pastor and father stated, "I think they got to see a lot of different ministries. When we took them to other places or to other churches and they could link with other pastor's children, and that sort of thing which was great for them." A pastor's wife stated that her kids were treated well due to the high respect that people had for their clergy parents. Another mother and pastor stated that she and her pastor-husband were very intentional in that. "Yes, we are involved in church life, which was quite demanding, but we also made sure that there was lots of the perks and benefits from that and actually communicated that to our children. We intentionally made sure that our kids saw the benefits rather than the burden of being pastor's kids." Another pastor stated, "It's such a positive thing now to be a pastor's kid, so I think they do get favored in a way. I think people are predisposed to like them in a church context, so that's really nice for them."

There are definitely great blessings that pastors' children enjoy due to their parents' involvement in the ministry. It is highly important that ministers and their spouses continue to be aware of these positive experiences that their children enjoy, and that they be intentional to continually highlight these blessings to their children. Such actions and attitudes will help their children to focus on the positives of ministry/family life rather than focus on the difficulties they experience at times due to their parents' ministry roles.

Leadership development for the family

The home of a pastoral family is very often a hotbed for leadership development. As the partners and children of pastors observe the leadership skills of their clergy family member, they learn much about leadership. Skills such as leading large groups of people, being a master of ceremonies at celebrations and events, preaching to the congregation, leading annual general meetings and the like are often learned through observation. One pastor's spouse stated, "Our boys have had a lot of positives out of our ministry life as they have learned much about leadership and about life due to our involvement in ministry in the church."

The ability to relate to people of different generations, cultures, and backgrounds is also learned through observation and experience. Family members also learn how to navigate difficult situations, such as crisis situations that arise in the church, difficulties with leaders or church members, responding to people who leave the church, and managing financial difficulties. As they observe their clergy family member responding to both pleasant and difficult situations that they as leaders within the church are confronted with, these leadership lessons are learned by the family members of the clergy by observation. Family members of the church are also exposed to other significant leaders, such as guest speakers in their church whom they get to observe personally due to such leaders coming into their home or sharing dinner with the family at a restaurant after church. A female pastor stated, "I really respect people in leadership a lot more and in a lot deeper way and respect what they do and I guess I can see the blessing of that as I have also instilled that into my children."

Pastors' families also have the opportunity for further leadership development as a result of attending pastors' conferences and pastors' meetings that are often geared to enhancing the leadership development of ministry leaders. A male pastor stated, "Ministry has just opened us up to a whole other world. Things such as leadership development and being able to meet the people that we have, and go on the journey that we have, the fact that we're regularly able to go to leadership conferences has been a great blessing." He continued, "I have to go to state conference and I have to go to national conference, and you're exposed to the bigger picture. I think just the journey of doing church life, where you are in the position that we are, it just exposes my kids to the bigger picture." Another pastor spoke about the confidence his children developed as leaders. "They have also had to develop their own confidence before people due to our ministry role." To conclude this concept of leadership development for the whole family, a pastor whose adult children are all employed in significant leadership roles attributes their leadership development to their ministry involvement: "We rejoice and praise the Lord that despite our significant challenges, our children prospered in terms of their social and educational development. Today they are each holding very responsible positions and leading very productive lives in adulthood." This positive benefit of leadership development due to the family's involvement in ministry can often be overlooked by ministers and their spouses. However, having an awareness of this benefit of leadership development can be a great advantage for ministry families to consider as they raise their children.

Fulfillment as a family

The blessing of enjoying fulfillment in ministry both as a family and particularly as a couple was identified as a great blessing. One pastor's wife explained, "I think this sense of fulfillment in doing God's will for you and your family is obviously a very positive one." A spouse of a female pastor also emphasized this blessing upon their family said, "I think both my spouse and I have a commitment and passion to serve God's purpose. Whatever that may require, whatever it may involve, I think our children want us to be fulfilled, to know that their parents are okay and happy. For us, happiness comes back to fulfillment in serving God's purposes." For many, the main motivator to continue to be in ministry is the fulfillment that they experience as people are converted, discipled, and then released into their own God-given purpose. Having an awareness of this blessing is a great motivator for families in their ministry, even during occasional stresses and challenges.

Flexibility with work hours

A final benefit that was revealed in my research, was the benefit of having flexible work hours as a pastor. This benefit allows pastors to get along to their children's school events. Events such as sporting events, school concerts, school excursions, or even picking up the children from school during the day, are opportunities that people without the flexibility of work hours can't do. One pastor likened his role as similar to a person who is self-employed. "I guess we do have a little bit of flexibility that we can take a little bit of time off if we need to. It's a little bit like being self-employed to a degree, I guess that's a positive." Having an awareness of such a benefit, and reminding the family of such, can help ministry families appreciate the blessings that being involved in ministry adds to them.

Spiritual Blessings of Ministry Involvement for the Family

Along with significant natural blessings that the minister's family experienced, there were also many spiritual blessings that positively impacted the minister's family. As the ministers and their spouses discussed the positive experiences and blessings that being involved in ministry brought to their family members, there were several benefits that the author categorized as spiritual blessings upon the family as it became very clear these were spiritual in nature. The following paragraphs identify and explain these spiritual blessings upon the minister's family as expressed by the ministers and their spouses throughout my research.

Developing a deeper faith

Perhaps the greatest desire of any minister and their spouse who are engaged in serving God through his church and other ministries is to see their own family members develop a deeper faith. One pastor stated that one of the most positive blessings of being involved in ministry is his wife and children are grounded in their faith. A female pastor said of her children, "They all have got a big faith in the possibility of change. You never hear anything about something being too hard or that's too difficult. So, I think that is the result of when you talk about testimonies and things, and they see God's presence and power is real. That big faith is because of the privilege of ministry."

Some pastors also spoke about their family's faith being deepened as a result of facing difficult times. A male pastor acknowledged the difficult times his family experienced in ministry were instruments for deepening their faith: "While there are tough times that the kids don't always understand, I think it actually gives them a wider and deeper faith when they mature. That has been something that has been a blessing for being in a ministry family." An awareness of the family developing a deeper faith in God due to the ministry is certainly something to celebrate.

Doing ministry together with the whole family

The idea of doing ministry together with the whole family was emphasized by many pastors and spouses as one of their aspirational ideals for their ministry/family journey. It was also identified as one of the spiritual blessings that pastors and spouses described when speaking about the benefits they experienced in their ministry/family journey. One pastor explained, "Because both my wife and I included each other and the wider family in ministry, there has been a time of common sharing. It wasn't just a Dad thing or a Mum thing, but something that we do as a family." A children's pastor stated, "A positive was that we were all together doing the children's ministry together when the children were younger." Also, "the sense together of feeling that we have made a difference as a family in people lives through ministry" was emphasized as a positive spiritual experience by another minister. A female pastor also commented "To have all three of my children come through Bible college is wonderful, because we can serve together and learn together. So, I think those things have been those priceless precious moments. So serving God together and going to church together has been amazing." This spiritual blessing of doing ministry together as a family was a very positive experience that many pastors and their spouses, as well as their children, enjoy due to the ministry.

Helping to grow the kingdom as a family

Following on from the spiritual blessing of doing ministry together with the whole family, was the positive experience of knowing that together as a family you are helping to grow the kingdom of God. This adds purpose to the practice, fulfillment to the function. The practice of doing ministry together as a family is a great blessing, however the purpose of what that ministry achieves adds even further blessing. A pastor stated, "A positive impact has also been for our family that we are a strong family, and we have discovered that ministry is a joy to us as a family. There are times when we all get tired, but it is a joy to see the products of what you have done in ministry affecting the lives of other people, so it's a joy to serve the Lord as a family." Another pastor commented on the joy and privilege of helping grow God's kingdom: "The sheer joy and blessing of serving the Lord can hardly be quantified. The overwhelming privilege of being used of the Lord and seeing firsthand his miraculous power at work in our own lives and that of those we minister to is beyond words."

Some female pastors also celebrated the joy of growing the kingdom as a family. One female pastor spoke of the spiritual blessing of the family seeing people set free and growing spiritually. Another female pastor also spoke of the rewards of growing the kingdom: "I think it's so rewarding as a family when you see someone either converting to Christ, or going further with God, or getting healed, or seeing those lifelong issues resolved due to the work of God." This spiritual blessing of helping to grow the kingdom as a family, adds great fulfillment to every family engaged in ministry.

The authentic modelling of the God-life lived in the home

Another spiritual blessing for the family was the authentic modelling of the God-life lived in the home. Pastors and their spouses recognized the value of the family being able to observe the authenticity of their ministry-involved family member, displaying the reality of their faith when it wasn't being observed by the public eye. A female pastor explained, "I think that with my kids, I can say that they are going on for God today because we have set the example." The wife of a pastor stated, "Another positive is that being involved in ministry has set an example to our children, by living it and not just saying it." A male pastor also added, "I guess the main one is seeing your kids watching you in private and then seeing you in public and noting that, so that's a real blessing to me." Another male pastor endorsed this same notion, "The biggest positive is the role model thing, that as the pastor of a church you have to be seen to be the example. So, we worked very hard at living our Christian life in an authentic way."

Vivian Grice, in his research regarding the adult children of Baptist pastors, found that PKs who had a positive spiritual experience stated that this was largely due to the examples and teaching of their parents.[3] The value of the authentic modelling of the God-life lived in the home cannot be overstated. This has been a key ingredient in helping pastors' children establish their own faith and develop a personal relationship with the Lord.

Positive role models in the church

God's church, though at times she takes a beating from within and without her walls, is a wonderful place for families to develop and grow in their faith and in every other aspect of life. Many of the participants in my research acknowledged the value that positive role models in the church had upon their immediate family members. A female pastor expressed her appreciation of the church by stating, "I think one of the great things for kids growing up in church is that they have so many people around them, like positive role models." Another female pastor expressed her excitement that her children were able to meet some of their heroes (role models): "They have had the opportunity to speak to people that they have regarded as heroes in the faith because of the settings that we have been in." Although, as we will discuss in the next chapter, some role models in the church are not always inspirational, there are certainly many positive role models in the church that have a profound effect upon the lives of a minister's family. An awareness of these positive role models helps ministry families count their blessings and appreciate the benefits of being a part of a family engaged in ministry.

Seeing the reality of God at work

Pastor's families are often more exposed to what happens in the church than the average family. Although this can be a hindrance when they are exposed to the negative aspects of church life, it can also be a blessing when they are exposed to the wonderful things that are happening in people's lives. Pastors' families often hear about the many prayer requests

3. Grice, "Pastor's Kids," 133.

that come to the pastor from church members. As a result, they are often the first to hear about God's answers to people's prayers. This exposure to answers to prayers can often encourage them in their faith and build their own faith to believe for even greater things for their own lives.

One pastor explained this blessing for his family: "I think it's the experience of seeing the reality of God working both within and without the church . . . to let them have the privilege of experiencing the blessings of that." A female pastor also expressed her appreciation of this blessing upon her family, "they have all got a big faith in the possibility of change . . . so I think when you talk about testimonies and things, and they see God's presence and power is real, part of that is because of the privilege of ministry." Another female pastor explained, "They get to be part of people's lives being changed."

A pastor expressed the blessing of the whole family seeing God working through their ministry by saying, "I think the positive experiences are probably fairly obvious, every time you see God do something really wonderful in someone's life you just know that it's God. Whether it be people that are saved or whose life has been transformed and knowing that you've made a significant difference in someone's life as a family." The blessing of being a part of a ministry family and being eyewitnesses of much of what God is doing in people's lives and in answer to their prayers should not be ignored. An awareness of this blessing should inspire pastors to celebrate the great things that God is doing rather than focus on the occasional negative happenings in the church.

The opportunity to hear amazing speakers

Amongst the many spiritual blessings that ministry families enjoy is the exposure to many of the great Christian personalities from around the world. Many ministry families have opportunities to attend ministers' conferences and other outstanding conferences due to being involved in ministry. The organizers of these conferences often invite guest speakers who are doing significant things in their particular part of the world. The by-product of this is that the ministry families that attend these conferences are impacted by these ministers.

One female pastor expressed her joy when speaking of this blessing: "The opportunity to hear amazing speakers, I just think the blessings far outweigh anything else." Another pastor expressed the family's privilege of not only hearing these guest speakers, but that his family has also been able to meet them: "Our children have had the opportunity to meet some great visiting speakers that have come to our church and some that they have met outside of the church at conferences and combined church meetings." This connection with God's servants whom God is using to do incredible things around the world inspires the minister's family to persist in their own ministry call. They also gain some wisdom and learn about key principles that are fruitful and fulfilling in ministry in the twenty-first century.

The blessing of people praying for the family

Many pastors and spouses spoke of the spiritual blessing of people praying for their family due to them being in ministry. Such an awareness gives the ministry family a sense of support from God's people and security that God is hearing and answering their prayers. One pastor's wife stated that her family felt supported and encouraged because of their church family's prayer support. Another pastor's wife also highlighted the blessing of people praying for them when she stated, "Obviously as pastors you get people praying for you, and I think that rubs off on the children as well." Still another pastor's wife explained, "We knew that people were praying for us. When there were dark times, you knew that you would never even have to ask because you knew that people would have been praying for us and for the ministry, and that's a wonderful thing to know."

As well as the appreciation that the above pastors' wives identified regarding the spiritual blessing of people praying for them, several female pastors also expressed their awareness of this blessing of prayer for their family. One female pastor expressed the value of, "getting prayer support from other people who just partnered with us unexpectedly, some that we hardly knew, and outside our denomination as well. We came across people that God led to pray for us, and I think that was a great unexpected blessing." Another female pastor also expressed this blessing, "And they've also received the benefit of people praying for them, as they pray for us as a family, whether the family know that that's why we're very blessed or not. I feel that those things have often been blessings as a result of being involved in ministry." An awareness of the value of people praying for the family is, again, not something to be treated lightly, as such prayer support expresses love and respect for the minister's family, not to mention the results of God answering their prayers.

God's blessings on us as a family

There were many general blessings that God brought to families due to their involvement in ministry. Several of the ministers and their spouses expressed the appreciation of God blessing their families overall. A pastor's spouse explained, "Definitely there have been many blessings from God because I think He blesses us for what we do, and the children have benefitted from that." Another pastor's spouse explained, "I just think the blessings far outweigh anything else. We just constantly tell the boys how blessed we are, and the boys can see that we live such a blessed life." A pastor also appreciated the blessing of being able to be a vessel that God has used: "It's a significant part of the reward of ministry, that you get to be God's vessel that God is using in some contexts. This is always rewarding for you and the family." There were many illustrations that the ministers and their spouses described as God's blessings upon them as a family. Both the ministers, their spouses, and their children were very much aware of these many and varied blessings that God had poured upon their lives due to their obedience to the call to ministry.

Our family loves God

The final spiritual blessing that many of the ministers and their spouses identified due to their involvement in ministry was that their family loves God. Although this was the final blessing in this list, for the majority it was the most significant and rewarding blessing that being involved in ministry provided for their family. When articulating their ideal aspirations for their family, the majority emphasized the ideal of their family's spiritual well-being. This blessing is at the very heart of my PhD research and this book. When speaking about the spiritual blessing that a family loves God, a pastor emphasized, "The positive experiences are that our whole family loves God, church, and that our children are grounded in their faith and have had experiences as a family serving God." A female pastor stated, "Well my kids know the word of God, they know the Lord." Still another female pastor explained, "They have developed great confidence in the Lord." Each of these pastors, who are also parents, along with many others have appreciated the blessing that their family loves God and rejoice in that blessing.

Chapter Summary

Having an awareness of the blessings that ministry bestows upon the family relates to the second recommendation of the "Triple A" Model, that of having a resolute awareness of the advantages and adversities that the family experiences as a result of their involvement with the ministry vocation. An analysis of the responses of those that indicated that they are satisfied with their children's spiritual outlook, compared to those that are not satisfied, was undertaken to reveal whether there are any clear indications of whether having a resolute awareness of the blessings upon the family due to ministry has any effect upon the spiritual outlook of their children. Data drawn from a comparison between the frequency of comments made by those that expressed that they were satisfied with their children's spiritual outlook and those that expressed that they were unsatisfied with their children's spiritual outlook reveals that participants from the satisfied group were more expressive overall regarding the benefits and blessings of their ministry upon their family. An awareness and appreciation of the blessings of being in ministry is more likely to lead to a positive outcome in regard to the family's spiritual well-being.

Summary List of the Blessings of the Ministry/Family Journey

Significant Natural Blessings

- The opportunities for travel and holidays
- Relationships that they formed in the church and through ministry connections
- Becoming closer as a family
- Social skills
- The provision of God
- Opportunities that came their way
- Enjoying some of the benefits of being a pastor's kid

Leadership development for the family

Fulfillment as a family

Flexibility with work hours

Spiritual Blessings

Developing a deeper faith

Doing ministry together with the whole family

Helping to grow the kingdom as a family

The authentic modelling of the God-life lived in the home

Positive role models in the church

Seeing the reality of God at work

The opportunity to hear amazing speakers

The blessing of people praying for the family

God's blessings on us as a family

Our family loves God

Personal Reflection

Add to the above lists some other blessings of your ministry/family journey.

Chapter 4

Ministry-Related Burdens

Heaven's Highway or Hell on Wheels?

WHILE THERE ARE MANY benefits and blessings experienced by families who are engaged in ministry, there is also a challenging side to ministry. One particular spouse of a male minister I interviewed regarding her ministry/family journey, who was obviously hurting, when describing her ministry/family journey, said, "Ahhh, it was hell on wheels. Some of it was great and some of it was 'Get me out of here.'" The realities of the challenges of ministry upon the family can often be a shock and in many cases a disappointment in the lives of those that have entered without an awareness of the issues that ministry families are confronted with. Having an awareness of these challenges is paramount to enjoying a flourishing family life while fulfilling the call to ministry.

As a leader within my Christian denomination, I conducted some round-table discussions regarding the ministry/family journey amongst pastors and their spouses within the areas I was responsible for. I discovered that many pastors and their spouses thought they were the only families that wrestled with the burdens that ministry places upon their family lives, and that most other ministry families seemed to have had an easy time. Many were relieved when they attended these round-table discussions to discover others also faced the same challenges. Realizing that these challenges weren't as unique and freakish as they thought, but were rather very normal for ministry families, lifted a heavy burden off many ministry couples' shoulders.

The purpose of this and the following chapter is to identify what these common burdens and challenges are in order to create an awareness of them, and to normalize them so ministry couples understand they are not alone or doing something wrong. As I analyzed the interview transcripts in my PhD research, I discovered the issues ministers and their spouses wrestled with were the same whether the ministry couple was satisfied with their family's spiritual outlook or not. In fact, overall, there seemed to be a greater awareness of these burdens and challenges amongst those who were satisfied with their children's spiritual outlook and stated all their children were still attending church and following the Lord.

When pastors overengage with their ministry responsibilities it can result in pastors and their spouses not being as aware of the challenges their families encounter, which can in turn result in not giving their families the attention they deserve. A key ingredient in the Triple "A" Model of Ministry Function and Family Fulfillment is to have a resolute awareness of the burdens the ministry family experience in order to mitigate such burdens by giving attention to help the family flourish as they are engaged in ministry together.

The blurring of home and work boundaries is common in pastoral life. David and Vera Mace, in *What's Happening to Clergy Marriages?*, discovered the major challenges clergy families are confronted with were: congregational expectations; the tyranny of time; regularity of moving geographically; and the battle of the budget.[1] Norman Blaikie, in his research regarding Australian mainline church ministers entitled *The Plight of the Australian Clergy*, revealed that many of the factors associated with the Australian clergy occupational context have a bearing on the clergy's marriage and family.[2] Factors such as unrealistic expectations placed on the spouse and children of the clergy, disrupted routines, lone-parenting, lack of privacy, mobility and resettling family, loneliness, financial restrictions, and lack of time for leisure, were identified as some of the difficulties Australian clergy families encountered.[3]

Cameron Lee and Jack Balswick, in their book *Life in a Glass House*, describe the responses of a group of clergy families who were asked to describe the greatest disadvantages of being in the ministry. Their answers

---

1. Mace and Mace, *What's Happening to Clergy Marriages?*, 48.
2. Blaikie, *Plight of the Australian Clergy*, 183.
3. Blaikie, *Plight of the Australian Clergy*, 183–84.

came down to five broad recurring themes: not enough family time together; high expectations; low pay; the difficulties of moving; and the lack of privacy.[4] Michael Morris and Priscilla Blanton's research also revealed five challenging factors of ministry life: mobility; financial compensation; time demands and expectations; family boundaries; and social support.[5]

These challenging factors from David and Vera Mace's research in the 1960s, Blaikie's research in the 1970s, Lee and Balswick's research in the 1980s, and Morris and Blanton's research in the 1990s regarding the burdens that ministry places upon the family appear to have similarities to the findings of my own recent research of ministry families from 2015/16. As the participants in my research discussed the issues that they wrestled with regarding their ministry/family journey, the most frequently emphasized ministry challenges that were identified will now be described in further detail. Many issues that were described are ministry-related, and many were family-related. I have focused on the ministry-related issues in this chapter and the family-related issues in the following chapter.

Ministry-Related Issues

Time constraints

Time constraints was mentioned frequently as an issue that the participants in my research wrestled with. David Goetz states that many ministers fall into the trap of spending excessive amounts of time at the church.[6] A wife of a male pastor lamented, "I think it's becoming really quite difficult in the amount of paperwork that he finds himself doing every day, so time is becoming less." Several other spouses of pastors also commented on the time constraints that the ministry role imposed on the family: "I think that sometimes you can't spend the time with your family that you would like to, even now with our children as adults"; "Time has always been a juggle and that's the big struggle, I suppose, to find that right balance between your ministry life and your family life"; and "Probably time was our greatest struggle in that you are on-call 24/7."

---

4. Lee and Balswick *Life in a Glasshouse*, 191.
5. Morris and Blanton, "Influence of Work-Related Stressors," 191.
6. Goetz, *Is the Pastor's Family Safe at Home?*, 39.

Many pastors also lamented the issue of time with their family: "Time is an issue. As the pastor of a small church you're responsible for everything and so there is a lot to do and to focus on, and so your family does tend to miss out"; "Time was the biggest issue, trying to find time to spend with the family was a constant issue due to the demands of the ministry"; "I think that probably the big one is time, there's been moments when there's been pressures on time"; and "In regard to time, there's probably been seasons where I have been out too much of a night, involved in too many things, when by the time I've got home the kids have already been in bed asleep, and you can get up and go first thing in the morning before the kids have woken up." Reduced time is also a common theme that was identified by Mace and Mace, "As everyone knows, Sunday is the pastor's busy day; Saturday is often sermon preparation time; and most of the important church meetings, and many counselling sessions, are scheduled in the evenings."[7] These time demands often impinge on the time when the minister's family are at home, and render she/he unavailable.

Such time issues are assumed to predominantly involve male clergy, however both the literature and data from my research indicate that the challenges of time are also issues that female clergy wrestle with. During the discussion of the ideal picture of ministry/family life, two female pastors suggested they would like a maid like an Alice from *The Brady Bunch*, who could do the washing, shopping, and cooking, so that when they arrived home after fulfilling their ministry responsibilities they could then spend more time with their family.

Susan Cody-Rydzewski adds that, "clergywomen are likely to experience conflict between work and family . . . In part, this is because ministers often report that they are on-call. Thus, unexpected emergencies or requests may interfere with scheduled family time."[8] Often the battle is not in their heart or their desire to be with their family, but rather in the demands that crowd out their time and attention that they would like to give to their family. A female pastor explained: "The issue is in regard to time, getting enough time together, and fulfilling the tasks and functions of both ministry, marriage, and work expectations. I find it very hard to say no when it comes to ministry because you feel that if say no that you are not only letting others down, but you are also letting God down."

---

7. Mace and Mace, *What's Happening to Clergy Marriages?*, 64.
8. Cody-Rydzewski, "Married Clergy Women," 273–89.

Still another female pastor commented, "Time, never enough, it is very difficult to prioritize time." The spouse of a female minister also conveyed how the issue of time affects his wife and therefore the whole family: "The issues that we have wrestled with particularly relate to the time demands upon my wife . . . even at times when we have had family gatherings she has received calls where she has had to drop everything for the sake of the church." Pastors, whether male or female, who do not pay attention to this vital area of making time for their family, will have families who will miss out on the time and attention from their ministry spouse/parent that they desperately need and deserve.

Unrealistic expectations

Another very prominent issue that was revealed was the unrealistic expectations placed on family members of the minister and the minister themselves. Pastors and their families constantly wrestle with unrealistic expectations, often from their congregations, peers, and many times from themselves. Lee and Balswick comment on such unrealistic standards that pastors can often place upon themselves: "By perceiving themselves as some nonhuman Christ figure, many clergymen are locked in a double bind. To themselves and to others they are not allowed the privilege of being human."[9] In this regard, a pastor stated, "My overwhelming struggle was with those unrealistic expectations that others so often place upon us. Admittedly, many of those expectations were also self-imposed."

The wife in a ministry couple spoke about the pressure of her own self-imposed expectations as she journeyed though an unusual family health challenge with her child:

> For me as a pastor's wife, and just out of Bible college, I really felt under the pressure that I had to just be smiley and trusting God, even though my baby had a major problem and people really didn't understand, because it wasn't a problem that was a common problem. So, I think that right from the very beginning I set myself up to wear a mask.

Another wife of a minister explained her misgivings about becoming a pastor's wife: "I would hear many people criticizing the pastor's wife for many petty reasons, so I was fearful of the expectations that people place on the wife of a pastor." Another pastor's wife described the pressure to

---

9. Lee and Balswick, *Life in a Glasshouse*, 123.

be someone other than herself: "Because of who I am, at times I felt pressured to be someone that I'm not. I'm not an outgoing kind of person, I'm a quiet person, rather than the outgoing pastor's wife type of person."

A pastor explained how people placed expectations on their kids, "people try to put unrealistic expectations upon our kids because they're the pastor's kid and therefore they need to conform to a certain way." A female minister whose husband was also a pastor commented, "In regard to family life, the expectations of people on the pastor's children were unfair: they should behave in the church, they should walk like this, they should dress like this, they should behave like this." Some other female ministers also commented on expectations that were placed on their children: "Sometimes there is a lot of pressure on our children to be perfect, a lot of expectation on them which is unrealistic, and I know my children have definitely felt the weight of that." One female pastor admitted allowing herself to place expectations on her children due to such pressure, "I did put pressure on my children when they were little and would put great expectations upon myself. And if my child did fail in some area, I would then feel quite guilty and ask myself where did I miss it? I would stress myself if they failed in some area."

Several male spouses of female pastors also discussed the expectations upon them and their clergy wives. One husband of a female minister commented on the tension that the church's expectations placed upon their home life: "The expectations upon her have at times been unreasonable and that has created some tension at times." Another female minister also discussed the challenge of expectations, "I find it hard at times in regard to the expectations people have of me, and the fact that sometimes our family time is interrupted."

The comments above are just a sample of the multiple comments regarding expectations from the interviews I conducted. I could write a whole book on the issues of expectations upon pastors and their families from these interviews. However, the comments above serve to instill an awareness for those who are beginning their ministry/family journey that being engaged in the vocation of ministry will entail expectations, often unrealistic ones, upon the minister and the minister's family. It is important to be aware of the potential of expectations to be imposed upon the family and to develop strategies of managing and mitigating them.

Limited finances

Limited finances were also highly emphasized by many ministers and their spouses when they were asked what the issues were that they wrestled with in their ministry/family journey. A pastor explained, "The issues that we have wrestled with have to do with financial challenges of church planting, where there is often the challenge of finances to do with the church, but also the family financial challenges that correspond with that." Another pastor stated, "The big one all through our early ministry life was probably financial pressure." In regard to the difficulty of finances due to the ministry vocation, Lee and Balswick state, "Quite simply, if they don't have enough money, their financial obligations become burdens and a certain source of family stress."[10]

An extreme illustration of the tension that financial pressure can cause in a minister's home is described in a news report in Christian Century, 2007, as explained in my introduction chapter.[11] The report describes the story of a pastor in Tennessee who was shot dead by his wife in March 2006 after a build-up of stress regarding finances in the family had erupted into an altercation with her pastor/husband.[12] Although this was certainly an extreme case, there are many ministry couples that can assert to the reality of the stress that financial limitations place upon the minister's family and the arguments such pressure generates.

The impact that the financial stresses of ministry had on the wife of a pastor was expressed as follows: "My wife has had to work pretty hard, I think because of the financial stresses and so on. She ended up getting cancer in her tongue even though she has never smoked or drank alcohol." This same pastor, whose children were now adults, lamented, "You've got to be careful from a resources point of view, that you don't put your kids at a disadvantage and that becomes a great challenge for the kids . . . So that's an interesting kind of tension between the call and parenting and providing for your family." Another pastor spoke about the financial loss of their home due to ministry relocation: "Finance has always been a major issue because of the investments into property that we made when we were younger. When we moved from the church where we had been in ministry for eight and a half years we lost everything, and we still haven't been able to recover from that."

10. Lee and Balswick, *Life in a Glasshouse*, 193.
11. "Slain Pastor's Wife Convicted."
12. "Slain Pastor's Wife Convicted."

Several pastors also explained the sacrifices that being in ministry placed upon their family due to limited finances. One pastor commented, "I think that everyone has certain struggles with finances, and we've had seasons when we've been a bit lean when it comes to money, as there have been certain things that we haven't been able to do." A wife and co-pastor with her husband explained the extreme pressure of providing food for their children as pastors, "In regard to finances, we always knew that maybe the situation would be a problem, but when that reality really hits and you don't have food to put on the table that becomes quite a stress." Another pastoral couple also commented regarding the pressure of finances on their family. The pastor/husband stated:

> Finances has always been a big issue as we have been pastoring in a remote area with a small amount of people in our church, therefore it's always been hard to be able to give our children everything that they needed. There were times when our children wouldn't even ask us for things because they knew that we couldn't afford them, so rather than putting more pressure on us they would prefer to not ask for the things that they needed.

Unfortunately, there are many in pastoral leadership who have received a call from God but have left the ministry due to the financial pressure that low income in ministry places on their family members. This is a tragedy, yet a common reality. Having an awareness of financial limitations that many pastors wrestle with is important in order to develop strategic plans to help mitigate such challenges that many ministry families wrestle with.

Competing priorities

Comments regarding having a hierarchy of priorities (with God first, then family, and then ministry) were discussed when the ministers and spouses reflected on their ideals and aspirations. This ideal has developed out of the challenge of competing priorities that are often pulling the minister and spouse in several directions. Douglas W. Boquist, in his dissertation, "Pastoring First Church: A Resource to Equip Pastors in the Spiritual Formation of their Children," illustrates the tension that pastors experience regarding competing priorities with the following illustration:

> A little-known, martyred saint of the Catholic Church, St Hippolytus, a disciple of Irenaeus, was martyred in Rome in the

early third century. The method of his execution is barbaric beyond words, but it does serve as an apt metaphor. His hands were tied to one team of horses, and his feet to another team of horses. He was torn apart when the horses moved in opposite directions."[13]

Boquist states that there are times when pastors feel pulled toward their family moving in one direction, with another, often stronger demand from the church pulling him/her in a different direction.[14] This challenge of competing priorities was emphasized by several participants throughout my interviews, mostly the female participants such as the ministers' wives and female clergy. On pastor's wife lamented, "Whatever was going on in the church would always have to come before the family. So, I think a balance there would have been good. I think a fair bit of pressure was on the family from that side of things." Another minister's spouse stated, "I think in the early years there was a struggle of trying to juggle family and ministry life." A female minister whose husband was also a minister commented, "I think the issues were in regard to those priorities of what God expects and what do our children need. So, at different times this was a wrestle." Another female minister confessed her struggle with competing priorities, "I think 'competing priorities' are an issue when you are torn between wanting to be part of a ministry activity or something that you can go to, and your family commitments . . . and you had to make those decisions, so that pressure is an issue."

The challenge of competing priorities was expressed by many of the ministers and spouses as being a major issue they wrestled with on a regular basis. It is important for ministers and their spouses to be aware of the tendency to lose focus of their family priorities. To assess and realign your priorities regarding your ministry and family on a regular basis is a healthy exercise. We will address this issue further in part 3 when we focus on giving attention to the family as we engage in our call to ministry.

The difficulties of relocation

The difficulties connected with relocation due to ministry were also regularly expressed by those who were interviewed regarding their ministry/family journey. Such difficulties are well worth being aware

13. Boquist, *Pastoring First Church*, 26.
14. Boquist, *Pastoring First Church*, 26.

of, particularly as they relate to the spouse and children of the minister. Regarding the challenge of relocation, a study was conducted in the US regarding relocation stress and coping among clergy and spouses. The results demonstrated that clergy spouses (wives in this study) in the United Methodist Church (USA) experience considerably more relocation stress than clergy, due to eight significant stressors: "an increase in the demand for household labour; a denial of the opportunity to own a home or personalise one according to the family's needs; a disruption of the children's social/friendship networks; assumption by the wives of the responsibility for re-establishing the family within the new community; a disruption of the wives' own employment patterns and career plans; an increase in financial burden due to moving expenses; a disruption of the wives' own informal social support networks; and lack of support from their clergy spouse who is often preoccupied with his own career transition."[15] Marsha Wiggins Frame undertook further research in this regard involving clergy spouses of United Methodist clergy that revealed that pastoral counsellors should address issues such as grief, powerlessness, loneliness, and clergy family reluctance to seek counselling services.[16]

In the profile questions, I inquired regarding how many churches the ministry couple had ministered at up to that time of their ministry. On average, participants indicated that they had ministered in three to four (3.5 on average) different churches over their ministry life. When the average years that the pastors stated they had been in ministry (21.6) is divided by the average amount of churches that pastors had ministered in (3.5), it can be seen that on average pastors have relocated their family every 6.2 years. Regular relocation would certainly have some impact upon the stability and well-being of the family.

When discussing the burden of relocation due to ministry, several ministers and their spouses discussed the price that the family paid due to this challenge. One pastor discussed the financial burden of relocation on his family: "The city to where we have come to created a challenge because to move from the country to the suburbs meant that the price of housing went up by at least $100,000. So, I think that was certainly a difficult thing, the moving costs both financially and emotionally and relationally for our family were significant." Another pastor also discussed this as a burden that they had to bear: "There has also been the challenge

---

15. Frame and Shehan, "Work and Well-Being," 196.
16. Frame, "Relocation and Well-Being," 415.

of relocation, moving churches, which also means moving home, schools, and everything else that goes with that."

Many ministers and their spouses lose meaningful contact with close, supportive friends, due to the relocation. A female minister who ministers alongside her pastor/husband lamented, "Moving several times also created some issues. From a family/life perspective, every time you move you sacrifice your support network and move into established church communities where it already has established loyalties. So, it takes time to create a support network. Yet you need support all the time." Another female pastor and mother added, "Having had to move the family has always been an issue. Taking them away from their friends and family and moving to a remote area has placed pressure upon them, as they have felt quite lonely at times." This is also illustrated in the following pastors' comments, "The kids didn't like to move when we needed to move and that was a challenge. So, mobility was an issue. Taking the kids out of the place that they felt secure in, and my wife was never one to move, she would rather stay in the same place for about 50 years if she could. So that was quite difficult for my wife and for my kids as well." This pastor continued to reiterate the impact of this issue: "Because when the kids were in their teenage years, to actually move them to a small church, when the kids were part of the youth group, was difficult for them." In a time in their life where their friends give them a sense of belonging and an understanding of their value in regard to who they are, a change of location and cultural setting away from the familiarity of their friends and surroundings can make it very difficult for ministers' children to resettle and find their way.

A wife, mother, and pastor exclaimed, "From the ministry/family perspective, with the little girl inside of me, I just wish some people in my church would understand how difficult this has been for us. Just to be understood, you know? You are carrying this load, and you just wish that somebody understood what an impact this has on your family, when you have to change." It is critical that ministers and their spouses have an awareness of the impact that relocation can have upon their spouse and children's lives and find ways to help them navigate through these difficulties.

Balance of ministry and family

Another frequently mentioned issue that affects the family due to being involved in ministry is the balance between ministry and family. In the postmodern world the boundaries between work and family can often be confused, particularly amongst those engaged in ministry. When commentating on the family in general, Viji George refers to the "permeable family" because the boundaries of the family today are much more porous and open than those of the nuclear family.[17]

The female spouses of ministers expressed their awareness that balancing ministry and family life is a big issue. One stated, "The biggest struggle I suppose is to find that right balance between your ministry life and your family life." Another spouse reflected on the small arguments that she and her pastor/husband had in regard to having a day off: "A big issue was navigating a day off, because pastoral ministry is very demanding and so I would have to be very strong. Oftentimes my husband and I would have little tiffs about it because he would take a phone call or visit someone on his day off and I would say 'no' the family is a priority."

The following pastor expressed the difficulty of finding a good balance between their ministry and family responsibilities: "Having that balance between switching off from pastoral mode into more of a family mode and being there for my family, I think that's a challenge." Another pastor also expressed a time when there was an imbalance of ministry and family that affected his family, "I remember when we had three kids under the age of three and it was a lot of work and late nights and not sleeping, and that was one of the flags that we were just doing this ministry thing that just wasn't sustainable, so we changed it."

Marsha Wiggins Frame and Constance Sheehan found that around 25 percent of female clergy find it a challenge to balance work and family life.[18] This difficulty was expressed by a male spouse regarding a female minister: "I feel in the early days she was quite driven and focused in an unbalanced way that meant that the family was neglected due to her passion to serve God. . . . She gave much more of herself to the church than into the family." Another spouse of a female minister stated, "I think that it's something that we all struggled with, to get to be at a place of balance, if there is such a thing. The first calling is to be the parent, and I think that it's something that we all struggled with to get to be at a place of balance."

---

17. George, *Reweaving the Fabric*, 5.
18. Frame and Shehan, "Relationship between Work and Well-Being," 15.

That balance of allowing time for family while remaining engaged in ministry also extends to allowing time to do something for your own well-being away from ministry. A spouse stressed the importance of having the balance of personal time away from ministry responsibilities, "The biggest issue in regard to balancing ministry and family life was time for myself. I was always there with my husband volunteering alongside him and that was a real problem for us. If you don't have that balance with something outside the church it can become too encompassing and can implode upon you." Having an awareness of the challenge to maintain balance between ministry and family and your own well-being is critical in order to ensure the total well-being of the family, including yourself, is attended to.

Ministry demands

Ministry demands are an enormous challenge for ministers and their spouses, especially when they intrude upon the minister's time with the family. Research in the USA regarding the occupation and health of clergy over recent decades has demonstrated that such a role involves many demands and stresses that are not as common for those who are employed in nonchurch work.[19] The changing expectations of the pastor's role in the last 25 years have become increasingly challenging and it is important to understand the growing demands being placed upon clergy with regard to their responsibilities and roles.[20] For many, the result of capitulating to these demands means the minister's family can be severely neglected. Lee and Balswick suggest, "Many clergy marriages need a high degree of marital cohesion to face the onslaught of congregational demands. Where marital cohesion is low, congregational intrusion can act like a wedge to drive a minister and spouse apart."[21] In a study of clergy families by Morris and Blanton, it was found that family boundary intrusion was a significant factor in predicting both clergy and their spouses' reports of marital and parental satisfaction.[22] Therefore, an awareness of the challenges of ministry demands is vital for those who have embarked on the ministry/family journey. As the pastor develops in his/her

---

19. Morris and Blanton, "Influence of Work-Related Stressors," 189.
20. Hagerman, "Occupational Stress and Clergy Support," 83.
21. Lee and Balswick, *Life in a Glasshouse*, 218.
22. Lee and Balswick, *Life in a Glasshouse*, 218.

ministry, these occupational demands and expectations often continue to increase.

In her study of the needs of clergy families, Linda Mileman observes that, "demands of the ministry, unlike almost any other profession, impact the whole family . . . There can be great joy, a sense of fulfillment and purpose, and also loneliness, frustration, and pain."[23] H. B. London, former vice president of Focus on the Family, and Neil B. Wiseman, in their book, *Pastors at Greater Risk*, which resulted from a study of pastors, revealed that 90 percent of the pastors felt they were inadequately trained to cope with ministry demands.[24]

My research revealed that one female spouse often felt her clergy husband seemed to be consumed with ministry demands, which affected the family in a negative way: "I think my husband would say that he was too involved in his mind, mentally. That he didn't put enough attention on the special things that the children were involved in during their early years." Cynthia Wilson and Carol Darling add, "Perhaps the best hope for dealing with the stressors of clergy life and their impact on clergy children is that clergy need to become more aware of how the demands of their jobs affect their families."[25]

In light of these challenges, respondents provided some insightful comments based on their own life experiences and observations. One pastor explained, "I think for me the challenge is that in regard to church life there are constantly people that have their own challenges and that want you to be available for them all of the time. So, they tend to demand you to rush to them and leave your family or neglect your family at times." Several female pastors also expressed their challenges that ministry demands imposed upon the family. One female minister explained, "sometimes you're really crazy busy where people have got demands on you." In this regard another female minister explained her strategy to handle such demands, "Due to the demands that the church can place on us in our roles, I've had to develop strong boundaries to stay within my call and not drift from that, and that's been the linchpin in keeping family life and church life in balance."

With all the demands pressing in on pastors, sometimes their families feel they don't always get the attention they need. Pastors! Many

---

23. Hileman, "Unique Needs of Protestant Clergy Families," 121.
24. London, and Wiseman, *Pastors at Greater Risk*, 20.
25. Wilson and Darling, "Understanding Stress and Life Satisfaction," 140.

churches may have had pastors before you, and will have pastors after you, but your families only have one husband and wife and your kids have only one mum and dad. It's so important you understand the issues at hand and not allow the demands to rob you of a flourishing family life whilst fulfilling your fruitful ministry life.

Church conflict

Another challenge that ministers and their spouses identified was experiencing and dealing with conflict in the church and the impact that had on their families. There has been an increased discussion amongst clergy regarding conflict issues. Ministry-training institutions and denominational leaders are including conflict management courses for the benefit of their pastors and leaders. Conflict between a church and its pastor, whether large or small, almost always results in a break in the relationships between the two. The results are often destructive, with both pastor and congregations suffering serious loss to their reputations and credibility.[26]

Unfortunately, the family of these pastors often become wounded in these conflicts, and as such are left with a bitter perception regarding the perpetrators of such conflicts and often resent the church or the ministry itself. A pastor from my interviews explained why his son resented the church: "When a child sees the demands that the church makes on the pastor and his wife, and some of the hurts that come as a result of small church politics and that sort of behavior, it's possible for resentment to occur."

Boquist speaks of the issue of tolerance of toxicity. "It is rare that a pastor resigns a church because the majority of the people want him or her to leave."[27] It takes a very small number of people to make life so difficult for a pastor that he or she wants to move on. It has been Boquist's observation that usually no more than seven people are responsible for a pastor prematurely leaving a church.[28] Boquist poses that "religious institutions are the worst offenders at encouraging immaturity and irresponsibility. In church after church, some member is passive-aggressively holding the whole system hostage, and no one wants to fire him or force her to leave

---

26. Hagerman, "Occupational Stress and Clergy Support," 98.
27. Boquist, *Pastoring First Church*, 75.
28. Boquist, *Pastoring First Church*, 75.

because it wouldn't be "the Christian thing to do."[29] In a mistaken notion of Christian love and patience, churches tolerate angry people who actively sabotage the pastor's work. It only takes a few saboteurs, when left unconfronted, to undermine a pastor's ministry.[30]

William Hulme states that religious professionals are the only professionals whose job includes a built-in community.[31] Yet the seemingly comfortable church community creates its own set of tensions for the clergy. Conflicts with members and conflicts between members flare up continuously.[32] Those who are really angry at God find a logical scapegoat in the pastor's symbolic role because it is easier and safer to attack someone who is tangibly human than to attack the Ruler of the universe.[33] In regard to clergy and congregational conflict, Hagerman concludes that: "there are some churches and congregations that are abusive; there are some pastors who are also abusive to churches; and there is an evil force causing conflict within the church, which must be faced and dealt with, using spiritual and other resources."[34] The key for pastors is to discern where the conflict is initiating from (i.e. hurting people, aggressive pastors, misunderstandings, spiritual attacks, etc.) and then respond quickly in order to eliminate or minimize the potential damage such conflicts can produce.

Vivian Grice discovered that the kinds of church problems that caused church conflict with the pastor were: difficult and obstructionist people; division over vision and direction; church politics; conflict caused by pastor being a change agent; church splits; and criticism by church people of the pastor's spouse or child.[35] Potentially, the pastor's children are exposed more to both the positives and the negatives of congregational life than the typical child in the congregation.[36] Such conflicts can affect the ministry family and lead to an increased frequency of

---

29. Boquist, *Pastoring First Church*, 76.
30. Boquist, *Pastoring First Church*, 76.
31. Hulme, *Managing Stress in Ministry*, 5.
32. Hulme, *Managing Stress in Ministry*, 5.
33. Hulme, *Managing Stress in Ministry*, 5.
34. Hagerman, "Occupational Stress and Clergy Support," 104.
35. Grice, "Pastor's Kids," 67.
36. Grice, "Pastor's Kids," 68.

relocations, isolation and peer dislocation, and disillusionment due to such church conflict.[37]

In my interviews, church conflict was stressed as quite a painful issue that participants and their families experienced. Several pastors described the challenges of dealing with church conflict and its impact upon their family. One pastor described the pain that church conflict inflicted upon his sons:

> We faced what I would only describe as a major betrayal within the ranks of our leadership. It's now behind us, we came out the other side, the congregation was minimally affected, but it did take a significant toll on my wife and me. Through that journey, even though our boys during that time were married and had left home and had their own family, it affected them big time to see Mum and Dad going through what we went through. I know that they had to deal with some anger issues over the people that were the instigators of that.

London and Wiseman's studies discovered that over 40 percent of the pastors reported serious conflict with a parishioner at least once a month.[38] This leaves pastors physically tired, spiritually weary, and even distant from God. Thus, they cannot properly minister or connect with their flock.[39] The difficulties of dealing with church conflict were also identified throughout my research as a ministry-imposed challenge for the children of ministers. The reality is that pastors will face congregational conflict within their church from time to time. An awareness of this reality should motivate ministers and their spouses to prepare themselves regarding how they will respond to such conflict and how they will protect their spouse and children from the damage that church conflict can inflict upon their family.

Small-church challenges

The majority of those that responded to the invitation to participate in my doctoral research were pastors from small- to medium-size churches, which represents the majority of churches overall. The larger and megachurches are more the exception rather than the rule, although I certainly

---

37. Grice, "Pastor's Kids," 120.
38. London and Wiseman, *Pastors at Greater Risk*, 20.
39. London and Wiseman, *Pastors at Greater Risk*, 20.

don't want to downplay the value that such churches bring to the kingdom in the twenty-first century.

Small-church issues are usually associated with the lack of resources that are available in churches their size. Issues such as the reality that some pastors can't be paid full-time due to the church's limited finances and therefore need to approach their ministry in a bivocational capacity are quite common. One pastor's spouse explained how she decided to work more in her employment role due to this issue: "When we moved to the small church, I decided that I would work more so that my husband could put more time into the church, as he wasn't being paid full time in the church." Her pastor/husband also commented on this issue in their small church: "in a small church there is not a lot of finances available to pay the pastor." Another pastor also commented on the need to be bivocational due to the limited finances in small churches: "One issue is finances, because there were times where we pastored in small churches, so it challenged our financial situation. But we were able to resolve that by getting jobs, so I decided that I would find other work while I was also working for the church in order to pay the bills."

Another small-church issue that many pastors and spouses had to contend with was the lack of youth in their small churches. The same pastor that mentioned the challenge of limited finances also commented on the painful journey of their children wandering from the faith: "It was a painful journey for us. In a small church there was no positive peer pressure for them. It was a pretty tough time for me and my wife running the church, and our teenagers were trying to find their way." A female pastor also discussed this small-church challenge: "The fact that there is no youth in the church of their age meant they didn't feel like they were a part of the church." Another pastor commented that it was hard moving to a small church when his children were teenagers: "I think if I was going to do a small church again I would have done it when the kids were younger, rather than when they were in their teenage years. Because when the kids were in their teenage years, to actually move them to a small church, when the kids were part of a good size youth group was difficult for them." The challenge of limited numbers and resources in the youth or children's ministries in small churches is quite substantial and certainly has an effect on the pastor's family.

Another small-church challenge is over-familiarity due to the limited amount of people in the church. One pastor mentioned this as a challenge for his family: "The location itself where we have been pastoring has been a challenge, as it's been so far away from anywhere and so remote that it's been hard to have good fellowship with anyone else apart from those in our small church, and this in itself has created problems of familiarity." Another pastor suggested such familiarity led to small-church politics: "There are the demands that the church makes on the pastor and his wife, and some of the hurts that come as a result of small-church politics." The spouse of this minister stressed her sense of isolation and lack of support as a pastor's wife in their small church: "When we were in a small church there wasn't a great network for pastors' wives. You had your regional meetings and that was about it. And I was working at the time, so it was hard to get to any meetings during the day . . . our pastoral experience was that we walked the walk very much alone."

Such small-church issues such as financial challenges, lack of numbers and resources for youth and children's ministries, and familiarity and isolation are realities for those that pastor small churches. An awareness of these challenges and a strategy to mitigate such challenges will serve pastors and their families in small churches (of which the majority of churches are) well.

Chapter Summary

An awareness of the ministry-related issues that ranged from issues such as time constraints to small-church issues were expressed. My research revealed that all participants encountered similar issues throughout their ministry/family journeys; no one was exempt from these realities. However, there seemed to be a greater awareness of these issues expressed by those that were satisfied with their children's spiritual outlook than those that were not satisfied. Such an awareness alerted and motivated the ministers and spouses to give attention to their family to help mitigate such challenges to help their families to flourish while they were engaged in ministry.

Summary List of Issues of the Ministry/Family Journey

Church-Related Issues

Time constraints
Limited finances
The difficulties of relocation
Ministry demands
Small-church challenges

Unrealistic expectations
Competing priorities
Balance of ministry and family
Church conflict

These were identified as the main issues that participants revealed throughout the semistructured interviews that were conducted.

Personal Reflection

List some other church-related issues you are aware of and consider how you plan to navigate them for the sake of your ministry/family journey.

Chapter 5

Family-Related Burdens

Family-Related Issues

ADDED TO THE CHALLENGES that affect the family in a general sense as discussed in the previous chapter, such as time constraints, limited finances, church conflict, and the like, ministers and their spouses also discussed issues that affect family members in a more personal way. These issues were identified in my research as family-related issues. A resolute awareness of these family-related issues would strengthen relationships within the family, as an understanding of the challenges the individual family members are confronted with would motivate pastors and spouses to give attention and support to help work through and overcome such challenges. The most frequently emphasized challenges will now be considered.

Impact on children

Many of the ministry couples I interviewed as a part of my research indicated their children had been impacted as a result of their involvement in ministry. There has been extensive research undertaken regarding the negative effect on children who have grown up in a clergy home. One such study was conducted by Grey Matter Research & Consulting (formerly Ellison Research) of Phoenix, Arizona. Pastors were asked about the health of their family and the pressures associated with being the family of a minister.[1] The study found that the vast majority of Protestant clergy believe there is additional pressure on pastors' families. Ninety-one percent also agree "There is extra pressure being the child of a minister."[2] Some further research found that life satisfaction of clergy children as adults is directly related to their life satisfaction and stress levels of living as an adolescent in a clergy home.[3]

Unfortunately, there are some challenging issues that children of ministers have to contend with as a result of the ministry vocation of their parent(s). There is often the pressure for children to project themselves in a way that doesn't necessarily feel authentic. One female pastor emphasized, "In general, I have observed the negative impact of requiring ministry children to wear masks." She continued, stating that, "sometimes there is a lot of pressure on our children to be perfect and a lot of expectation on them which is unrealistic. I know my children have definitely felt the weight of that." Other issues also affected the children of pastors negatively where one pastor explained the impact that going to a regular yearly conference had on his son: "Our second son's birthday always falls during Hillsong conference week, and we would always be at the Hillsong conference for his birthday. He never really felt that he was able to celebrate his birthday on his birthday, it had to be either before we went away or after we got back." These very real and heartfelt comments reflect just a few of the comments that ministers and their spouses expressed throughout the interviews of my research.

Challenges with children

Many Christians and non-Christians alike have challenges with their children. However, when pastoring a church there seems to be a greater focus on the pastor's children and the outcomes of their lives. Such focus can add pressure to the pastor, their spouse, and their children, and can result in extra challenges. The issues regarding challenges with the children of the minister was brought up many times. A male pastor who was a children's pastor spoke of the resentment his two sons felt as a result of his ministry role: "They would be hanging around till late, especially if we had a camp and we had to put the camp gear away, and they were

---

1. Grey Matter Research, "Pastors and the Health of their Family."
2. Grey Matter Research, "Pastors and the Health of their Family," 7.
3. Wilson and Darling, "Understanding Stress and Life Satisfaction," 136.

still there after all of the other kids had gone home with their parents. So those extra responsibilities on our children were an issue as the kids began to resent having to hang around later than they wanted to." Unfortunately, both of this pastor's sons (now in their adult years) no longer attend church or follow the faith of their father and mother.

Among the issues that were brought up in my interviews were their children struggling to find their own way and finding it hard to embrace the faith of their ministry parents. These parents also brought up the painful journey they personally experienced as a result of this. A pastor who experienced the painful journey of their children wandering from the faith explains: "It was a painful journey for us. In a small church there was no positive peer pressure for them. It was a pretty tough time for me and my wife running the church, and our teenagers were trying to find their way." In regard to the comments that their children found it difficult to embrace the faith of their ministry parents, participants who had children that were no longer attending church or following the Lord mentioned this issue much more often than those whose children were still attending church and growing in their faith in God. Such challenges are important for those who are just starting out in ministry to be aware of in order to determine ways that will mitigate the prospect of these challenges with their children. We will consider the challenges that ministers' children have to contend with on a deeper level in a further chapter that focuses solely on ministers' children.

Impact on wife

Throughout this book I have tried to be gender-neutral as much as possible as there was an increase in the participation of female ministers in the latter part of the twentieth century which has continued into the twenty-first century. However, when it comes to analyzing the responses of those who participated in my research interviews, there was a clear concern by the male ministers regarding the impact that the ministry had upon their wives, whereas the amount of comments from the female ministers regarding the impact of the ministry upon their husbands was minimal. Therefore, the responses regarding the impact upon the wife of the minister warrants some definite consideration. As with the minister's children, I have devoted an entire chapter regarding the minister's marriage and spouse later in this book. However, some of the participants' comments regarding the impact upon the wife of the minister necessitates some further discussion in this chapter regarding having an awareness of family-related challenges that ministers and their spouses wrestle with throughout their ministry/family journey.

As both the male and female participants told their stories about their ministry/family journeys, the negative impact that the ministry had on the wife of the ministry couple was frequently identified. A pastor discussed the weight of the ministry that his wife has carried: "My wife sees and feels firsthand the blows that fall upon her husband, yet she has no escape; no way to resolve what she is privy to. The pain, frustration and hurt she feels on my behalf is often crushing, yet cannot finally be shared or resolved." Another pastor spoke about the loneliness his wife sometimes feels: "[T]here are times when I wish my wife would go out with some of the girls in the church, but that doesn't always happen. There have been times that she has shared where she has felt lonely." In Boquist's study, one pastor's wife states, "I'm supposed to listen, smile, listen, bring lots of food to pot lucks, listen, go to all baby showers, listen, help in vacation Bible school, listen, entertain, listen, go visiting with my husband, and listen. But no one wants to listen to me!"[4]

A pastor's wife also expressed the challenge of people imposing themselves on her because she was the pastor's wife: "I'm not pastoral, that is not my gifting. My gifting is more with administration. But as a pastor's wife, I find the challenge of people imposing themselves upon me and my time to be quite a challenge." Norman Blaikie, when speaking about the demands that are placed upon pastors' wives by their congregations, states that there can hardly be another occupation in which a man's wife is as conspicuous to his clients and in which there is the same degree of opportunity to place demands upon her.[5] I have presented just a few examples of the impact upon pastors' wives due to their husband's ministry role. However, there are multiple things that impact their lives which we will discuss further in the next chapter regarding the minister's marriage and spouse.

The importance of male ministers being aware of how their wives are impacted (mostly negatively) due to their ministry role cannot be overstated. When comparing those who stated that all of their children are still attending church and following the Lord with those who stated

---

4. Boquist, *Pastoring First Church*, 75.
5. Blaikie, *Plight of the Australian Clergy*, 183.

they have at least one child no longer attending church and following the faith of their parents, there was evidence of a contrasting awareness between the two groups. Those who stated that all of their children are still attending church and following the Lord seemed to express a greater awareness of the negative impact the vocation of ministry had upon their wife compared to the frequency of comments from those who stated they have at least one child no longer attending church and following the faith of their parents. Awareness in this regard leads to attention to the needs of the pastor's wife.

Care for spouse

The challenges regarding the impact upon the pastor's spouse due to ministry involvement was specifically focused upon the female members of the pastoral ministry couple. In regard to this issue of care for the spouse, focus is not so much about the gender, but rather about the spouse of the minister, whether male or female. Participants in my research stated that one of the issues they wrestled with in their ministry/family journey was in regard to having adequate care for their spouse. The assumption is normally that the majority of spouses are female; however, several comments were related to caring for the male spouses of female pastors.

Several female pastors commented on the impact their involvement in ministry had upon their male spouses. One female pastor spoke about the uncertainty her husband experienced at a function she was leading:

> I feel that there was one time when my husband felt a little out of the loop when we are at a function that I was particularly involved with and was organizing. He was conscious that he didn't want to disappoint me in regard to how he was to behave at that particular function. Therefore, he placed expectations upon himself that created more pressure than was necessary, because the limelight was pretty much on me because I had organized this event.

Another female pastor spoke about the burden her husband carried for the family on her behalf due to her ministry role: "I would go alone to ministry dinners after church events. But my husband couldn't come with me. . . . He would take the kids home, because it was better to do it that way for our children. So that caused separation at times, but I think for our children it was a right thing to do and helped them cope." A female itinerant pastor also spoke about the price her husband paid financially so she could fulfill her ministry: "My husband supports me being in ministry by managing his own business, because very few women are able to manage a sustainable income as an itinerant." Each of these female ministers were aware of the price their husbands paid for them to fulfill their ministry, and several stated the need for their spouses to also receive some support as the spouse of the minister.

The female spouse of a male minister stressed her lack of support as a pastor's spouse. "We didn't have any support. When we were going through the really hard times, we didn't have anybody. My husband always had people that he could go to, guys that he knew in ministry, but I didn't have that, which means that you carry the load alone." In light of these realities, there is a great need for ministers' spouses to receive specialized support for their ministry/family journey. The story of the participant above who had no real support in the midst of their own ministry/family crisis is multiplied throughout the ministry world. Michael Morris and Priscilla Blanton discovered that clergy and their spouses find it difficult to obtain relief from stress due to the absence of social support, with feelings of loneliness and isolation by clergy families being a common experience.[6] The importance of being aware that your spouse also needs support, rather than them just giving support to your ministry and support to the many other congregational members of the church that need her/his support, is critical for safeguarding the spiritual well-being of the family while fulfilling the ministry call. Seeking such support for their spouse is not an option for those in ministry. It is the responsibility of the minister to ensure their spouse receives support that brings both joy and comfort for their ministry/family journey.

Impact on marriage

The negative impact that their involvement in ministry had upon their marriage was also discussed throughout the interviews. Morris and Blanton state it is almost impossible to separate the occupation of the clergy from the clergy person's marriage and family.[7] David and Vera Mace state that "the impact of decline in family and marital quality is not unique to secular society; it is also taking its toll upon those in the church and also

---

6. Morris and Blanton, "Influence of Work-Related Stressors," 189.
7. Morris and Blanton, "Predictors of Family Functioning," 27.

those within clergy families."[8] Therefore, an awareness of these challenges is vital for those who are engaged in the ministry/family journey.

Several pastors and spouses expressed how they felt their involvement in ministry had impacted upon their marriage. One female pastor whose husband was also a pastor explained, "As far as our marriage, I think that the ministry has made us tired at different times. So rather than being refreshed or really enjoying each other's company, we've actually been exhausted in each other's company. . . . I don't know if there's always been a joy there. It's not as if there was ever a time that we thought it would end, but it wasn't always super-duper happy." Another female pastor who was married to a pastor expressed her awareness of how the ministry could negatively affect their marriage and how they endeavored to turn the tide in that regard: "I think that we had seen and heard of many casualties where the couple in ministry had marriages that had fallen apart or marriages that were still together but only were just existing and not flourishing. So, we said that we wanted to change the tide of that. We don't want that to happen with our situation." This pastor and wife continued: "So we would be investing into our lives, into each other, and into the church. So, after twenty or thirty years we didn't want to be a trainwreck, so we set some strong frameworks in place when we started out. So that's kind of evolved and changed according to the different seasons."

Two female pastors who had husbands that were not employed in ministry spoke about how they had to be sensitive to their husbands in regard to their ministry role within the church. One female minister explained, "I think that in the early stages it was difficult. Being a pastor in the church and being in leadership in the church where my husband actually came under my leadership, and then when you come home, and your husband then leads you as your husband. There's been some challenges in that because my husband is a strong choleric and I also am a strong choleric. So, we've had to battle those issues over the years, but I think as time has gone on the balance has become better." Another female minister also expressed a similar scenario: "I think it's been challenging for my husband, I think at times he found it challenging because often the direction would come to me from the senior pastor, and then I would find myself having to tell him what to do as he was a lay leader in the church. That didn't always go down so well." A research study conducted

---

8. Mace and Mace, *What's Happening to Clergy Marriages?*, 100.

by Grey Matter Research & Consulting found that 94 percent agree with the statement, "There is extra pressure being married to a minister."[9]

As the ministers and spouses from those who were satisfied with their children's spiritual outlook told their stories about their ministry/family journey, an awareness of the impact the ministry had on their marriage was mentioned often. However, those who stated they weren't satisfied with their children's spiritual outlook or had at least one child no longer attending church or following the Lord seemed to display less of an awareness in this regard. The results from my research confirm that a resolute awareness of the impact of the ministry upon their marriage is vitally important for ministers and their spouses who desire to be fruitful in their ministry and flourish in their family.

Being present with the family

Another issue that directly affected the family was the issue of not being present when they were with their family. Many ministers spoke of their experiences that when they were with their family physically, they struggled to give their family their complete attention due to their mind and thoughts still being consumed by ministry concerns. One female minister who was also the senior pastor of her church described this challenge:

> I think the challenge is having your head full of so many responsibilities that you're not present sometimes. So, you come home, or someone texts you with an issue, or you're thinking about how you can deal with the problem in your leadership team, and so your mind is quite full. So, I think that that's been a challenge for me to turn off from ministry and responsibilities and has affected our family, definitely.

Another female pastor who was also a senior pastor of a church explained, "There are times where physically you might already be home, but emotionally you've already checked out. So maybe I wish that I could have somehow pulled back so that my family didn't get the leftovers. I think I would at times be at home with the family, yet in my mind was dealing with some of the stuff that I had to deal with at church."

In one interview, a female spouse often felt her clergy husband seemed to be consumed with ministry demands that severely affected their family: "I think my husband would say that he was too involved

---

9. Grey Matter Research, "Pastors and the Health of their Family," 7.

in his mind, mentally. . . . He was always thinking about the next thing rather than living in the moments when the children were growing up." This spouse's husband, who was a pastor, admitted he lost focus on his children while he was engaging with the challenges of his ministry: "I remain deeply regretful that I was so often present physically, but absent from their day-to-day lives. While each of them still has a faith in God, it may explain their present disenchantment with the experience of Church." This pastor and his spouse acknowledged in the interview that only one of their four children regularly attended church at this time, due to being affected by these unfortunate experiences of overfocus on the church and not being present with his children.

Another male pastor expressed this same challenge: "Having that balance between switching off from pastoral mode into more of a family mode, and being present for my family, I think that's a challenge." Yet still another male pastor struggled with this issue. "There have been times when I've been with my children and wife physically, but in my mind, I was somewhere else. The children have sensed this at times, that they haven't had my full attention, that I haven't always been present with them even though I was physically with them."

Later in my interviews, several ministers and their spouses expressed that being more present with their family as a key initiative was something they would do differently if they had their time over again. Comments like "I try to be present when I am with them" were common, particularly from the female ministers. The importance of having an awareness of being present with the family and giving them focused attention is imperative for those who desire to see their family flourish as they pursue and fulfill their ministry responsibilities.

Family intrusions and lack of privacy

There are times throughout the ministry/family journey where the minister's family feel they are owned by the church. As participants discussed the issues that can be imposed upon them due to the ministry vocation, issues such as intrusions into the home by church members as well as a lack of privacy were both mentioned. Family intrusions and lack of privacy are very real issues that tend to inhibit the private lives of the ministry family. Lee and Balswick affirm that "the boundaries between the congregation and clergy family are often too defuse, which is usually not the case in other professional occupations."[10] When a group of clergy families were asked to describe the greatest disadvantages of being in the ministry, their answers came down to five broad recurring themes, and a lack of privacy for the family was one of these five issues.[11] Clearly there is a need to address the concerns of the family intrusions and lack of privacy with tangible resources.

Blaikie's research also demonstrates that many clergy families experienced extreme strain due to the physical and relational context in which the clergyman works.[12] Factors such as disrupted routines and lack of privacy were identified as some of the difficulties that Australian clergy families encountered.[13] In regard to this challenge that female spouses have to deal with, Blaikie states: "Some wives feel they lack adequate privacy, either because of the location of the house beside the church, or because it is regularly used for meetings and functions."[14] A female pastor whose husband was also a pastor spoke about the challenge of letting too much of their ministry activity overflow and intrude into their home. "We've been involved with people with many needs over the years and I think we may have gone a bit far with that by bringing too many people into our home. I don't know, but I think that the kids had to pay a price for that I guess."

David and Vera Mace emphasize that the lack of privacy is a real difficulty for ministry families, particularly for families who live in a manse or other property close to the church grounds.[15] In my research interviews, a pastor whose family lived in the church manse spoke about an intrusive instance where a board member came into the house (manse) without knocking while this pastor's wife was getting changed. She was the only person in the house, so she had left her bedroom door open while she was changing, only to be greatly shocked and embarrassed when this male board member saw her. When the board member was questioned as to why he didn't knock on the door before entering the manse, the board member explained (without apologizing for his intrusion) that the house belonged to the church and he as a board member didn't need to knock.

10. Lee and Balswick, *Life in a Glasshouse*, 75.
11. Lee and Balswick, *Life in a Glasshouse*, 191.
12. Blaikie, *Plight of the Australian Clergy*, 184.
13. Blaikie, *Plight of the Australian Clergy*, 183–84.
14. Blaikie, *Plight of the Australian Clergy*, 161, 184.
15. Mace and Mace, *What's Happening to Clergy Marriages?*, 40.

Another pastor's wife had a similar intrusive experience into her home, which happened to be the church manse on the church property. In this case she was the wife of a youth pastor who was paid by the church two days per week for his services to the church. His pay was the value of the rent of the church manse in exchange for the two days that he worked for the church, therefore no money exchanged hands. Consequently, his two days plus voluntary hours in the church added up to around fifty hours per week. There were several experiences in the case of this couple's first ministry appointment that helped shaped how they would treat their ministry team members in their future ministry.

In one instance, on a very hot day in which the youth pastor was working in his secular employment, he dropped in to see his wife and very young children during his lunch break. Being such a hot day and the fact that the manse didn't have air-conditioning, he suggested to his wife that he would drop her off at the nearby indoor air-conditioned shopping complex which was much cooler for her and the children. He would then pick them up from there on his way home from work. His wife quickly changed the youngest child (a five-month-old baby girl) and headed out to this much cooler place along with her two-and-a-half-year-old son. She had to rush out the door so that her husband could get back to his secular employment on time. In her rush, she left a wet nappy (diaper) on the change mat which was on the floor.

While she was at the indoor shopping mall, the senior pastor of the church decided to show someone through the manse without warning the youth pastor's wife that he was coming. As he had his own key to the manse, he showed these people through the house and there was the wet nappy (diaper) on the change mat where the youth pastor's wife had changed her baby. This youth pastor's wife was embarrassed by this intrusion into the privacy of her home. Rather than apologizing for the intrusion into the youth pastor's private home and apologizing to the youth pastor's wife for invading her privacy while she was out, the senior pastor counselled the youth pastor about how the youth pastor's wife needed to improve in regard to her housekeeping habits if he was to become a pastor of significance in the future.

Without naming this youth pastor who is now a senior minister, and who has become quite significant in his ministry, as has his wife in her ministry, they both learned greatly from this experience. Along with many other lessons they learned from this their first ministry appointment, the importance of respecting the privacy of their ministry team members has become very much a part of their ministry team focus. This couple decided to never accept a ministry role that demanded that they live in a church manse again. This is also a lesson for pastors, churches, and board members that have church manses to not intrude on the privacy of the pastor who lives in the church manse. This manse is also the pastor and his family's private home.

This now-senior pastor spoke of an experience years later where he and his wife had applied for a mortgage to purchase their own home, as they decided to never live in a church-owned manse again. The treasurer of the church told this pastor that as the church was paying their salary, therefore the money to pay the mortgage came from the church offerings, therefore their home belonged to the church. The pastor replied by suggesting that the treasurer's employer must also own his house as his employer paid the salary that paid the treasurer's mortgage.

This issue of having a lack of privacy was regularly raised by participants in my research. Apart from the family intrusions and lack of privacy due to living in the church manse, there were also other instances that were emphasized in regard to the desire for ministry family members to have their private space respected. The cry for privacy of one ministry wife who works alongside her husband in a small country town was passionately emphasized. "A big challenge is that there is really nothing to do in our country town. So, if I go out for a coffee or wherever I go, people are there and people feel they have a right to you at any time. So, for my sanity I just need some space to do something else away from the church, and away from the people, but I don't get that time to feed my social self."

Another intrusive issue has arisen due to the invention of the mobile phone. One pastor explained, "I was in another city with my middle son when he was competing in a sports event. During the first two days, my phone just wouldn't stop ringing, so it got to the point where he complained and walked away from me." A pastor's wife also bemoaned the intrusion into family time that can arise due to people's access to the pastor via the telephone. "People would ring up at any time and ask my husband to come and pray for them at all times, and he would go racing off rather than just praying with them over the phone or asking to come the next day."

In an innovative line of research in 2003, Lee et al. applied family boundary ambiguity to experiences of intrusion between clergy families and their congregations in the United States.[16] Lee proposed that a unique type of boundary ambiguity exists when external family boundaries are intruded upon by extrafamilial systems, and discovered that boundary ambiguity related to the intrusiveness of congregational demands was associated with clergy members' reports of well-being, burnout, and life satisfaction.[17] In a study of clergy families by Morris and Blanton in 2001, it was found that family boundary intrusion was a significant factor in predicting both clergy and their spouses' reports of marital and parental satisfaction.[18] The findings of Hill et al. confirm that such intrusions interrupt the privacy of pastors' lives and families and negatively affect the quality of life for clergy families.[19]

Being aware of the potential for the church and congregation to intrude into the privacy of their home and family life is critical regarding the health and well-being of the pastor, the spouse, and their children. Many who lack an awareness in this regard lack the capability to be able to give attention to their family and protect their family's privacy from the intrusive demands of the congregation and community in which they live.

Personal challenges

Participants in my research expressed some personal issues they wrestled with in their ministry/family journey. Some of the major personal challenges that were emphasized were the issue of self-comparison with other pastors' wives, the myopic lifestyle that is at times attached to being in ministry, getting enough rest and relaxation, making personal sacrifices, health issues, and not always feeling personally fulfilled in the ministry role. A pastor's wife stated the following in regard to self-comparison with other pastors' wives: "Another thing is that I, and I think most women, do the self-comparison. I used to look at people like my senior pastor's wife and other pastors' wives and compare myself and feel less than I was because I felt that I didn't compare or match up to them."

In regard to personal fulfillment, a male minister explained, "At the close of each and every day, I could never feel that I had completed the

---

16. Lee and Iverson-Gilbert, "Demand, Support and Perception," 249.
17. Lee and Iverson-Gilbert, "Demand, Support and Perception," 249.
18. Lee and Iverson-Gilbert, "Demand, Support and Perception," 249.
19. Hill et al., "Understanding Boundary-Related Stress," 147.

work and to find that 'rest' in the Lord so necessary to really hearing his voice.... While I am not unique, I found that I do need to see some tangible evidence of my efforts for the day." This minister continued, "Emotional exhaustion rather than physical exhaustion meant that sleep was rarely sound or refreshing." Many pastors have difficulty in understanding what their role is, due often to the ambiguity of their job descriptions. They also find it difficult to separate this often-ambiguous role as ministers from who they are as people and family members. Research also suggests ministers experience higher levels of guilt over family issues than other groups.[20] The challenge also comes when clergy are also faced with the very real dangers of secondary traumatization in the line of professional duty, which can significantly alter the life direction of a minister.[21]

Having appropriate support structures in place is a very important element for ministers on their journeys. Research has found that poor support networks are a major reason ministers face burnout.[22] Social isolation and interpersonal or relational difficulties are major reasons for high levels of anxiety in clergy.[23] Yet, Trihub et al. found that many denominations provide insufficient support and training for clergy regarding personal and health issues.[24] Having an awareness and understanding of the minister's personal challenges enhances the possibility of a healthy ministry function and flourishing ministry family.

Bringing church issues home

Another issue that directly affected the family was bringing church matters home to the family. A male pastor admitted this was a mistake he and his ministry wife made in regard to their family: "My wife and I would be discussing something at home that probably was in earshot of the kids at times, and probably that issue at times was something that we would regret in hindsight that we did do that at times, and brought the ministry into the home a little bit too much."

---

20. Rickner and Tan, "Psychopathology, Guilt, Perfectionism," 29.
21. Hendron et al., "Unseen Cost," 61.
22. Grosch and Olsen, "Clergy Burnout," 619.
23. Trihub et al., "Denominational Support for Clergy Mental Health," 101.
24. Trihub et al., "Denominational Support for Clergy Mental Health," 102.

A female pastor also lamented the fact that she didn't define the boundaries between the church and home, "So you come home and someone texts you with an issue, or you're thinking about how you can deal with the problem in your leadership team, so your mind is quite full. I think that that's affected the family, and so that's been a challenge for me to turn off from ministry responsibilities." Her husband also commented on this issue concerning the church/home foray:

> It's hard for her not to bring it home. In a different sense she is not bringing home administrative stuff or reports or anything like that, but she was bringing home the relationships. She was bringing home the issues and the troubles or whatever that had been heaped upon her during the day. Bringing that stuff home affected us all because the problems at the church would come home and they would become a part of our life.

Another husband of a female pastor mentioned his ministry-ordained wife struggled with the same issue:

> There were great responsibilities that she had with the long hours and the frustrations that she experienced. It is probably good that she is not here listening to me, because even though she would say, 'No I didn't bring that home,' yes, she did. The kids and I would hear her coming up the steps of the house that we were in, and you knew by the time she got to the top of the stairs whether we would be in for a good night or not at times. There were definitely times of spill-over of her ministry into the family atmosphere.

A pastor made the following statement: "You've got to keep the church issues out of your home, and certainly not around the dining room table either." Another minister whose children were still in the church made a clear emphasis in regard to protecting his children from unhealthy church issues: "We would never talk church business or politics in front of the children." In a study of adult pastors' children conducted by Kimberley Strange and Lori Shepherd, it was revealed that, amongst other things, if their parents had maintained boundaries between church and home, they were more likely to be religiously committed.[25] My research revealed that those who focused on keeping their home as the family home, rather than an extension of the church office or church

---

25. Strange and Sheppard, "Evaluations of Clergy Children," 53.

auditorium, were more likely to enjoy a flourishing family life as they fulfilled their ministry calling.

Chapter Summary

An awareness of family-related challenges due to involvement in the ministry was considered throughout this chapter. Family-related issues such as the challenges with the children, bringing church issues home, family intrusions and lack of privacy, and the needs of the minister's spouse were explored. The research revealed that all participants encountered similar issues throughout their ministry/family journeys; no one was exempt from these realities as such. However, there seemed to be a greater awareness of these issues expressed by those who were satisfied with their children's spiritual outlook than from those who were not. An awareness of these issues alerts the participants to respond and give attention to their families so they can flourish while they are engaged in ministry.

Summary List of Issues of the Ministry/Family Journey

Family-Related Issue

Impact on children	Challenges with children
Impact on wife	Care for spouse
Impact on marriage	Being present with the family
Family intrusions & lack of privacy	Personal challenges
Bringing church issues home	

Personal Reflection

List some other church-related issues you are aware of and consider how you plan to navigate them for the sake of your ministry/family journey.

Chapter 6

The Ministry Couple

IN HER FASCINATING STUDY of the needs of clergy families, Linda Mileman observes that, "demands of the ministry, unlike almost any other profession, impact the whole family . . . There can be great joy, a sense of fulfillment and purpose, and also loneliness, frustration, and pain."[1] This chapter brings focus to the ministry couple and observes how each spouse handles the ministry/family journey. In a later chapter we will examine some of the positive things that ministers and their spouses discussed in regard to what they did that works for their marriage while engaged in the ministry. In this chapter I want to raise an awareness of the challenges the ministry couple wrestle with throughout their ministry/family journey.

The Impact of Ministry upon the Minister's Marriage

As participants discussed their ministry/family stories, they discussed the impact their ministry calling had upon their marriages. An awareness of these potential challenges is vital for couples in ministry. David and Vera Mace state that "the impact of decline in family and marital quality is not unique to secular society; it is also taking its toll upon those in the church and also those within clergy families."[2] Ministry marriages demand more than mere obligatory commitment; they, like any other marriage, require quality time, communication, and affection. An awareness of the impact that ministry has on their marriage is so important for

---

1. Hileman, "Unique Needs of Protestant Clergy Families," 121.
2. Mace and Mace, *What's Happening to Clergy Marriages?*, 100.

ministers and their spouses in order to be able to give attention to their marriage before they get to the point of irreparable damage due to an imbalanced ministry focus.

The challenge of beginning ministry and marriage at the same time

The majority of those that I interviewed regarding their ministry/family journey began their ministry around the same time they were married. For many couples, the challenge of adjusting to being married places a certain strain on the relationship as they are getting used to living with another person. Although they love their new spouse, they also discover there are some habits and issues regarding their new spouse that need to be navigated. When these new couples have also recently engaged with the wonders and challenges of public ministry life, further tension can be expected.

One pastor explained the journey into ministry as quite similar to entering into marriage:

> It's been both stable and unpredictable. It was nothing like I thought it would be. Sort of like the person who thinks that they know everything about marriage while they are still single because they watched it on a soap opera. There were unexpected elements that I would not have anticipated. Overall it was a good experience, but I'm just saying that I wouldn't have anticipated some of the things that I experienced, and I had some idealistic expectations.

Another pastor spoke about being converted, married, beginning Bible college and having their first child in a very short period of time: "I went to an interdenominational Bible college for two years, and we had our first child while we were at Bible college. It wasn't necessarily a good experience, as it was a high-pressure situation with a lot of demands and very little in the way of resources." Yet another pastor confirmed this phenomenon: "My wife was a personal assistant to a pastor at a church when we married, and I was also involved on a ministry team as a pastor at that time. So, we entered married life as a ministry couple. Not long after our marriage we then planted a church together which was both exciting and challenging."

There were many other comments similar to the comments above that described how couples began both their ministry and their marriage around the same time. These new experiences were also mostly followed by the new experiences of becoming parents. One pastor explained, "I started when I was still single, and then we married and when the children were born, we were already in the ministry." Another pastor and wife expressed their beginnings: "So we got married and then we had our first child, and then we checked out a few Bible colleges and ended up going to Bible college in Sydney." Yet another wife said, "So we got married and then we went to Bible college within the second year of getting married before we started a family. We knew that was what we wanted to do." The children of these couples were born into ministry families that were endeavoring to establish themselves in their ministry, marriage, and family all at the same time.

Such scenarios are bound to result in certain consequences. While many of these couples wouldn't have it any other way, many of them also lamented that they weren't really prepared for any of these new responsibilities they entered into in their early years. One female pastor explained, "I was involved in every aspect of the church ministry without being paid, such as hosting, women's ministry, I was running church marketing, and much more. We had another baby in that time as well, and I went back to work. So, I guess I was navigating ministry/family/work. I guess I was managing the tension of those things, because although we wanted there to be a flow, there was also a tension." An awareness of such tensions that juggling ministry, marriage, and family can bring to the ministry/family journey is vital for couples who are called to ministry, especially for those who enter the ministry soon after they are married. If you are not aware of the potential challenges, you can't prepare and give proper attention to your marriage in those early critical moments.

The challenge of having some ministry-free couple time

Another ongoing challenge for ministry couples at any age and stage of their relationship is the challenge of giving time and attention to each other away from their ministry responsibilities. The wife of one ministry couple spoke of the frustration of being consumed with ministry in every aspect of their relationship. "As far as our marriage is concerned, my husband and I have been in ministry together, so in some ways there's been times when we can never get away from it. There's always that talk in every room of your house, when you're in the car, it totally absolutely consumes you, so there's no getting away from it really, because it's the call of God." She continued, "As far as our marriage, I think that the ministry has made us tired at different times. So rather than being refreshed or really enjoying each other's company, we've actually been exhausted in each other's company.... We've always been strong as far as our marriage, but I don't know if there's always been a joy there." This couple are still very strong in their marriage and have two married children and several grandchildren who are all still strong in their faith. However, the tragedy is that it seems that there was a season in their marriage that was so consumed by an obsessive focus on ministry that they were robbed of the joy and happiness that their marriage deserved.

My wife and I realized we didn't want to lose the vitality of our love in our marriage in the midst of our ministry. So, after six years of marriage—three at Bible college and three in ministry—we decided to leave our children with their grandparents so that we could have a weekend away together. We went out to a restaurant together and set the rules that we wouldn't talk about the church we were leading or about the children, but rather we would focus on each other.

For quite some time we didn't know what to talk about. Then I suggested we share our dreams for our future. We were renting a house at the time, so my wife began to talk about the dream home she would love to live in one day. I knew we couldn't afford anything like that on a small-church pastor's income, but it was about dreaming about the future, not about purchasing it straight away. Now, over thirty years later, we can look back and see she has been able to live in her dream home in two different locations. However, she has also willingly left them behind to follow the leading of the Lord to where he has wanted us to further minister. Currently we are renting an apartment while I am teaching at our national ministry training college and someone else is renting our dream home in another city.

I also shared one of my dreams of travelling to other nations of the world, both for ministry purposes and leisure holidays. Again, we had no money in the bank at the time and lived week to week off a very scant pastor's income. Yet again we can look back and note that we have had the privilege of travelling to over thirty different countries for both ministry and holidays, with many more countries yet to explore. Since that first weekend away from our children and ministry responsibilities, we have tried to get away at least once a year and dream about our future as a couple. The key was to continue a life of love and dreams beyond the world of our ministry responsibilities. This was not about neglecting ministry responsibilities, but about fulfilling marriage, family, and personal responsibilities. It's not this *or* that but rather this *and* that. We are blessed to still be in love and enjoying each other's company, while still fulfilling God's call upon our lives by living a balanced and focused life in our marriage, family, and ministry.

The challenge of structuring some boundaries around ministry

Many couples in my research interviews stressed that it was difficult to have quality time together due to the unpredictable nature of the ministry. Often they would find plans had to be changed due to ministry-related issues. They would plan to have a quiet meal together and then the phone would ring, someone needed to talk to the pastor about some personal issue. They would plan to go on holidays and just before they were about to leave, an emergency or crisis would arise that meant the pastor couldn't leave at that time or had to return midway through the holiday break. These intrusions into ministry couples' relationships can do irreparable damage to their marriage if not managed. A female pastor who ministered alongside her husband explained how they set some structures in place for their marriage and family in the early years of their ministry.

> We got married and then we went to Bible college before we started a family. A couple of our lecturers were brilliant, and they were a married couple and they had a great family, and they spoke to us about marriage and ministry when we were at Bible college. So, when we came back from college ready to go into ministry, we made some really strong decisions of how we wanted our family to function in ministry. We wanted to survive. I think that we had seen and heard of so many casualties where marriages had fallen apart, or marriages that were still together but were only just existing and not flourishing. So, we just said we wanted to set some strong frameworks when we started out, so that's kind of evolved and changed according to the different seasons.

The importance of putting some boundaries in place so the ministry couple can still enjoy a flourishing marriage in the midst of their ministry calling is nonnegotiable. Although God's people are to be valued, and their needs are incredibly important, it is also important that ministers and their spouses give priority to their relationship with each other. An awareness of this challenge should motivate ministers and their spouses to be intentional about structuring some boundaries in their lives that will enhance their marriage relationship in the midst of their many ministry responsibilities. We will see what has worked for pastors and their spouses to maintain a vibrant marriage relationship in the midst of their ministry responsibilities in a later chapter.

The challenges faced by the pastor's spouse

Added to the impact the ministry has upon the ministry couple, some empirical research demonstrates that the occupational role of a minister also adds further stress to their spouse and influences their quality of life.[3] Scottie Samper found that isolation and resentment are the key causes of mental health issues among clergy spouses.[4] Michael Morris and Priscilla Blanton's research revealed that clergy and their spouses find it difficult to obtain relief from stress due to the absence of social support, with feelings of loneliness and isolation in clergy families being a common experience.[5] Essential ingredients for healthy family functioning are the availability of the clergy as spouse and parent and their authority over time, particularly for clergy spouses.[6]

Morris and Blanton's study indicated both clergy and their spouses reported that intrusiveness, lack of social support, mobility, and time demands/expectations impacted their competence in family functioning, with spouses being more affected by these stressors across several family-functioning dimensions.[7] Congregational expectations are often the highest stress factor for the minister's spouse. Many clergy spouses experience many and varied stressors due to their spouse's ministry role.

The majority of the literature regarding clergy spouses relates to females, i.e., spouses of male clergy, although it is acknowledged, especially more recently due to the rise in the ordination of female clergy, that there is an increasing number of male spouses of female clergy. Marsha Frame and Constance Sheehan found that around 25 percent of female

---

3. Darling et al., *Understanding Stress and Quality of Life* 261.
4. Stamper, *Clergy Spouse Well-Being*, 77.
5. Morris and Blanton, "Influence of Work-Related Stressors," 189.
6. Morris and Blanton, "Influence of Work-Related Stressors," 194
7. Morris and Blanton, "Predictors of Family Functioning," 37—38

clergy find it a challenge to balance work and family life.[8] While marriage has been a valued resource for occupational success among Protestant clergymen, particularly where the minister's wife serves as an unpaid co-worker, the occupational effects of marriage and family have been assumed to be negative when the minister is female due to disproportionate domestic and childcare responsibilities faced by women.[9]

Hanna Papanek coined the phrase, "two-part single career,"[10] whereby clergy wives are assumed to be working unpaid alongside their husbands in the ministry. Norman Blaikie, when speaking about the demands that are placed upon pastor's spouses (wives in his research) by their congregations, states that there can hardly be another occupation in which a man's wife is as conspicuous to his clients and in which there is the same degree of opportunity to place demands upon her.[11] Blaikie stated that "family life is not only disrupted, but in many cases is also very restricted, and some wives find that they are left to bring up children on their own, largely because of the extent to which their husbands are out or busy in the evenings."[12]

Lee and Balswick state that the tug of war between the many roles a minister and spouse have to fulfill adds to their many stressors.[13] The responses from minister's spouses are clear: the higher the level of family stress, the more they desired to leave the ministry.[14] It is also evident that ministers who experienced higher levels of family stress were, overall, less satisfied in their ministries.[15] One pastor's wife states, "I'm supposed to listen, smile, listen, bring lots of food to pot lucks, listen, go to all baby showers, listen, help in Vacation Bible School, listen, entertain, listen, go visiting with my husband, and listen. But no one wants to listen to me!"[16] Many ministers and their spouses enter ministry with high ideals regarding how they will fulfill their ministry roles alongside their family

---

8. Frame and Shehan, *Relationship between Work and Well-being*, 15.
9. Nesbit, "*Marriage, Parenthood, and The Ministry*, 397.
10. Papanek, "Men, Women, and Work," 852–72.
11. Blaikie, *Plight of the Australian Clergy*, 183.
12. Blaikie, *Plight of the Australian Clergy*, 184.
13. Lee and Balswick, *Life in a Glasshouse*, 164.
14. Lee and Balswick, *Life in a Glasshouse*, 219
15. Lee and Balswick, *Life in a Glasshouse*, 219
16. Boquist, *Pastoring First Church*, 75.

responsibilities. The difficulty arises when the realities of the ministry/family journey begin to unfold.

Male minister's appreciation of their female spouse

When presented with the question regarding how their spouse handles the ministry/family journey, an overwhelming majority of the male participants responded positively. One pastor stated, "She handles it really well, my wife is an angel from God and a very peaceful person." Many also responded by saying their wife was their greatest strength and that she has flourished. Other comments, such as those below, were also expressed regarding the minister's spouse:

- Up until now my wife has been the rock, she has really been the centerpiece that has kept the home and family probably on track more than anything.
- My wife has been incredibly sacrificial in regard to the ministry/family journey, because at times I've had to work in a secular job in order to pay the bills because the church can't afford to pay me at times, so my wife has carried the responsibilities of the church during the day, things such as the administration of the office and dealing with people's needs during the day, yet at the same time she has been a brilliant wife and mother, and has always stepped up to the mark in regard to the family.
- She always took the attitude that she was there to support me in the ministry, and if we were doing something that demanded of us as a family that was part of the sacrifice. A wonderful lady with a great attitude.
- She was very supportive and put up with a lot of my unbalanced approach to ministry and family.

The power of the minister expressing their appreciation of their spouse would have a very positive impact upon the spouse, resulting in a very high satisfaction factor for the minister's marriage and family.

The concept of a calling for the spouse

The concept of a calling also arose as the male participants considered the strengths of their female spouse regarding their successful navigation of their journey of ministry and family. Katherine Brookes, when describing the difference between a job, a career, and a calling, describes calling in the following manner:

> Individuals with a calling orientation often describe their work as integral to their lives and their identity. They view their career as a form of self-expression and personal fulfillment . . . individuals with a calling orientation are more likely to find their work meaningful and will modify their duties and develop relationships to make it more so. They are found to be more satisfied in general with their work and their lives.[17]

Provided there is a realistic aspiration regarding the ministry calling, it can lead to ministry/life fulfillment for both the minister and their spouse. Many participants emphasized the importance of a calling. Comments that their female spouse has always had a strong sense of a ministry call were frequent. The importance of the spouse having a sense of calling to the ministry undoubtedly would greatly affect how the family perceives the ministry/family challenges they contend with from time to time. A pastor, when explaining the call of God on his wife, stated that "She has always had a strong sense of a ministry call from a younger age for her own life. We have always ministered together, as I've often been involved in the worship area in most churches and she's got involved in more pastoral ministry." Another pastor stated that his wife "carries a call in her own life, rather than just being the minister's help-meet."

Those who indicated that all of their children still attended church and were continuing in their faith commented three times more often on the importance of God's call to ministry upon their female spouses than did those who indicated they had children no longer in the faith. Perhaps this awareness and understanding of the call to ministry and the commitment to such a call has had an influence on the children of these ministry couples. This was expressed as a key ingredient for those who experienced a sense of satisfaction with their children's spiritual outlook.

---

17. Brooks, *Job, Career, Calling*

An awareness of the ministry-imposed difficulties that ministers' spouses encounter

As the male participants discussed their female spouse's handling of the ministry/family journey, they expressed an awareness of the various difficulties their spouses had to contend with. Ministers' wives and female ministers face certain challenges that are unique to their gender, which male ministers or the spouses of female ministers do not necessarily have to contend with. An awareness of the ministry-imposed challenges the female ministers and female spouses encounter is imperative for the ministers and spouses to be able to give the appropriate mitigating attention these challenges demand.

Although they stated their spouse had handled the ministry/family journey well, many male participants in my research stated it had been a challenge for their female spouses. The data in my research confirms some previous research conducted by Michael Morris and Priscilla Blanton, who state that it is almost impossible to separate the occupation of the clergy from the clergy person's marriage and family.[18] A striking 80 percent of American pastors say they have insufficient time with their spouse.[19] Such research has demonstrated there are consequential stress factors upon the spouses of those who are involved in the vocation of church ministry.

The difficulty of financial constraints was also discussed as a stress factor for ministers' spouses. Living up to the expectations associated with being the spouse of a minister arose again in the interviews. Carol Darling et al. have written about the intangible ways in which congregations can intrude upon the boundaries of the clergy family. The intangible intrusion of criticism directed at the pastor and/or their family can often be more harmful than tangible boundary intrusions.[20] It has been discovered that clergy spouses had higher levels of physiological and psychological stress than did the clergy member due to boundary intrusions.[21] One pastor explained how he would add to his spouse's psychological stress by unloading his burdens on her. "The sheer loneliness of ministry life can be crushing as one cannot possibly take any other

---

18. Morris and Blanton, "Predictors of Family Functioning," 27.
19. London and Wiseman, *Pastors at Greater Risk*, 88.
20. Darling et al., "Understanding Stress and Quality of Life," 261.
21. Darling et al., "Understanding Stress and Quality of Life," 261.

individual from the church into one's confidence. Unfortunately, the only option may be to unload onto your long-suffering spouse."

The need to rely on God due to the difficulties of the ministry/family journey was also recognized as a challenge for their spouses. Loneliness was also highlighted as a challenge for the female spouses. A pastor whose wife is also credentialed stated that "there are times when I wish my wife would go out with some of the girls in the church, but that doesn't always happen. There have been times that she has shared where she has felt lonely." According to research conducted by Wayne Cordeiro, 56 percent of pastors' spouses say they have no close friends.[22] An awareness of such statistics is paramount for pastors to help their spouses who have social needs beyond their husband's ministry responsibilities. One male pastor encouraged pastors to focus more on the needs of their wives particularly to help them overcome the loneliness factor: "Schedule quality time that gives priority to your wife that is nonnegotiable. Make every provision for her to make a life of her own, maintaining and prospering long-term friendships outside of your ministry obligations."

Another imposing challenge was where the minister was described as being imbalanced regarding her ministry/family life. This difficulty was expressed by a male spouse regarding his ministry-employed wife, who stated, "I feel in the early days she was quite driven and focused in an unbalanced way that meant that the family was neglected due to her passion to serve God. This was then expressed in her commitment to the church, as she gave much more of herself to the church than to the family." This spouse also placed much of the responsibility of his wife's imbalance on the senior pastors of the church she was employed by: "At times when we have had family gatherings, she has received calls where she has had to drop everything for the sake of the church. The expectations upon her have at times been unreasonable and that has created some tension."

Although the male spouses of the female ministers overall responded positively regarding the question of how their spouse handled the ministry/family journey, there were also some challenges regarding being married to a female minister, as described above. Overall there were many imposing challenges the male participants have identified as a part of their spouses' ministry/family journey. Although the contrasts vary, neither the female spouses who had all their children in church and committed to their faith, or those that didn't have all their children in church

---

22. Cordeiro, *Leading on Empty*, 32–33.

and committed to their faith, were exempt from these challenges. The reality is that all ministry spouses are confronted with imposing challenges due to the vocation of ministry. The key is to identify what these ministry-imposed challenges are and to then give appropriate attention to the spouse to help alleviate such challenges.

A positive awareness of the male spouse's handling of the ministry/family journey

The question regarding how their spouse handles the ministry/family journey was also presented to the female participants in my research interviews. Their responses to this question were also analyzed. Although the responses were not as high in frequency as the male responses regarding their female spouses, there still seems to be quite a positive response to the question regarding how their male spouse handles the ministry/family journey. One spouse said, "He is just amazing! Really, he is a pastor, and so because of his pastoral heart, number one is foremost for his family, and so he has really navigated that beautifully." Another spouse of a minister stated, "My husband has handled the ministry/family journey extremely well. He has included me in all of the ministry decisions and honored and loved me and our family while being very busy with his ministry." Still another female spouse stated, "I think my husband has handled it really well and gave as much as he could to the boys and into the family whenever it was possible." These are just a sample of the many initial positive responses the female spouses expressed. Their love and respect for their husbands was consistently evident throughout my research interviews.

The challenges that male spouses wrestled with throughout their ministry/family journey

As we have observed above, the female spouses spoke of their male spouse very positively and with great admiration and respect. However, there were also some very honest reflections regarding how their ministry focus at times caused them to lose sight of what matters most in their lives—their family. As I mentioned in chapter 2, it appears from my interviews that the danger of an obsessive focus on ministry is prevalent among male pastors particularly. The most frequently discussed issue by the female spouses was that ministry demands took their toll on the minister and his family. Another issue mentioned was that the male spouse struggled with time limitations. Their spouse struggling with ministry/family balance was also mentioned often.

Research reveals that ministry couples often pay an unseen, unacknowledged and unappreciated heavy price for dedicating their lives to ministry. One study found that pastors often feel owned by their congregation.[23] Another study discovered that many ministers fall into the trap of spending excessive amounts of time at the church.[24] A wife of a male pastor lamented, "I think it's becoming really quite difficult in the amount of paperwork that he finds himself doing every day, so time together is becoming less." The struggle for time is one of the main complaints of ministers and their spouses, according to Norman Blaikie: "Many said there was insufficient time to do everything they felt should be done, or in fact, to do anything properly. Constant, varied, and often trivial demands on their time meant some tasks were frequently left uncompleted, and others did not receive adequate attention."[25]

Another challenge that consumes many male ministers has to do with their self-esteem or need for recognition within their denomination and amongst their peers. Linda Hileman suggests male pastors can often fall into the trap of competition in order to "climb the ecclesiastical ladder" of success.[26] Such a trap can cause pastors to become preoccupied with growth, success, and promotion, and become severely sidetracked from the focus they should be giving to their spouses and families. Many pastors have inflicted severe damage on their marriage due to the pursuit of their egocentric ambitions and unrealistic aspirations. Having God-inspired aspirations for ministry fruitfulness is a positive objective for ministers; this is much better than having no aspirations and just existing in ministry without any vision or productivity. However, when these aspirations are motivated by human insecurities and the need of approval by one's denominational leaders or peers to the point that they become obsessive and all-consuming, great damage to their relationships can occur.

---

23. Morris and Blanton, *Predictors of Family Functioning Among Clergy and Spouses*, 28.

24. Goetz, *Is the Pastor's Family Safe at Home?*, 39.

25. Norman W. H. Blaikie, *Plight of the Australian Clergy*, 161.

26. Hileman, "Unique Needs of Protestant Clergy Families," 129.

Some male ministers embrace their ministry as if they were still single. Rosemary Radford Ruether states that the roots in regard to the depreciating of marriage and family are not just discovered in recent modern times, but such devaluing of marriage and family stem back to first-century society.[27] Ruether states that despite the centrality of the family to ethnic identity and social maintenance, both the Greco-Roman and the Jewish worlds of the first century contained movements and ideologies that were anti-family. In the Greco-Roman world, for example, there was a misogynist tradition that saw wives as so great a burden that men were better off not marrying at all. The philosophers of the first century also encouraged single life.[28] It seems at times that some ministers are still in the first-century mindset, living with an obsession for ministry that devalues their marriages and families.

A comparison of the comments made regarding an obsessive focus on ministry revealed that overall the male spouses of participants who had at least one child no longer attending church or following their faith were more obsessive in regard to their ministry focus than were the participants that still had all of their children following the Lord. Such an obsession would no doubt lead to marriage and family neglect, where the excessive aspirational, ambitious minister is unaware of the issues that his/her family encounter, which then means they cannot give the appropriate attention the family requires. The importance of having an awareness of the dangers and challenges the male ministers wrestle with, as confirmed by the data in my interviews, is imperative for ministers and their families to flourish in the twenty-first century.

The pastor's husband

Not all of the male spouses that were described in the interviews were ministers; some were the male spouses of female ministers. Due to this variance, it is also important we recognize the unique characteristics of female ministers' husbands. With the increasing number of female pastors working full-time in church contexts, it has been noted that male spouses tend not to have the same high level of participation expected of them.[29] When the husband of a female minister attends meetings out-

---

27. Ruether, *Christianity and the Making of the Modern Family*, 21.
28. Ruether, *Christianity and the Making of the Modern Family*, 22.
29. Taylor and Hartley, *The Two-Person Career*, 354.

side the normal Sunday church services, such as mid-week Bible studies, prayer meetings, men's meetings, and the like, there is often great encouragement expressed by the congregation for the wonderful way in which they support their wife's ministry. On the other hand, when the wife of a male pastor attends mid-week meetings, outside of the normal Sunday services, as well as running the women's meetings and the children's church or Sunday school and being a part of the worship ministry, no encouragement is usually expressed, as many would say she is expected to do those things as she is the minister's wife. If she didn't support her husband's ministry in that way, many would complain and say she is not a true minister's wife.

Therefore, in regard to expectations on the spouse of the minister, the husband of the female minister finds himself better off. However, one spouse of a female minister explained that although this is true, there is also a downside to being the husband of the female minister. Firstly, he explained he left his employment position of many years to relocate the family so his wife could fulfill her call as a senior minister. He found another employment role in this new location that required learning some new skills and settling into a new employment environment and culture.

Secondly, he explained that the ministry often impinged on their family time. He felt he only had a one-day weekend due to the responsibilities he assumed in order to get the family prepared for the week on a Sunday afternoon, as his wife was busy with ministry responsibilities all day on Sunday. He stated,

> She would come home later after church on Sunday afternoon, but I would be making lunches for the week, and then I would be cooking up meals for dinner for the week due to her getting home late during the week from church. So, it wasn't uncommon for me to be spending Sunday afternoon cooking up meals for the week so that they would be just there ready to go.

He continued,

> Yes the guys get it easier on that level of expectations, but it's interesting that nobody is offering any help to me. I've got to go home and spend Sunday afternoon cooking up meals, and I do all of these other things on top of my full-time employment, et cetera, et cetera. But nobody is saying to me, 'how are you coping with your wife working all of these hours?'

He also explained that when they were part of another church, when the pastor's wife was ill, everybody rallied and made meals for her and offered to do her laundry and offered great help to her. However, when he became ill, and was bed-ridden for three weeks, nobody called or offered to bring meals home or offered any other help at all.

There are also many other issues that are unique to the spouse of a female minister that are not always evident to the local congregation. Yet these are very real to the spouse and family of the female minister. Due to the recent growth and development of female ministers throughout the church worldwide, further research needs to be conducted to more effectively understand this phenomenon and support both female ministers and their spouses.

Chapter Summary

The purpose of this chapter has been to provide some insights regarding ministry couples. My interviews were conducted individually, however each spouse, whether male or female, exemplified a healthy respect for each other throughout the interviews. My research regarding how the vocation of the ministry impacted the marriage of the minister was described. There was also an analysis of how each spouse handles the ministry/family journey. The responses of the participants were divided into two categories—male responses and female responses—for this part of the chapter. The imposing challenges that the ministry vocation presents to ministry spouses were also identified.

Personal Reflection

What issues are you aware of that affect your lives as a ministry couple and how do you plan to navigate them for the sake of your marriage.

Chapter 7

The Minister's Children

THIS CHAPTER GIVES FOCUS to the children of ministers. The perceptions of the ministry parents in my research regarding the benefits that their children enjoy due to ministry life, as well as the parents' perceptions regarding the ministry-imposed difficulties which their children wrestle with, will be discussed. Ministers and their spouses who have a greater awareness of the benefits and burdens that their children experience due to being pastors' children, and who give their children further attention in this regard, will more likely be satisfied with their relationships with their children throughout their ministry/family journey.

Surprising Findings Regarding Minister's Children

Although most investigations regarding the effects of growing up in a minister's home found that the strongest negative stressor was "expectations" due to being a pastor's child, there were surprising positive outcomes revealed in my research. A study by Kimberley Strange and Lori Shepherd investigated both ministers' children and nonministry children to ascertain whether a negative stereotype really exists, as many people tend to assume. To their surprise their research revealed that a positive stereotype may actually exist.[1] The findings indicated pastors' children are certainly bombarded with stress and high expectations from congregational and community members. However, 78 percent of pastors' children stated their experience as a PK was positive overall, and

---

1. Strange and Sheppard, *Evaluations of Clergy Children versus Non-Clergy Children*, 53.

95 percent disagreed that their experience as a PK was negative overall.[2] The findings of Strange and Sheppard revealed that the plight of pastors' children is more positive than the stereotypes have led us to believe.[3] This is comforting news for pastors and spouses who are concerned that their involvement in ministry may cause damage to the spiritual and social well-being of their children.

Further research regarding the effects that growing up in a minister's home has upon the religious commitment of the adult child was conducted with 574 adult PKs in the USA by Carolle Anderson. From those that were surveyed, 70.8 percent were of a high educational level, completing at least a four-year college degree; 25 percent stated they were in health professions, while many other categories such as teaching, religious, clerical, and homemaking occupations were identified.[4] The research I have conducted also reveals there are many positive benefits of growing up in the home of a pastor. Being a PK is actually an advantage overall rather than a disadvantage. For pastoral parents that think they are disadvantaging their children by raising them in a ministry home, be assured that you are actually setting your children up to succeed.

Ruth Hetzendorfer's research into the attributes and stressors of American Assemblies of God pastors' children concludes that these children, when compared to the general population, exhibit higher levels of strength in certain areas.[5] They are more likely to be people gatherers (46 percent), possess a healthy self-concept (55 percent), are more optimistic (55 percent), creative (54 percent), mission-oriented in the sense of allowing their work-life goal to be the criteria they followed in life (27 percent), and decisive (55 percent).[6] This research had similar findings to Strange and Shepherd's study. Though there are challenges that may be unique to the ministry family, which we will discuss further in this chapter, there are also unique benefits. Growing up in a pastor's home adds much to the life of the pastor's children.

In chapter 3 we discussed the many blessings that enhanced the lives of ministers' children. A large proportion of the participants commented

2. Strange and Sheppard, *Evaluations of Clergy Children versus Non-Clergy Children*, 59

3. Strange and Sheppard, *Evaluations of Clergy Children versus Non-Clergy Children*, 58.

4. Anderson, *The Experience of Growing up in a Minister's Home*, 393.

5. Hetzendorfer, *Assessing the Positive Attributes of Preachers' Kids*.

6. Hetzendorfer, *Assessing the Positive Attributes of Preachers' Kids*.

that their children handled the ministry/family journey really well. Other positive comments were that their children realized they were blessed to be part of a ministry family. Some commented on the positive experience the ministry endowed upon their children in regard to the wonderful people God has placed around them and they said their children love meeting significant leaders and going to ministers' conferences.

Further blessings and advantages due to being raised in a ministry family were expressed, such as the blessings of travel and holidays due to the minister's vocation; relationships they formed in the church and through ministry connections; becoming closer as a family; social skills developed as a result of being exposed to people in the church and community of all generations, backgrounds, and social statuses; the provision of God for the family as a result of prayer; opportunities that came their way due to being the pastor's child, such as ministry opportunities and the like; and the occasions when their children often enjoyed some of the benefits of being a pastor's kid. Finally, participants recognized the advantage of their childrens' opportunity to develop as leaders due to their exposure to the leadership culture in their home and denomination.

Strange and Shepherd's research, along with that of Carolle Anderson and Ruth Hetzendorfer, revealed many positive outcomes in the later lives of adult children of ministers. Overall, though they are raised in a glasshouse under the eye of the congregation and community as described in Lee and Balswick's book, *Life in a Glass House*, ministers' children are also raised in a leadership greenhouse.

They have the privilege of observing the leadership skills and characteristics exemplified by their parents. This hotbed of leadership development is also fertilized by the influence of many other significant leaders that the pastors' children are exposed to. Leaders such as visiting ministers that pastors' children have the opportunity to meet have significant influence on the leadership development of pastors' children. This influence is also enhanced by the speakers at ministers' conferences they attend with their ministry parents. Unbeknownst to their parents, these leadership insights are often caught rather than taught and become a part of the leadership development of the pastor's child. Their ministry parents are often inadvertently training their children to be effective leaders of the future.

In their research, Lee and Balswick found that "though there are hazards that may be unique to the clergy family, there are also unique advantages. Preacher's children have access to people, cultures, and experiences that would enrich the life of any child."[7] In one survey study, for example, the minister's wife wrote the following: "We have had people in our home whom other children have never had the benefit of knowing: African pastors, foreign missionaries, evangelists, other preachers. Our kids have been able to talk to them, play games with them, and find out more about the world and what makes people tick."[8] A pastor and personal friend of mine said his children had travelled the world without leaving their dining room table due to having meals with ministers and missionaries from around the globe. Pastor, your ministry can have an incredibly positive impact upon your child's future.

An inspiring spiritual focus

The notion of an inspiring spiritual focus was also identified in my research as the participants described their children's spiritual passion. Comments regarding their children being in ministry with them were the initial remarks regarding this spiritual focus. Further comments that their children made good spiritual life choices were expressed. In line with other studies, the capacity for ministers' children to make good choices is becoming more evident in the research landscape. Brian Jones recently undertook a pilot study using semistructured interviews with six adult clergy children from different denominational backgrounds who are now ministers in their own right. The results of his study demonstrated their upbringing in the home of a minister played a major role in their own vocational decision.[9]

Participants in my research also mentioned their family members developed a deeper faith as they saw the reality of God at work in the church and other people's lives. The benefit of people praying for the family and positive role models in the church was also emphasized. The notion that they draw on the experience and values of their parents was also highlighted. During the discussion regarding the authentic modelling of the God-life lived in the home, a minister stated, "I guess the main blessing is seeing your kids watching you in private and then seeing you in public and noting that, so that's a real blessing to me." Another spiritual

---

7. Lee and Balswick, *Life in a Glasshouse*, 163.
8. Lee and Balswick, *Life in a Glasshouse*, 163.
9. Jones, *Exploring the Impact of Parental Church Based Ministry on the Lives of Clergy Children*.

indicator was they support their parent being in ministry. Other ministry parents commented that their children were going through Bible college, which was further evidence of the inspiring spiritual focus of their children. Comments that their children had developed godly character were also expressed. The spouse of a minister spoke positively about her children's experience in a ministry home:

> Both our children are doing very well, and I think that it's such a wonderful thing when you can look at your kids and see that they've enjoyed your ministry life and they've been involved in everything from the start. They've grown up in such a wonderful environment and they're both going on for God, so that's a really great thing.

Ministry-Imposed Difficulties

Though there are many natural and spiritual blessings and benefits that accompany growing up in the home of a minister as we have noted above, there are also many difficulties experienced by their children that ministers and their spouses need to consider. Vivian Grice explains that "while children of pastors share some factors in common with other children of other professions such as magistrates, police, and ambassadors that have unique spill-over effects into the family setting, the particular stressors in each occupation differ."[10] He continues, "There are many stressors common to the helping professions, but some unique ones such as a conflation of professional, moral, social and spiritual expectations that not only make the pastoral role unique but the experience of the pastors' child unique also."[11]

Lee and Balswick suggest that "although all children must learn to adapt to social expectations, the expectations placed on preacher's children may be more intensive than most."[12] "In addition to an expectation of great piety, clergy children are also expected to attend every church function and to volunteer more readily than their peers."[13] They continue, "the pastor is not the only member of the family that feels the pressure of unrealistic expectations. Their children feel pressure to live to a higher

---

10. Grice, "Pastor's Kids," 32.
11. Grice, "Pastor's Kids," 32.
12. Lee and Balswick, *Life in a Glasshouse*, 163.
13. Lee and Balswick, *Life in a Glass*, 91.

standard than their peers."[14] One minister's child wrote, "I think the pastor's children's parents realize their children are the same as others, but I don't think the community/congregation realizes this."[15] The special status of being the pastor's child carries with it greater moral and spiritual expectations than those of nonministry children.

Research conducted by Cynthia Wilson and Carol Darling revealed that life satisfaction of clergy children as adults is directly related to their life satisfaction and stress levels of living as an adolescent in a clergy home.[16] Wilson and Darling added, "Perhaps the best hope for dealing with the stressors of clergy life and their impact on clergy children is that clergy need to become more aware of how the demands of their jobs affect their families."[17] In one study pastors were asked about the health of their family and the pressures associated with being the family of a minister. The study found that 91 percent agreed that there is extra pressure being the child of a minister.[18] In my research interviews, a significant amount of comments were expressed regarding how their children were negatively affected as a result of their involvement in ministry. Unfortunately, there were quite a number of challenging issues the children of these ministers had to contend with as a result of the ministry vocation of their parent(s).

Lee and Balswick state: "Positive and negative expectations alike can be experienced by the pastor's child as unrealistic or restrictive, with possible dangerous consequences for his or her emotional adjustment."[19] Research regarding relocation stress and coping among clergy and spouses in the United Methodist Church found that relocation due to ministry can cause a severe disruption of the children's social/friendship networks.[20] In a time in their life where their friends give them a sense of belonging and an understanding of their value in regard to who they are, a change of location and cultural setting can make it very difficult for clergy children to resettle and find their way.

---

14. Lee and Balswick, *Life in a Glass*, 91.
15. Lee and Balswick, *Life in a Glass*, 168.
16. Wilson and Darling, "Understanding Stress and Life Satisfaction," 136.
17. Wilson and Darling, "Understanding Stress and Life Satisfaction," 140.
18. Grey Matter Research, "Pastors and the Health of their Family."
19. Lee and Balswick, *Life in a Glasshouse*, 173.
20. Frame and Sheehan, *Work and Well-being in the Two-Person Career*, 196.

The most frequently emphasized challenge by the participants in my research regarding their children's experiences was the challenge of them having to deal with other people's expectations. These results confirm similar findings in previous studies regarding minister's families. Such difficult expectations and experiences in church life are often due to congregational members not being aware of their boundaries in regard to their scope of authority with the children of the minister. Lee and Balswick suggest that "some pastors' children may grow up with the sense that the church members, not the clergy parents, are the ones who defined the limits, who decide what is right and wrong for them."[21] Another challenge participants expressed was the difficulty of their children having to deal with financial constraints. I remember one of my children stating that she wanted to serve the Lord but also wanted to get a job where she could earn lots of money. She later became a schoolteacher but is now also a children's pastor in her church.

Another major emphasis was the comment by participants that their children had difficulties trying to find their way. Further challenges expressed regarding their children were that their experiences in church weren't that great. The difficulties of dealing with church conflict was also identified as a challenge for the children of ministers, which is possibly linked to the previous emphasis that their experiences in church weren't that great. The fact that ministry demands restricted family time was also mentioned. In Lee and Balswick's study, one minister's child poignantly wrote, "our father is always too busy to be with us."[22]

Another critical issue was the fact that some found it difficult to embrace the faith of their ministry parents. The parents expressed the painful journey they personally experienced as a result of this, which was exclusively related to those who had at least one child no longer attending church. A pastor who experienced the painful journey of their children wandering from the faith explains: "It was a painful journey for us. In a small church there was no positive peer pressure for our children. It was a pretty tough time for me and my wife running the church, and our teenagers were trying to find their way." Another minister shared his child's experience in regard to them having to deal with other people's expectations:

---

21. Frame and Sheehan, *Work and Well-being in the Two-Person Career*, 178.
22. Lee and Balswick, *Life in a Glasshouse*, 215.

My middle son has found it incredibly difficult. When he was at school, he went to a Christian school, and because he is not a high intellect, he is a tradesman, he is a doer, he is an outdoors man, he's a rough guide, they would expect, because he is a pastor's kid, that he should know everything in Christian studies and so on. They would say 'You should know. Your dad's a pastor. You're a pastor's kid. You should know that sort of stuff.' We didn't indoctrinate him. Yes, he grew up with Christian movies and so on, and has heard a lot of preaching, but he's not a reader and he's not a high intellectual, so he found it incredibly hard going to school, being a pastor's kid, particularly because of the stigma of being a pastor's kid and having to have had the answers . . . So, the expectation upon my son from about a five-year-old and onwards because he was a pastor's kid was very unfair and he rebelled against it.

Overall the participants who were unsatisfied with their children's spiritual outlook and stated that at least one of their children was no longer attending church or following their faith expressed a greater frequency of comments regarding ministry-imposed difficulties upon their children. The pain that was expressed by these ministry-engaged parents in regard to the difficult journeys their children had experienced was evident throughout the interviews. Ultimately, they would have liked to have started their ministry/family journey all over again and applied many of the lessons they had learned along the way.

Vivian Grice's research with pastors children aged 18 to 35 revealed that the vast majority of the interviews completed raised the issue of availability, either directly or indirectly, by commenting on the time cost of ministry and parental absence from the family because of ministry work.[23] The participants' assessment in regard to Grice's research was that parental influence on current belief was high and often influenced the child's choice of vocational church ministry.[24] Grice's research also affirmed that the positive spiritual impact upon the pastor's child was largely because of the example and teaching of their parents.

Research that focused on the importance of the home environment (particularly the influence of the parents, and especially of the mother) in influencing the later religious orientation (whether positively or negatively) discovered that parental influence is critical for the spiritual

---

23. Grice, "Pastor's Kids," 42.
24. Grice, "Pastor's Kids," 119.

well-being of young people.²⁵ This also aligns with previous research by Carolle Anderson when researching adult children of pastors. She found that the children were

> more likely to be religiously committed: if their parents had established a warm, loving, relationship with them; had given them the freedom to be themselves and make choices; had made them feel important and spent time with them; had portrayed a genuine and consistent spiritual role model, and, finally, had maintained boundaries between church and home.²⁶

In terms of negative impacts upon the pastors' child in regard to spirituality, Grice found that actions by the church appear to bear the greater weight. It would appear from Grice's research that in the perception of pastors' kids it is church behavior (or rather misbehavior) rather than parents' failure that is more to be borne in mind when it comes to allocating blame for negative impacts upon them in terms of the role the parents have.²⁷ It is these factors that are seen as the responsibility of the church, such as (perceived) mistreatment of parents, church conflict, and unrealistic demands that the pastors' kids found most to complain about.²⁸ The children of pastors are often spiritually vulnerable due to the effects the ministry vocation can impose upon them, and an awareness of these difficulties is imperative for ministers and spouses. A resolute awareness of these ministry-imposed burdens would assist ministers and their spouses to identify what areas of attention they need to give to their children to alleviate such burdens.

Chapter Summary

Being the child of a minister brings both blessings and burdens. The blessings are many and should be highlighted by pastoral couples and enjoyed by the pastor's child. However, there are also many burdens and difficulties that ministers' children experience. Many of the participants' responses in my interviews regarding how their children handled the ministry/family journey were positive. There were many comments

---

25. O'Connor et al., *The Relative Influence of Youth and Adult Experiences on Personal Spirituality*, 725.
26. Anderson, *The Experience of Growing up in a Minister's Home*, 404.
27. Grice, "Pastor's Kids," 134.
28. Grice, "Pastor's Kids," 134.

describing the blessings that being in ministry bestowed upon their children. There were also some very positive comments regarding their children's inspirational spiritual focus. However, the participants in my research also discussed the negative effects ministry had upon their children. Throughout these interviews the importance of being aware of both the blessings and the burdens their children experienced due to being part of a ministry family was affirmed so parents can give their children the appropriate attention they need throughout the ministry/family journey. Such attention has great value to either celebrate the blessings or mitigate the burdens children of ministers can often experience.

Let me conclude this chapter with a personal ministry/family story. When I first became a father, I was a student in my final year of Bible college. I was passionate about serving the Lord in ministry, but also concerned that being in ministry may have a negative impact upon my newborn child and future children. I had a friend who was the son of a pastor and was passionate for God who also had a brother that had drifted away from his faith at one time. Being curious as to what the difference was between he, who pursued God passionately, and his brother, who had drifted away from God, I asked him what he thought was the difference. His answer was that his brother resented the attention that being the child of a pastor brought to his life, whereas he relished the opportunities that being a pastor's child provided.

With such an understanding, I decided I would highlight the blessings and opportunities that being a pastor's child added to my children but would also try to shield them as much as possible from the burdens and difficulties that being a part of a ministry family can impose. Therefore, when we had lunch out with a visiting minister, I would highlight that privilege to my children. When they would travel with me for preaching appointments or when I would speak at youth camps (when I was much younger) I would emphasize the great joy it was to serve God in that way and travel to different places. They also had the privilege to travel to Christian conferences, such as Hillsong Conference and other minister's conferences, where they would meet other children of pastors and engage in exciting children's and youth activities. Often attending these conferences meant they had some time off from school (another advantage). The key was to celebrate the blessings that being children of a minister afforded them and also try to minimize a focus on the burdens, although there were always some issues they experienced that required us to mitigate.

The reality is that being a minister will mean your children will experience many great blessings and opportunities due to your ministry role. A further reality is your children will also experience some of the negative aspects that come with being a child of a minister. The key ingredient to a flourishing family life in the midst of a fruitful ministry life is to have a resolute awareness of such blessings and burdens and to celebrate the blessings and mitigate the burdens.

Personal Reflection

What blessings do your children enjoy due to your ministry role?
What issues are you aware of that affect your children as minister's children, and how do you plan to mitigate them for the sake of your children?

Part 3: Attention

PART THREE IS MY favourite section of this book as it focuses on the solutions to the many challenges that ministers and their spouses have discussed. Part 1 focused on the aspirations and ideals that the pastors and their spouses discussed throughout the interviews, including obsessive aspirations of some pastors and spouses. Part 2 focused on having a resolute awareness of the blessings and burdens that ministers and their spouses experience as a part of the ministry/family journey. This section also gave focus to the ministry couple and the minister's children. This third and final section will bring focus to the things that ministers and spouses discussed in regard to what works for them in their ministry/family journey, what they would avoid or do differently if they had their time over again, what resources and support structures are necessary to have in place in order to navigate the ministry/family journey well, and recommendations for couples and families starting out in ministry. This section is presented to enhance the journey of ministers and their family to enjoy fulfilled and flourishing family lives as they pursue fruitful ministry lives.

Chapter 8

Things that Work for the Family

THE QUESTION REGARDING WHAT ministers and their spouses do that works for them in their ministry/family journey was discussed by the participants in my research. Their responses to this question provide some outstanding insights and ideas for couples in ministry to activate in their own ministry/family journey. Couples reading this will also discover many things they may already do in their current ministry/family journey which will confirm they are on the right track. Overall, this chapter regarding what ministry couples do that works for them aims to encourage those who are already doing many wonderful things. It also aims to offer ideas that will further enhance the ministry/family journey of many ministry couples.

The Importance of Giving Attention to the Minister's Marriage

As participants in my research discussed the things they do that work for them in their ministry/family journeys throughout the interviews, the focus of their own marriage relationship surfaced, and discussions continued around how they have kept their relationship revitalized. A female pastor whose husband is also a pastor explained the importance of having creative quality time together on their day off:

> I have a bucket list, so I love doing different things . . . so I kayak out of the harbor, and we've got pushbikes and motor bikes . . . On my bucket list I want to go to every coffee shop in our city, so we go to a different coffee shop whenever we go out, so that

it's a coffee shop that's not the same as the last one . . . We are probably more in love now than we were when we first married.

Another pastor expressed a unique way of spending their time together in the midst of their ministry stresses:

> One thing we do, we pull the blinds down and we turn on the television and we watch a video series of something like CSI or something that interests us, and we watch 3, 4 or 5 episodes. So, we do that sometimes, and that helps us to recharge ourselves and strengthen our relationship.

Supportive marriages have been found to be one of the important factors in ensuring satisfaction in the ministry/family journey.[1] The importance of having a healthy marriage was a recurring theme during my interviews. The value of giving attention to maintaining a healthy marriage relationship is of extreme importance for all involved in ministry. The foundation of a fulfilled and flourishing family life is a fulfilled and flourishing marriage relationship. Several relational emphases were evident, such as comments regarding keeping their marriage healthy as they fulfill their ministry call. The value of the couples going on dates was also touched on. Being present when the participant was with their family was also emphasized. The notion of supporting their spouse was also discussed as something they did that worked for them. Further comments regarding strengthening and encouraging each other and speaking positively to each other were also articulated. We will now delve a little deeper into these frequent comments that participants expressed regarding what they did that worked to enhance their marriage relationship.

The value of keeping your marriage healthy

The most frequent response when asked the question regarding what they did that worked for their ministry/family journey was they kept their marriage healthy. Although this is a general response which was covered in more detail in their following responses, this is a clear affirmation of the value that participants placed upon their marriage relationship. This is a worthy goal for every ministry couple and demands due consideration in this book. The participants then continued to express how they kept their marriage healthy, which we will discover in the following pages.

1. Kerrick, *Positive Coping Practices among Wives of Male Christian Clergy*, 54.

The value of ministry couples going on dates

The excitement of courtship should not end once a couple is married, whether they are in ministry or not, yet many couples lose sight of the importance of courting their spouse and can easily fall into the trap of pursuing numerous other goals in their married and employed lives and forget about the necessity of giving attention to each other. Going on dates together was a great way of getting to know each other and establishing a loving and meaningful relationship together when couples first started going out together. This should not cease just because a couple get married and begin their ministry. The joy of continuing to go on dates with their spouse was expressed as both a significant and enjoyable moment in the lives of the participants.

The value of being present when with their spouse

Many of the ministers and spouses also expressed the importance of being present when they were with their spouse. Their meaning behind this was not just about being physically present, but also mentally and emotionally engaged with their spouse when they were together. It can be a trap to be physically present but be somewhere else mentally and emotionally, thinking about church and ministry issues as your spouse is trying to talk to you. I'm sure we have all been guilty of this from time to time. Added to many of the ministry distractions that demand our attention away from our spouse, we also live in a technological age where the screens of our devices are screaming for our attention, possibly at a higher volume than anything else. I have been at restaurants with my wife and observed couples sitting across from each other consumed by their devices and not communicating with each other at all. Ministry couples who desire healthy marriages know how to be present with their spouse by fully engaging with them in conversation with their minds and emotions, know when to turn off their minds from other distracting voices, and also know when to turn off their devices for this same purpose.

The value of supporting their spouse

Most of the comments regarding supporting their spouse were expressed by the spouses of ministers in that they supported the minister in fulfilling their ministry, and this is a very important part of a healthy ministry marriage. However, several participants also expressed that they supported their nonministry spouse in their endeavors, whether it was regarding their career or their nonministry pursuits such as sports, hobbies, and other interests that their spouse was engaged in. Supporting your spouse is about each spouse supporting the other in their lives and interests, rather than just a one-way support system that focuses on ministry alone. Healthy marriages are established on mutual support for each other.

The value of strengthening and encouraging each other

The demands and challenges of ministry certainly call for the need for spouses to strengthen and encourage each other. One pastor in my research stated: "My wife handles the ministry/family journey brilliantly. She is my secret weapon and my greatest strength." Another pastor also expressed his appreciation of his wife's strength and encouragement and the fact that they strengthen and encourage each other, as was also expressed by several other participants in my research. Again, this goal of strength and encouragement needs to be mutually assumed by both spouses, rather than just directed and focused from just one spouse to the other. Strength and encouragement are vital in any marriage, however in a marriage that is associated in ministry their value are appreciated in an even greater way.

The value of speaking positively to and about each other

As participants continued to discuss what they did that works for them in their ministry/family journey, several commented that they spoke positively to each other and about each other. Some ministers fall into the trap of using their spouse as the butt of their jokes while they are in the pulpit without understanding how deeply they can wound their spouse in doing so. I have noted some male ministers feel if they speak positively about their wives in public they would be considered weak. Therefore they speak harshly or sarcastically to or about their wife. The consequences of such actions can drive a wedge between the spouses that can expand further into a larger chasm in their relationship as time goes by. Those in my research that desired to keep their marriage relationship healthy explained that they spoke positively to and about their spouse, and this was a significant factor that worked well for their ministry/family journey.

Overall, being intentional regarding having a healthy marriage relationship enhances the ability to enjoy a flourishing family while pursuing a fruitful ministry.

Giving Attention to the Minister's Family

Knowing the potential for their families to be neglected due to ministry demands, or the potential for their family members to become discouraged or hurt by well-meaning congregational members, participants in my research emphasized the importance of giving attention to enhance their family well-being. I will now highlight the participants' deliberate focusing on their families which they discussed throughout their interviews. An intentional attitude toward the family was revealed to sustain health and wholeness within their family while they engaged in their ministry.

The importance of keeping the family as a priority

Many of the participants stressed keeping their family as a priority as something that worked for them while they engaged in their ministry call. This is a challenging process as many demands on the pastor can cause the pastor and spouse to lose sight of their familial priorities while fulfilling their ministry responsibilities. The wife of a pastor stated, "He is a wonderful father to the children, and very focused when it comes to both the vision of God and his family."

The value of prioritizing time with the family was highlighted by a female minister as she explained how she deliberately sets aside time for her family: "I've learned that I don't need to justify my reasons to spend time with my family to other people. I've learned to just say that I'm not available at that time, or 'That won't work for me' without giving any other personal reasons as such." This female pastor developed a way to spend time with her family without having to justify her reasons. This approach helped her sustain a heathy family experience rather than settling for a mediocre family existence due to not giving them the priority they deserved. Another pastor, who is a mother and wife of a pastor, commented on how she prioritized her family by using a calendar:

> I'm a very good planner and so we have a diary and we have a calendar up on the fridge with everybody's activities on there and I really keep that up to date to see if we are doing too much. We definitely tried to have at least one night when we are all at home together, one night where we watch a movie or do something fun as a family.

Other comments along these lines of keeping the family as a priority as they engaged in ministry noted that their spouses maintained a clear focus on the family, and that they maintained balance between ministry and family. A husband, whose wife was also in ministry, stated that his wife, "has really been the centerpiece that has kept the home and family probably on track more than anything." Another pastor, when speaking about his wife, stated, "She has been a brilliant wife and mother, and has always stepped up to the mark in regard to the family." The importance of keeping the family as a priority as they engaged in ministry was most frequently cited by participants who indicated they had all their children still attending church and pursuing their faith. This confirms the value of intentionally prioritizing your family while engaging in your ministry responsibilities.

A hierarchy of priorities

Following on from the importance of being intentional regarding keeping the family as a priority as they engaged in ministry, several participants in my research expressed comments regarding having clear priorities in their ministry/family lives, such as: God first, family second, and ministry third, which I defined as a hierarchy of priorities. This concept was frequently emphasized by those who had all their children still attending church and pursuing their faith. Although many might react to this as being an ultraspiritual formula, it was evidenced in the data that those who emphasized this pattern seemed to have had a more successful and satisfying ministry/family journey. Perhaps it was not so much the formula that worked for them but rather the fact that they were deliberate and intentional regarding prioritizing the family in the midst of their ministry responsibilities.

An alternative to this emphasis was the emphasis that their ministry and family responsibilities were complimentary to each other, meaning they were all-inclusive rather than compartmentalized. Unfortunately, the evidence within my data regarding those who postulated this approach was that these comments came from ministers and spouses who indicated some of their children no longer attended church or pursued their faith. Perhaps the intentionality of prioritizing the family in the midst of their ministry demands was lost in the "all is ministry, all is family, all is God" complimentary approach in these cases.

Maintaining clear lines of communication

Many of the participants in my research also expressed the importance of maintaining clear lines of communication. A pastor explained, "With my wife and myself, we've just lived it every day. We do talk a lot. We debrief most days. We just talk about where our lives are at and pray together every day." A female pastor when speaking about what works for their family revealed, "Open communication works for us, sitting down and having a time when we do communication, where we communicate well and communicate our expectations of one another. Yes communication has been the key." The spouse of a female pastor stated, "we communicate in a way that helps each other understand each other and support each other."

Some practical applications of ensuring good communication were presented by some of the following pastors as they explained what works for them. One pastor described their mealtimes together, "We don't eat around the TV, we have always kept the dinner table fairly sacred, not because of an issue with TV necessarily, but just that we've wanted places where the family communicated as a family with food." Another pastor described an open-door approach for his family. He explained, "What I mean is that I talk to them and if they wanted to talk to me, I would drop everything to listen to them. If they wanted to interrupt me when I was at work, then they could interrupt me if they wanted. So clear lines of communication are extremely important."

Several wives of couples that were both employed in the ministry emphasized the importance of honest communication with their clergy spouses to enhance their relationship and not allow small things to grow into larger issues. One female pastor commented, "We would go down to the beach and talk about how we were going and how we were feeling and made sure that we communicated, even though they may have been hard conversations." Another pastor and wife explained, "we would sit down and talk it through and say this is how I'm feeling at the moment, so communication was very important between us." In addition to the importance of communicating honestly, even when at times such honesty was confronting, a female minister emphasized the importance of communicating to their family how much they love and valued them:

> I would encourage pastors and their spouses to verbalise to your children and verbalize to your spouse that they are important to you. Therefore, you won't answer that call, because your time with them is very important. So, I think you need to verbalize those things to your family to help them to understand how valuable they are to you.

The value of having trips away together (holidays and conferences)

Having trips away was another thing many pastors and spouses discussed as something that works for their ministry/family lives. A female pastor expressed how important family holidays have been to their family: "We try to have a yearly holiday, even if it's just a few long weekends where you're just together as a family having fun together away from the church. So yes, having a break, going away somewhere just with the family is something that we do regularly that works well in our ministry/family journey." Another pastor also stated the value of holidays as a key ingredient for the health and well-being of their family:

> We always have had great holidays. When we were younger obviously the holidays were a lot simpler than they have been in the last few years. In more recent years we started to plan every year to have an annual time away together. We've always found that such planning has been refreshing for several reasons. It is not just the time away but it's the preparation. I find that's part of relaxing for me and so it's the whole thing. It's not just the couple of weeks away, it's the whole thing that is something that refreshes, the planning and preparation, the holiday itself, and the memories that you make together that last a lifetime.

In addition to regular holidays, many ministry couples also expressed that another thing that worked for them was that they took their family with them to pastors' conferences. This was an opportunity for the family to travel together and exposed the family to other ministry families that would bring added support and enhance their lives and relationships. The value of taking your family to pastors' conferences, even though it may be inconvenient and costly at times, cannot be overestimated. Such experiences for the family help them to understand that they are a part of a much larger purpose, as well as exposing them to other ministry families with whom they can develop some lifelong friendships.

The value of having regular family meals together

Having family meals together was also expressed by many ministers and their spouses as something that worked for them to keep their family flourishing as they fulfilled their ministry calling. A pastor explained the following in regard to the intentional approach that he and his ministry spouse initiate with their children:

> We always have dinner at the table to make sure that we always eat together and have a meal together. For us that's our special time. We will share a devotion at the dinner table and we always ask about something that was positive about the day and something that they struggled with and how can we help them with that. That can always be fun because of the age difference between our kids having a six-year-old, a twelve-year-old, and a sixteen-year-old, especially the six-year-old and what he comes out with.

A female minister also stated the value they place on having regular meals together as a family:

> Every second Sunday afternoon I would have all the family over for afternoon tea, or a barbecue, or something like that. We have made it that everyone comes together and we have specifically bought a house with some land so that the kids can go out and play, and the grandkids can go and feed the chickens, so that we are creating a specific family time together.

Just like any family, as the children grow older, they have many friends and other responsibilities such as study, employment, etc. that draw them away from the home. The danger in the midst of all of these things is the family becomes disjointed and ceases to connect on a level that enhances good communication, respect, and loving relationships.

Before long, the pastor's family can become be so fragmented in a collective sense that their relationships also become fragmented and strained due to a lack of connection and communication. Many of the ministers and spouses in my research were aware of the potential of such fragmentation happening and therefore intentionally established family meals together to enhance their family lives and mitigate the negative potential of the family disintegrating. To conclude this section regarding having family meals together, a pastor's wife explained how she developed a family tradition that involved food, fun, and opportunities for her family to flourish by making their weekly family meal one which they would look forward to every week.

> When they were little, because we have three children, we used to have three jars. We would get them to write down what they would like at our family nights and place the piece of paper in their respective jar. One jar represented an activity that we would do, one jar was what the main meal was going to be, and the third jar was what desert we were going to have. So, when it came to the family night, having three children with three jars, they all got a chance to choose either what activity we were going to do, or what main meal we were going to have, or what desert we were going to have, and we would rotate this choice every week.

The value of doing things together as a family

The importance of doing things together as a family was also emphasized by many ministers and their spouses as something that worked for them. Activities such as having meals together, going on holidays and to conferences together, doing ministry together, and just being together have been spoken about throughout this chapter as important to enhance the family lives of ministers and spouses. Such family time need to be inspiring memory-making moments rather than routine, obligatory, mundane moments. A female minister explained some of the emphasis that their family placed on doing things together:

> We had great holidays, we'd go camping and things like that, and the boys have always gone bike riding and always had their friends around to the house. Also, my sister has three children and my brother has four children, so we have done a lot together with family over the years... Now that they have grown up and

married with children, we have a regular family dinner where we are all together, and we have our grandchildren, and that's something that we both really enjoy immensely. We do more outdoors types of things than indoors, just because there's many more of us now.

Other pastors and spouses also emphasized the importance of doing things together as a family. One pastor's wife explained, "We always get together for every birthday, every Christmas, and Easter, and anything that is happening in someone's life, we love to get together and celebrate. We've had engagements and weddings of late, so there's always something to get together as a family. It probably wouldn't be two or three weeks gone by when we don't gather together for something, so we try and do that and make sure we do that regularly now." Being together was also emphasized by another pastor "We spent time together, we went out together, we had lots of holidays, and we would go away as often as we could, so that kept us sane. So, we would play together and pray together and make decisions together."

Another female pastor stated, concerning the value she and her husband placed upon doing things with her family, "I think definitely we made family priority, we did lots of things that would create memories for the kids outside of church too. We had lots of picnics and bike rides, and even now we still have family dinners and we'll get together and have a lot of fun and laughter because family is a precious time for us." Another pastor stated, "I think that number one is that we always planned time together as a family and set a schedule for family time as well is ministry time. And so, every week we would have a specific family day." Another female pastor whose husband was also a pastor explained, "We look for regular points of connection, we have flexibility with that, but we make sure we have the intentionality of that still happening. Also, we would look for those special moments where we would have the whole day together, or a whole weekend together, and maximized those special moments." A pastor spoke about how he spent time with his children when they were young: "We would do things with them on our day off when they weren't at school, to make sure we do things together. You take the time out to get on the floor and play with them and be a dad."

There was much discussion by pastors and their spouses regarding the importance of doing things with their family as something that worked for them. This example is something every pastor and spouse should note and put into practice as many pastors and spouses get so involved in spending time with the many members of their congregations that they can neglect the important time they need to spend with their family.

The emphasis of making time for fun

Many ministers and spouses emphasized the value of making time for having fun and laughter with their family as something that worked for them and brought the family closer. It is a true statement that a family that prays together stays together. It is also true that a family that laughs together enjoys staying together. A female pastor explained the joy of making time for fun with her family: "We are all very engaged in our lives, but on a regular basis we go out to dinner. Our kids are foodies so that is a lot of fun. When we are together, there will always be impassioned talk about something or other. We can laugh till we are sick. We are very connected. We are a tight family." Another female pastor commented, "We enjoy getting together and have a lot of fun and laughter." The spouse of a pastor enthusiastically stated, "We would go and do something spontaneous and something fun and something creative." Another pastor's wife stated, "We do make time for fun. We like to go on dates, go out for coffee, ... we work at having a balance so it's not just all ministry."

A male pastor also explained the importance he and his ministry-employed spouse place upon having spontaneous, weekly, random fun with the family: "We have yearly holidays just with the kids. Spontaneous, weekly, random fun, and we are daily looking for moments to be together." Another male pastor also emphasized the importance of having fun in the ministry and with the family: "I think that you need to have a lot of fun with the ministry and the family and even if you tell really bad jokes you have a lot of fun and that's really important to keep your sense of humor." Unfortunately for many ministry-involved families, fun and laughter get lost due to the many responsibilities that are connected to the ministry. Yet the Bible tells us a merry heart is as good as medicine. Families that laugh together and keep a sharp sense of humor often enjoy being together and enjoy the ministry/family journey. Don't take yourself too seriously or be so serious that your family don't enjoy being around you.

The importance of protecting the family

The emphasis of protecting the family from being exposed to the various ministry challenges that arise within church/ministry life was also identified as something that worked for ministers and their spouses to maintain a healthy ministry/family journey. In this context, the participants spoke about shielding their children and spouses from the human side of ministry involvement, whether it was political, personal, or relational issues with which the minister often had to deal. A male minister made a clear statement about protecting his children from unhealthy church issues: "We would never talk church business or politics in front of the children." This intention of protecting the family from being exposed to the various challenges that arise within church/ministry life was also expressed by a male participant: "With the children I've done my best to protect them from the burdens of the ministry." We will make further comments regarding the importance of giving attention to the family by protecting them from the ungodly and burdensome problems of church life in chapter 9.

Giving Attention to the Spiritual Well-Being of the Family

Having noted the importance of giving attention to the minister's marriage and family, we will focus on giving attention to the spiritual well-being of the family. This was emphasized in my research as another area of focus that worked for many ministers and spouses. When discussing their ideals, the blessings upon the family, the issues they wrestled with, how their spouse and their children handled the ministry/family journey, what works for them, what they would do differently, and what recommendations they would make to those starting out in the ministry/family journey, the focus on the spiritual well-being of their family continued to surface. When discussing their ideal picture regarding ministry/family life, the participants highlighted a clear desire for the spiritual well-being of their family.

Such a desire for the spiritual well-being of their family is grounded in their call to bring salvation to all people through the ministry in which they are called. However, due to the close relationship they have with their family members, such an ideal is an even higher priority. For those ministers and their spouses whose children have drifted away from their faith, such a situation weighs heavily on their hearts and minds.

The importance of maintaining spiritual health in the family

In regard to maintaining the spiritual well-being of the family, a female minister voiced the deep desire of her heart for her family's spiritual well-being: "I guess my ideal picture is that my family would have a positive spiritual outlook, that the church and ministry would inspire them to love the church and love God for themselves, and to feel that that's a really positive thing."

Those who indicated their children still attended church and were still pursuing their faith expressed the highest frequency of comments regarding giving attention to their family's spiritual well-being. A female minister stated her desire for her children's spiritual welfare as follows: "As for my kids, I'm protective of my kids because of the situation and the expectations that other people put upon them, I just want them in an ideal setting to first and foremost have a very real relationship with God."

When participants discussed the things that work in their ministry/family life, the theme regarding a spiritual focus for the family continued to become evident in their responses. Sometimes, because ministers and their spouses are engaged with the spiritual dynamics of others in their church on a regular basis, it is easy for them to assume those closest to them on this journey, namely their family, are progressing well spiritually by virtue of proximity. When this is simply assumed, the resultant neglect can have serious consequences, even eternal ones. My research revealed that those who focus on maintaining the spiritual health of their family, including their children, are more likely to experience satisfaction and fulfillment regarding their children's spiritual stance. The wife of a couple who were both credentialed in ministry explained:

> There are different things that we have done depending on the season. So, when they were young we were very deliberate to sow the scripture into their lives and to really utilize that season that they were in, and sow in a love for Jesus, and to bring them up understanding not just that church was normal but having their own faith in Jesus is important. Therefore, you frame everything else around that.

Another female pastor, mother, and wife stated:

> I have developed a strong prayer life to pray for our family, this is a very big part of our life, as the children know that we are often praying for them and the situations that they find themselves in. They often ask for us to pray for them when I'm catching

up with them on the phone, or when they are with us. I write a devotion and post it online to them every week to let them know what I feel God is saying to us.

This value of focusing on the spiritual health of the family was highly emphasized by many.

The importance of being involved in ministry together

As a pastor and preacher who has preached in many different churches, one of the things that strikes me is the amount of ministry families that do ministry together. Often the pastor's spouse is involved in the worship team, welcoming new people to church, organizing rosters, or sharing the pulpit duties. Many ministers' spouses are authentically involved and committed. The children of the minister are also conspicuous in their involvement in the life of the church. Whether they are involved on the sound desk, the video projector, the music/worship team, or leading the youth group or children's work, the minister's children contribute greatly to the function of the church's ministry.

When presented with the question regarding what they do that works for them in their ministry/family journey, many ministers and spouses stated they involve their whole family in doing ministry together. A spouse of a female minister celebrated being involved in ministry with his clergy wife: "I think it's our involvement in ministry together that keeps us pretty well balanced." Another spouse also explained how he "gets involved and tries to support his wife as much as he can." A further comment from a female pastor's spouse was, "Our family have seen many lives turned around and I think it's exciting for them to be a part of that, and I think they also aspire to help people."

A pastor of four daughters explained, "We intentionally disciple the girls in work ethics, church involvement, schooling and family life." Each of this pastor's four daughters are very passionate about their church, their faith, and their life, as well as being a tight-knit family. Involving the whole family in doing ministry together was emphasized as something that works well for ministers and their spouses as they live out their ministry/family journey. This involvement also helps each family member to have a reason to develop a healthy spiritual life.

The importance of setting (living) an authentic example

As ministers and spouses in my research discussed the importance of focusing on the spiritual well-being of their family, the need for setting an authentic example or model was also discussed. A male minister remarked that "Hopefully they would be able to see what Dad and Mum preached on Sunday was lived out throughout the week." Participants recognized the value of the family being able to observe the authenticity of their ministry-involved family member displaying the reality of their faith when it wasn't being observed by the public eye. This authentic modelling of the God-life lived in the home was viewed as a spiritual benefit for the family by many. Another minister commented, "The main blessing is seeing your kids watching you in private and then seeing you in public and noting that, so that's a real blessing to me."

A female minister stated the importance of staying authentic as a recommendation to those starting out in ministry:

> I would tell them to stay authentic, because the thing that I experienced over many years was the disconnect between my real self and my public self, and that can lead to finding yourself in a place where you are no longer enjoying what you are doing. Because you're not being your real self and you're trying to perform rather than minister. You need to be who you are, who you are all the time, rather than having two different versions of who you are.

The importance of setting an authentic example before the family not only works toward maintaining a healthy spiritual focus for the family, but also works toward maintaining a healthy personal integrity that sustains the spiritual well-being of the minister themselves.

The importance of making church a very special thing

The importance of the family experiencing the church as a special place to attend and a positive place to be around is nonnegotiable if you want your family to continue to attend church at their own initiative, and genuinely seek God and worship him. The secret behind such an experience for the minister's family is in how the minister and spouse portray the church to their family. If they portray the church in a negative light, eventually their spouse and children will see the church in that same negative light and develop a negative attitude toward the church. Many pastors' children eventually stop attending church because they view it as an organization that treated their parents poorly. Others cease to attend church due to their perception of the church being boring and irrelevant. Much of these insights stem from their parents' conversations and behaviors in the home, which are observable by the minister's family.

Several of those who indicated they were satisfied with their children's spiritual outlook and had all of their children still attending church and pursuing their faith indicated they made church a very special thing as something that worked for their ministry/family journey. A mother and pastor of a ministry couple stated she deliberately made church a very special thing for her children. According to Grice's study, the advantages of a Christian upbringing was expressed as the greatest advantage of growing up in a pastor's family:

> Six potential advantages of being a pastor's child in order from the highest to the lower score were as follows: gained a basic Christian upbringing; met many interesting people; knew some things better than many in the church; cared for in special ways; position of recognition, status and influence; felt positively special with elevated status.[2]

Special moments of encountering God were also discussed as a special experience at church for the family. Another female pastor explained, "I always wanted to present the positives of being involved in ministry and how that blesses the family, so my grandkids absolutely love going to kid's church and being involved because I make it a very special thing. So, I think that having them seeing church as a positive, a real positive experience, has worked well for me."

The importance of making church a very special thing, rather than portraying the church as a place of negativity and pain, needs to be heeded by ministers and their spouses whose desire is for the spiritual well-being of their family. The value of characterizing the church as a very special place in the eyes and ears of their family members should not be underestimated. This principle is not just true for ministry families but is also true for Christian families at large. The value you place upon the church as a parent and spouse will also be reproduced in your family members, with eternal results.

---

2. Grice, "Pastor's Kids," 98.

Chapter Summary

When comparing those who indicated they were satisfied with their children's spiritual outlook with those who indicated they were unsatisfied, there was a vast difference in the number of comments made by participants from the satisfied participants compared to the unsatisfied participants regarding the endeavor to maintain spiritual health in the family. According to my research, those who gave attention to the spiritual well-being of their family are more likely to have a satisfied outcome regarding the spiritual outlook of their children.

The third feature of Attention in the Triple "A" Model for Ministry Function and Family Fulfillment encourages ministers and their spouses to give continual attention to their family. Such attention creates strength and support for their family and particularly their children. In this chapter, the research identified keys that respondents found to have worked in their ministry/family life, which included giving an intentional focus to their marriage relationship, their family life, and also the spiritual well-being of their children. My research concludes that being intentional about their focus on their family builds their family relationships and family unity, and helps each member of the family to understand they are valued. Giving such attention to their family while engaged in ministry will result in children wanting to continue to follow the faith of their ministry-engaged parents.

Giving Attention to the Minister's Marriage

The value of keeping your marriage healthy

The value of ministry couples going on dates

The value of being present when with their spouse

The value of supporting their spouse

The value of strengthening and encouraging each other

The value of speaking positively to and about each other

Giving Attention to the Minister's Family

The importance of keeping the family as a priority

A hierarchy of priorities

Maintaining clear lines of communication

The value of having trips away together (holidays and conferences)

The value of having regular family meals together

The value of doing things together as a family

The emphasis of making time for fun

The importance of protecting the family

Giving Attention to the Spiritual Well-Being of the Family

The importance of maintaining spiritual health in the family

The importance of being involved in ministry together

The importance of setting (living) an authentic example

The importance of making church a very special thing

Personal Reflection

What are some things you do that have a positive effect on your marriage?

What are some things you do that have a positive effect on your family?

What are some things you do that have a positive effect on the spiritual well-being of your family?

Chapter 9

Reflective Evaluation, Insightful Decisions, and Proactive Protection

THIS CHAPTER WILL CONTINUE to focus on the third feature of the Triple "A" Model regarding giving careful Attention to the minister's family. An imbalanced focus on ministry and church growth, when allowed to become an extreme preoccupation, can at times conflict with the minister's responsibilities as a spouse and parent. The purpose of this chapter is to reveal how the minister's journey toward ministry/family fulfillment can be aided by evaluating what the minister and spouse would avoid or do differently if they had their time over again, what decisions they would make, and the importance of being more protective of their family while they are engaged in their ministry.

Reflective Evaluation

As the question was posed to the participants in my research regarding what they would avoid or do differently in their ministry/family journey, they focused their responses primarily on what they would do differently rather than what they would avoid. In the midst of this discussion, participants demonstrated an intentional devotion to their family. Such a devotion was balanced with the many demands these clergymen and women must contend with. Research has discovered that, in addition to the issues of nonstandard work schedules, long work hours, the helping nature of the profession, and numerous but varied responsibilities, clergy experience boundary ambiguity between the domains of their work and family.[1]

Susan Cody-Rydzewski adds that, "clergywomen are likely to experience conflict between work and family . . . In part, this is because ministers often report that they are on-call. Thus, unexpected emergencies or requests may interfere with scheduled family time."[2] Often the battle is not in their heart or in their desire to be with their family, but rather in the demands that crowd out their time and attention that they would like to give to their family. In response to the question regarding what they would avoid or do differently in their ministry/family journey, the ministers and spouses in my research emphasized several things they would do differently as follows:

I would intentionally spend more time with the family

One of the great challenges of many ministers and their spouses is the challenge of spending quality time with their families. As we have read in a previous chapter regarding what issues coupless wrestle with in their ministry/family journey, lack of time together as a family was a major issue they identified. Many pastors are in demand outside of normal business and school hours. Most church, board, small group, department, and other church-related meetings occur when congregation members are available. These hours when congregation members are available are usually in the evenings and on weekends. The great dilemma is these are the hours when the pastor's family are at home. One pastor stated he would "make Saturdays a day when I don't do church associated activities in order to spend Saturdays with the family." Another pastor also emphasized the importance of preserving their Saturday to spend with the family, "I would target the weekends to spend more time with my family, on Saturdays in particular when the children are at home."

When a group of clergy families were asked to describe the greatest disadvantages of being in the ministry, their answers came down to five broad recurring themes: the first and foremost disadvantage was there was not enough family time together.[3] Reduced time is also a common

---

1. Wells et al., *Work-Related Stress and Boundary-Related Stress Within the Clerical Profession*, 216.

2. Cody-Rydzewski,. *Married Clergy Women*, 273–289.

3. Lee and Balswick, *Life in a Glasshouse*, 191.

theme in the literature on church health. In Lee and Balswick's research, a minister's child touchingly wrote, "Our father is always too busy to be with us."[4] In Norman Blaikie's study, *The Plight of the Australian Clergy*, a number of clergy complained that the long and irregular hours they have to work, particularly in the evenings, leave them little time to spend with their families.[5] A spouse of a male pastor in my research stated she would "like to have one day a week when you spend time together and don't have to use that time to get the groceries for example, and just relax and be together."

There were many comments regarding the desire to spend more time with their family as something they would do if they had their time over again, however I can only include a few more in this chapter. This pastor above summed up what he would do differently in a short sentence: "Not be so consumed by the church, spend more time with the kids, and be more balanced and not so neglectful." A pastor's wife expressed her regret that she and her pastor/husband didn't spend more time with her family:

> When the kids were young and growing up, life was just crazy and busy, and there was a lot of pressure on my husband at that time. So, I particularly would have liked to have spent a lot more time as just the two of us. Probably more time with the children as well, like even mealtimes, having my husband there with us at mealtimes so that the children could just talk. I think looking back that would have been good for us.

The lack of time given to the family due to being consumed by ministry responsibilities is something most pastors regret later in their lives. Such a regret can be rectified now by determining and actioning this desire by scheduling for more time in your diary to spend with your family.

I would communicate with the family better

Another thought expressed as pastors and their spouses discussed what they would do differently was they would communicate with their family better. Communication is not just a one-way conversation; it takes more than one person to have good communication. Open and honest communication between the minister and spouse, as well as between the parents and children, can create a pathway to mitigate the many

---

4. Lee and Balswick, *Life in a Glasshouse*, 194
5. Blaikie, *Plight of the Australian Clergy*, 183.

ministry-imposed difficulties associated with being a part of a ministry family, and to identify and celebrate the many blessings as well.

Many married couples in ministry find daily relationship stress occurs because of a lack of communication, often due to being consumed with ministry responsibilities. This, in turn, leads to negative assumptions and misunderstandings and therefore creates further stress in their relationship. The case studies undertaken by Thomas Ledermann et al. revealed that "both relationship stress and marital communication in conflict situations have an effect on the quality of intimate relationships."[6]

A spouse of a female minister stated the importance of maintaining communication between himself and his clergy wife: "I think good communication is so important, so that before anything festers, we communicate about things so that they don't fester and become poisonous. So rather than leaving things in the dark we bring things out into the light before they get too difficult." Another pastor stated, "I have learned about the use of language. I have learned to use the language of grace and would use that much sooner regarding how we communicate with the family."

Ministry marriages demand more than mere obligatory commitment. They, like any other marriage, require quality time, communication and affection. Dennis K. Orthner et al., in their research article entitled "The Resilience and Strengths of Low-Income Families," discovered that one of the key factors that has been linked to more positive outcomes of family resilience is the effect of positive communication.[7] Many married couples in ministry (who are also usually on low incomes) find that daily relationship stress occurs due to a lack of communication. The statement that "I would communicate with the family better" is an indication of ministers' and their spouses' desire to give further attention in this regard to relieving some of their marital and family stress.

I would put my family first above everything else

Additional frequent comments regarding what they would do differently focused on how they would put their family first above everything else. One pastor emphasized, "I would certainly put my family first above everything else and structure family time into our weekly schedule." A

---

6. Ledermann et al., "Stress, Communication, and Marital Quality in Couples," 199.

7. Orthner et al., "Resilience and Strengths of Low-Income Families," 160.

pastor's wife also stated the value of prioritizing their children: "I would also make our children feel like they were first priority." Another female pastor stated, "If I had my time over, I would have made more of a focus on our family time. So, I would make it a priority, even if it feels that it's an appointment in a calendar. But I would make family a priority and be proactive to do something fun. That would make all the difference."

I would be more present with my family

Another thing the participants indicated they would do differently was be more present with the family. Participants spoke about how when they were with their family physically, they struggled to give their family the attention they would like to give them due to their thoughts still being consumed by ministry concerns. A female minister, a senior pastor of a church, explained her dilemma of not being more present with the family:

> There are times where physically you might already be home, but emotionally you've already checked out, so maybe if I could have somehow pulled back the number of work hours or somehow got some relief in my head so that my family didn't get the leftovers. I think I would at times be at home with the family, yet in my mind was dealing with some of the stuff that I had to deal with at church.

Another female pastor also described this same scenario as something she would do differently: "If I had my time over again, I would be in the zone more. It's so important to be present with the family, to focus being off the clock from work and having time out. Therefore, doing that and being present with the family and turning off from work is something I would do differently." A male pastor also explained what he would do differently: "I would make sure that I give more attention to my children and wife when I am with them rather than letting my mind continually wonder about the other issues that are happening in the church at any particular time."

A regrettable account from another male pastor who had several of his children drift away from church and from their faith, is the explanation of how he lost focus of his children while engaging with the challenges of his ministry. His reflections have a bittersweet tone to them:

> We rejoice and praise the Lord that despite our significant challenges, our children prospered in terms of their social and

educational development. Today they are each holding very responsible positions and leading very productive lives in adulthood. This is despite my neglect of them due to my preoccupation with the pressures of ministry life. I remain deeply regretful that I was so often present physically but absent from their day-to-day lives.

The comment that "I would be more present with my family" received the highest number of comments by the female ministers who consciously desired deeper relationships with their family. These female pastors felt some regret in being consumed with their ministry thoughts in their minds while they were physically present with their family. A key to being more present with your family, whether you are a male or female pastor or spouse, is to turn off your mobile phone before you enter your home and leave your church responsibilities at the front door before you enter the domain of your family.

I would be more intentional about planning and doing things with my family

There is a saying that if you fail to plan, you plan to fail. This often applies to ministry families who allow life and time to just transpire or even expire rather than being intentional about making specific plans for the health and well-being of their family. The necessity to be deliberate about making plans to spend quality time with the family is essential if you are serious about having a flourishing family, as well as a fruitful ministry. A pastor who is also the father of two boys (now adults) stated, "I think I would probably be more intentional about our days off. Especially in our early time when our boys were younger. I would be more intentional about planning and doing things together rather than just sort of waiting and seeing, and then doing things on the spur of the moment." Another pastor explained, "I think what we would do differently is definitely take specific times for ourselves. We felt that we had burnt ourselves out because we didn't. Even if it was just an overnight time together somewhere just to refresh ourselves." Another pastor stated, "I would certainly take holidays, and I would actually block in those holidays."

These are descriptions of actions that ministers and their spouses in my research interviews indicated they would take if they had their time over again. They stated they would do these things differently and would intentionally give attention to these factors of their ministry/family journey. Such descriptions were emphasized from hindsight reflections of ministry couples regarding their family lives. They also discussed decisions they would make differently if they had their time over again, which we will now consider.

Insightful Decisions—The Desire to Have Made Better Life Decisions for the Family

As participants in my research discussed what they would do differently they emphasized their desire to have made better life-related decisions for the sake of their family. There have been many studies recently on mental health support for clergy and the importance of making wise life choices for sustained harmony in the home.[8] Each of the respondents' life decision comments began with "I" as participants reflected on decisions they personally would have made differently if they had their time over again. We will now reflect on these decisions that could have made a more positive impact upon their family.

I would have made better financial decisions

David and Vera Mace, in their pioneering study *What's Happening to Clergy Marriages?*, discovered one of the major challenges clergy families are confronted with was the battle of the budget.[9] Comments that they would have made better financial decisions reflects an ongoing challenge for most ministry families—limited finances. This issue of limited finances was highlighted in several places throughout this research. A minister stated, "If I was to say that if I could do something different, I would say, to get yourself a strong financial base early in life that will stand you in better stead to what God calls you into. . . . I think that personally I would probably try to structure my financial life a little bit better, a little bit earlier." Another pastor also commented along this same theme: "In hindsight, I would do some things differently in regard to financial decisions." Another pastor explained, "I would try to avoid exposing the financial pressure, or stress part of that, to our kids, I don't know if we

---

8. Weaver, et al., *Mental Health Issues Among Clergy and other Religious Professionals*, 395.

9. Mace and Mace, *What's Happening to Clergy Marriages?*, 48.

were actually successful but that's something I would try to avoid." A pastor's spouse also expressed their challenge of financial constraints in the ministry as she explained, "We were very stretched financially at times, so I would like to have had more finances available to us."

I would seek more guidance regarding time management

Another frequently mentioned decision was how they would seek more guidance regarding time management. William H. Willimon, in his book, *Clergy and Laity Burnout,* states that, "Poor time management wears down many in the church. Many pastors are sinking in a tangled web of trivial, unimportant, poorly organized commitments and activities that rob them of the time they need for more important ministry."[10] Pastors who do not pay attention to this vital area of their ministry/family lives will not only be candidates for burnout in their own lives, but their families will also miss out on the time and attention from their ministry spouse/parent that they desperately need and deserve.

I would avoid going ahead too fast

These statements were linked to discussions regarding being impatient and issues regarding making decisions in the ministry that weren't necessarily bad decisions but were premature in their timing. It is likely that going ahead too fast was also potentially caused by an extreme desire of seeking approval and recognition from fellow ministers and ministerial leaders.

I would avoid being isolated and would seek support when needed

Several ministers and spouses lamented that they felt like they were very much alone in their ministry/family journey and would not want that to happen again. They would instead initiate supportive relationships with other key leaders and pastors. One pastor made a telling statement regarding the need to be supported in ministry, with regard to avoiding being isolated and seeking support when needed: "If I had known then what I know now, I would have been far more forthright in seeking out some

---

10. Willimon, *Clergy and Laity Burnout,* 31.

form of immediate oversight to which I could be accountable. I would certainly avoid being isolated." Those who stated they had adequate support for both their ministry journey and their family had a much higher satisfaction rating concerning the spiritual well-being of their families.

All of the above statements regarding making better decisions for the family were made by multiple participants when reflecting upon what they would avoid or do differently in their ministry/family lives. The following statements were made by single individuals regarding making better life decisions for the family. I have also included these individual statements without further comments as many of these resonate with many pastors and spouses.

- "I would work hard at finding my comfort level in God, and flow with that."
- "I would have recognized that there are seasons."
- "I would have started a lot of the things that I do now, earlier on."
- "I would probably give back all of the transfer, headache, church members to their old pastors."
- "I would avoid a renovation straight up when taking over a ministry."
- "I would not go into a church where the previous pastors are still there."
- "I would probably focus on my health better."
- "I would do further studies sooner rather than later."

Overall, participants who stated they were satisfied with their children's spiritual outlook were more expressive regarding making better decisions for the family. The wisdom of making better decisions would obviously lead to greater family well-being.

Proactive Protection for the Family

When discussing the things that work for them in their ministry/family lives, the concept of a protective focus for the family was highlighted, as we briefly discussed in the previous chapter. This focus of protecting their family was also discussed regarding what they would avoid or do differently if they had their time over again. One pastor's wife explained,

"With the family I would have protected them a little more. With the kids growing up I should have taken more notice of their after-school friends, maybe I could have got a little bit more insight." A pastor explained, "I could have been more protective and spared my wife from a lot of anxiety."

We will now give this focus deeper consideration as many families, and particularly children, can be greatly damaged by church politics, church leaders, and congregational members (often unintentionally). The experience of one spouse of a male minister was expressed with irritation regarding having to protect her child from an unreasonable congregation member: "We had one of our boys being choked by a congregational member telling him not to run around, when all of the other children were also running around. So, I asked him if he was going to treat the other kids in the same way, because you have to protect your kids." Throughout the interviews, participants discussed the importance of protecting their family from the issues that can be imposed upon them due to the ministry vocation.

Protecting the pastor's family from unrealistic expectations

The first aspect within this concept was the emphasis that participants wouldn't allow other people to put expectations on the family. Others stated they would avoid the expectation scenarios. The spouse of a male pastor who had her child being choked by a congregation member as discussed above also explained how people placed different expectations upon her once her husband had been employed as a pastor.

> When we first entered the ministry, I was told that I can't be the same person that I was before I was in the ministry and that I had to change, and that I had to go to Bible college. I like to have fun, so I was told that I couldn't have as much fun, and I'm not studious so that weighed heavily upon me. Then one day I was praying about it and God revealed to me that I created you to be you, you are not to be someone else. So, you've got to learn to walk on the path God has called you to, not the path that someone else expects you to walk in.

Another pastor's spouse explained her desire to avoid comparisons and expectations:

> I would avoid comparisons that put a lot of pressure on me, comparisons with myself and our family with other pastors' families and what other families are doing. I would also avoid comparisons with the ministries in the church because it always seems to be that someone always seems to be doing better than yourself. I would also avoid trying to put expectations on our kids.

A female minister stated her desire to protect her children from expectations in order to ensure her children's spiritual welfare: "As for my kids, I'm protective of my kids because of the ministry situation and the expectations that other people put upon them." There have been times where church leaders and congregational members feel it is their right to place expectations on the minister's family and often feel they have the right to correct and discipline the pastor's children.

In my research, those who were aware of this possibility and placed protection boundaries around their children tended to enjoy a flourishing family life. Whereas those who were unaware of such challenges their spouses and children faced, and therefore gave no attention to protecting their spouse and children from such unrealistic expectations, tended to experience resentment and frustration within their family as they engaged in their ministry.

Protecting the family from unhealthy church issues

As much as the church is the bride of Christ and is being purified and prepared for the return of Jesus, there are still many imperfections within the present institution that can have an unhealthy effect upon pastors and their families. Many pastors and spouses discussed the need to protect their families from some of the unhealthy, humanity-generated church issues. One male minister reflected on a conversation he had with a more mature minister in his early days regarding shielding his family from church issues:

> The strange thing is that I sat under a ministry, where the guy said, don't share everything, why burden your loved ones, you should be protecting them and not burden them with every silly thing and silly action that people in the ministry/church context might do. But I didn't listen to that, and we paid a price. So, I learned the lesson, and I've done my best to be protective,

and tried not to burden my family when they have no ability to contribute to a solution.

This same pastor who endured some challenging times in the early years of his ministry emphasized his desire to have been more sensitive in regard to what he shared with his wife: "I have learned the lesson since, as I learned this over 25 years ago, that I would shield my wife from the nastier, unattractive experiences that I had seen in the church context, and not share so much with her." This pastor made the following recommendation regarding not bringing the negative church issues church into the home:

> You can't bring the church into your home; you know the problems that go with it. You can't spend all your time at home talking about it because your spouse and children hear that, and it does affect them. If someone gives you a hard time in the church, and your spouse and kids hear about it, then they get very resentful and angry and protective, then the situation gets sorted out, but they are still left with all that anger and dislike toward those people. So, you've got to keep the church issues out of your home, and certainly not around the dining room table.

Many who participated in my research also discussed their desire to protect their family from unhealthy church issues such as church crises, the politics of church life, and criticism from church members. In this context, the participants spoke about shielding their children and spouses from the human side of ministry involvement, whether it was political, personal, or relational issues with which the minister had to deal. Carol Darling explores the intangible ways in which congregations can intrude upon the boundaries of the clergy family and finds that intangible intrusions of criticism directed at the pastor and/or their family are more harmful than tangible boundary intrusions.[11] One might call these psychological boundary intrusions. Darling discovered that clergy spouses had higher levels of physiological and psychological stress than did the clergyperson due to boundary intrusions.[12] These issues also affect the children of ministers if the parents don't protect them. The intention of protecting the family from being exposed to the various challenges that arise within church/ministry life was expressed by many in my research as something they would avoid or do differently.

11. Darling et al., "Understanding Stress and Quality of Life," 261.
12. Darling et al., "Understanding Stress and Quality of Life," 261.

I would learn to say "no" more and manage people's demands better

The comment that I would learn to say "no" more was expressed as a time and stress-protection issue. A female minister stated, "I became very strong in boundaries, I developed the skill of how to say no." The desire to manage people's demands more effectively was also emphasized by many of the ministers and spouses in my research.

Due to the spiritual call upon ministers and their spouses, many feel an obligation to say "yes" to every demand the congregation or community places on them. Often these demands come at times when the pastors and spouses are planning to spend some quality time with their family. The outcome of many that haven't learned to say "no" and protect their time with their family, is their families feel they are not valued and are not given the priority they require by their ministry spouse/parent. The question to ask when demands are made on your time is: "If I say "yes" to this, what or whom am I saying 'no' to?" Many ministers constantly say "yes" to the congregation demands and "no" to their family responsibilities. The findings of Wayne Hill et al. were that time intrusions negatively affected the quality of life for clergy families.[13]

Of course, there are unavoidable situations that demand the pastor's time and attention, such as the sudden death of a church member or a serious event that suddenly occurs. However, there are also many demands that are made on the pastor that can be dealt with at a time that doesn't impinge on the pastor's time with his/her family. A key attentional ingredient to ensuring a flourishing family life while engaged in ministry is to protect the family by learning to say "no" to demands that can be dealt with at a time that is not detrimental to the family's well-being.

I would keep our home our home

Many pastors commented on the need to keep a healthy balance between their home and their ministry so their family could come home and enjoy a healthy home life, while at the same time experience the joy of being a part of a ministry family that loves God and his people. Several of the ministers and their spouses emphasized they would protect their family

---

13. Hill et al., "Understanding Boundary-Related Stress," 147.

by keeping their home as their home, and not as a church drop-in center, or an extension of the church office.

The blurring of home and work boundaries are common in pastoral life. Lee and Balswick state that the boundaries between the congregation and clergy family are often too diffuse, which is usually not the case in other professional occupations.[14] When a group of clergy families were asked to describe the greatest disadvantages of being in the ministry, their answers came down to five broad recurring themes, one of these was the lack of privacy.[15] In a 2001 study of clergy families by Morris and Blanton, it was found that family boundary intrusion was a significant factor in predicting both clergy and their spouses' reports of marital and parental satisfaction.[16]

Many ministry families use their home as a base for counselling, prayer meetings, board meetings, leader's meetings, men's breakfasts, and many other church-related activities. One female pastor mentioned they would be more conscious in regard to not making their home the center for ministry in regard to counselling, prayer ministry, and other church-related activities that impinged on their children's freedom to relax in their own home. Blaikie highlighted this need for protecting the home regarding the challenges that female spouses have to deal with due to the ministry vocation: "Some wives feel they lack adequate privacy, either because of the location of the house beside the church, or because it is regularly used for meetings and functions."[17]

Of course, in the early days of a church's existence, perhaps in a church-planting situation, the church office is often based in the minister's home. However, this situation should be only temporary and a suitable church office outside the pastors' home should be organized as soon as possible. Being able to maintain boundaries between the church and home is vital for maintaining the health and enjoyment of ministry families, therefore the protection of keeping your home as your home can enhance the well-being of your family.

---

14. Lee and Balswick, *Life in a Glasshouse*, 75.
15. Lee and Balswick, *Life in a Glasshouse*, 191.
16. Morris and Blanton, "Influence of Work-Related Stressors," 189.
17. Blaikie, *Plight of the Australian Clergy*, 161.

The importance of protecting some time for solitude and privacy

Although there are times when ministers and their spouses can feel quite lonely throughout their ministry, there are also times when they need some solitude and privacy to refresh themselves and recharge their lives. There were some frequent comments in regard to the importance of protecting some time for solitude. The cry for privacy of one minister's wife who works alongside her husband in a small country town was passionately emphasized: "If I go out for a coffee or wherever I go, people are there and people feel they have a right to you at any time. So, for my sanity I just need some space to do something else away from the church and away from the people, but I don't get that time to feed my social self." Protecting time for solitude and privacy to refresh and recharge your life individually, as a couple, or as a family, is something that is nonnegotiable for those who desire to have a flourishing family life in the midst of a fruitful ministry life.

Overall there was a higher frequency of comments regarding the protective focus for the family by participants who were satisfied with their children's spiritual outlook compared to those who weren't satisfied. The data from my research confirms the value of giving attention to the family by intentionally protecting the family while fulfilling their ministry call.

Chapter Summary

In summary, giving Attention to the family, which is the third feature of the Triple "A" Model of Ministry Function and Family Fulfillment, is vital to enhance the spiritual well-being of the family while you are engaged in ministry. The importance of learning from pastors' and their spouses' reflections is imperative for both current and future ministry families. The wisdom of evaluating what they would do differently and what decisions they would make differently, as well as protecting the family while engaged in ministry, is wisdom that can't be ignored.

Reflective Evaluation

I would intentionally spend more time with the family

I would communicate with the family better

I would put my family first above everything else

I would be more present with my family

I would be more intentional about planning and doing things with my family

Insightful Decisions—The Desire to Have Made Better Life Decisions for the Family

I would have made better financial decisions

I would seek more guidance regarding time management.

I would avoid going ahead too fast

I would avoid being isolated and would seek support when needed

I would work hard at finding my comfort level in God, and flow with that

I would have recognized that there are seasons

I would have started a lot of the things that I do now, earlier on

I would probably give back the transfer, headache, church members to their old pastors

I would avoid a renovation straight up when taking over a ministry

I would not to go into a church where the previous pastors are still there

I would probably focus on my health better

I would do further studies sooner rather than later

A Protective Focus for the Family

I would protect the pastor's family from unrealistic expectations

I would protect the family from unhealthy church issues

I would learn to say "no" more and manage people's demands better

I would protect some time for solitude and privacy

Personal Reflection

Evaluate what things you would do differently if you had your time over again regarding your ministry/family journey.

What are some decisions you would make in regard to the health and spiritual well-being of your family?

What are some things you would do that would be more protective of your family?

Chapter 10

Stable Support Structures and Sustaining Resources

Stable Support Structures

Having appropriate support structures in place is a very important element for ministers. Research has found that poor support networks are a major reason that ministers experience burnout.[1] Social isolation and interpersonal or relational difficulties are major reasons for high levels of anxiety in clergy.[2] As the participants in my research reflected upon the support structures from which they drew strength and wisdom along their ministry/family journeys, several insights were identified within the interviews. Most expressed that they had no structured support; some expressed that they received a certain amount of support from their family and friends; a few expressed that they had received some limited ministry related support from their denomination's leadership; and approximately one-fourth commented that they receive some support from mentors.

The Tyranny of No Support

It is alarming to discover that almost half (46 percent) of the participants indicated they had no structured support for their ministry/family journey. Those participants who indicated they had some support explained

---

1. Grosch and Olsen, "Clergy Burnout," 619.
2. Trihub, et al., "Denominational Support for Clergy Mental Health," 101.

the support they received was for their ministry world. Yet, very few indicated they had reliable support structures in place for their family while they engaged in their ministry. This highlights the need to give attention to developing reliable support structures for both their ministry and family.

The family in a general sense, with all of its complexities, needs social support, educational support, psychological support, medical support, and the list continues ad infinitum. If that is the case with the complexities of the family in general, how much more do the families that are confronted with the complexities of the ministry necessitate even more support? The very essence of marriage and family involves loving and respectful relationships; interdependence; personal and collective well-being; provision of emotional, physical, and material needs; and the social and spiritual enhancement of each member. Such a concept can also be anticipated as a reasonable expectation for members of clergy families to assume. The reality that many of the pastors and spouses indicated they had no reliable structures in place to support their families is a very real concern.

Morris,and Blanton highlight a study in the USA that confirmed the lack of support available for ministers and their families. "Research of 28 Protestant denominations of over 200,000 members in the USA discovered that although the majority of denominations (including clergy, their families, congregations and denominational leaders) were aware of the stresses that clergy and their spouses experienced, only a minority provided professional support that was adequate for their needs."[3]

In my research, those who indicated they were satisfied with their children's spiritual outlook and had all of their children still attending church and engaged in their faith more frequently expressed that they have support structures in place for their ministry/family journey than those who were unsatisfied regarding their children's spiritual outlook. The spouse of a minister from those who indicated they were unsatisfied stressed her lack of support as a pastor's wife in ministry:

> We didn't have any of that. When we were going through the really hard times, we didn't have anybody. My husband always had people that he could go to, guys that he knew in ministry, but I didn't have that, which means that you carry the load alone. . . . Our pastoral experience was that we walked the walk very much alone.

3. Morris and Blanton, "Denominational Perceptions of Stress," 345.

There is a great need for ministers and their spouses to receive specialized support for their ministry/family journey. The story of the participant above who had no real support is multiplied throughout the ministry world. Morris and Blanton discovered that clergy and their spouses find it difficult to obtain relief from stress due to the absence of social support, with feelings of loneliness and isolation by clergy families being a common experience.[4] The question for all ministry couples is whether you have stable support structures for your ministry and family well-being. If the answer is no, then you need to seek some help in establishing such support structures to sustain you in ministry and more importantly to ensure your family can continue to flourish.

The Value of Having a Mentor as a Part of the Stable Support Structure

Throughout the interviews, the participants discussed some practical and helpful recommendations for ministers and their spouses who are just beginning their ministry/family journeys—we will see more of these responses in the following chapter. Analysis of this data has proven useful as it reveals that continual attention to building reliable support structures is at the heart of these pastors and spouses. They themselves made recommendations regarding areas they see as important from their own ministry/family experiences and saw giving attention to building reliable support structures as vital.

The highest recommendation was to find good mentors. A pastor recommended they "definitely get someone who is experienced, to draw from their experiences with their ministry and their family." A renewed focus on the need for mentors has risen within the ranks of the ministry, where pastors and their spouses are becoming more aware of their need for a mentor to guide and develop their lives and ministries. A male pastor explained, "I didn't have a lot of mentors growing up in the ministry, I probably didn't have a lot of mentoring or coaching." A female minister highlighted her need of a mentor to support her in her ministry/family journey:

> I probably think that that's what I'm lacking, and I think that that's part of the tiredness that I have been feeling recently, and so that idea of having a mentor, especially a female mentor,

---

4. Morris and Blanton, "Influence of Work-Related Stressors," 189.

would be something that I would like. So you know you've got peers and good friends, but somebody that is fully two steps ahead of you, that I could have that as someone a little bit wiser, that is a little bit more ahead of me, that I could go to and receive wisdom from.

George Barna, from his research regarding ministers in the USA, suggests the development of mentoring programs for pastors.[5] Because ministry is not meant to be conducted alone, such a need for mentors, as revealed in the recommendations in my interviews, and also recommended by Barna, is not to be ignored. Mentoring in the secular world of business and education has proven to be of great assistance, and such would be the case in the ministry/family world. A female minister stated the necessity of regularly seeing her mentor:

> I have my own professional supervisor that I see on a regular basis. I see her monthly, so I think that is vital, because that's not only for support, but also learning about myself and helping me with my direction and how I see both ministry and my personal needs and value. So, I've made that very intentional, because I believe that if you don't intentionally develop those relationships that go the distance, then it's very hard to develop relationships with people that you are leading that will go the distance.

Lonnie Inzer and C.B. Crawford suggest there are benefits of mentoring for the protégé, the mentor, and the organization, such as promotion opportunities, higher wages, and personal growth in a non-threatening environment.[6] They also explain that mentors share and take pride in their protégé's accomplishments, which invigorates and renews their commitment to their job and their profession and provides them with an ongoing legacy.[7]

Whether you are just starting out in ministry, or whether you are somewhere along the ministry/family journey timeline, the recommendation to find good mentors is now recommended to you. Identifying a mentor to provide guidance and support has also proven to be a key to satisfaction in a minister's spiritual journey.[8] If you don't have a mentor/

---

5. Barna, *Today's Pastors*, 18.
6. Inzer and Crawford, "Review of Formal and Informal Mentoring," 36.
7. Inzer and Crawford, "Review of Formal and Informal Mentoring," 36.
8. Doolittle, "Impact of Behaviors among Parish-Based Clergy," 89.

confidant in place, make it a priority to find someone whom you can trust and from whom you can receive wisdom and guidance.

The Value of Structured Ministry-Related Support

During my research interviews the ministers and their spouses also discussed the structured support they received in the process of attending to their ministry responsibilities. They discussed the various relationships they developed while engaged in their ministry. Support from their peers, such as other pastors and their spouses, was highlighted. Evidence suggests pastors who fostered healthy peer friendships are more likely to maintain a healthy work-home balance.[9]

The practice of attending ministry-related conferences was another avenue of support, although, as a spouse of a male minister explained, "There were conferences and things like that, but they were mainly support structures in regard to doing ministry, not so much for helping us with our family lives." Another spouse of a male minister spoke about going to monthly pastors' meetings for ministry support: "We would go to pastors' meetings once a month where we would get to meet other pastors and catch up and see how each other is going. Apart from that we didn't have a lot of support for our family as such."

Another source of ministry-related support was the participants' eldership or board within their church, and support from the ministers' pastoral teams. Others emphasized supports from ministry networks and from state and regional leaders. A pastor emphasized his appreciation of being able to receive support from his state executive leaders:

> Just being able to talk to someone and completely dump things on them, not worrying about how it could affect them by what you say is extremely important. Otherwise you don't ever get a chance to really release the burden you carry, and that's really important. And I've got a chance to spend time speaking to some of our state executive members, and they have been happy to have a good long chat with me and I think I've really needed that.

A female minister who is in her first pastorate as a senior pastor in a country town explained the value she placed upon her support structure from within her denomination:

---

9. Meek et al., "Maintaining Personal Resiliency," 339.

I have connected with the district meetings in a city that is a four-and-a-half-hour train ride away, to connect with that district leader and his wife. Also, I have connected with other leaders and pastors that are females and pastors' wives, where we can connect every three months for a coffee to support one another in ministry. My board have encouraged me to connect with a counsellor to talk about ministry issues. So, I do have that network and I still have some relationship with other female ministers that we connect with relationally. At any time, I've probably got three to five people that I can call, and some male ministers as well, that I can call on if I need to talk through some issues.

Research suggests clergy experience higher levels of guilt over family issues than other groups.[10] However, Bobby Trihub et al., in their study "Denominational Support for Clergy Mental Health," found many denominations provide insufficient support and training for clergy regarding personal and health issues, including family issues.[11] There is certainly a demand for some further structural support systems to be developed within all denominations that will undergird the ministries and families of ministers within the church.

Whether it be the minister, the spouse, or the children, each family member needs to be able to lean on someone else in times of difficulty, distress, or confusion. Although the family are a great source of strength and comfort, there are times when the minister and spouse's family will not suffice due to the intimacy or vulnerabilities within the family. One wife of a minister explained she would often download some of her frustrations within her church and ministry onto her sister. She felt her Christian sister was a safe place to unload the weighty thoughts and concerns she and her husband wrestled with. Unfortunately, due to her sister not understanding the weight that ministers and their spouses carry, the sister lashed out at this hurting pastor's wife telling her she was unspiritual and had no faith. This pastor's wife once again retreated into her lonely shell to suffer in silence, with her feelings and frustrations remaining internal with no opportunity for release or relief.

Several participants explained they relied on their church board or eldership for support, which can be a source of strength and encouragement. However, although relying on the church eldership or board may

---

10. Rickner and Tan, "Psychopathology, Guilt, Perfectionism," 29.
11. Trihub et al., "Denominational Support for Clergy Mental Health," 102.

be convenient, it is not necessarily always expedient. There are times when the eldership/board can be the source of unrealistic expectations, financial limitations, and other stressors the pastor and spouse deal with. An overfamiliarity with board members or elderships who haven't experienced the responsibilities of ministry firsthand has the potential to lessen the respect they have for the pastor/leader. This is often due to their unrealistic expectations that pastors and their spouses should always be highly spiritual, full of faith, and without personal challenges or limitations. Many pastors have made the mistake of becoming overfamiliar with their boards or elders, to the detriment of their ongoing ministry in their local church setting.

The satisfaction factor that ministers and their spouses indicated regarding the spiritual outlook of their children largely depends on having reliable support structures in place for each member of the family. The highest response regarding ministry-related support from participants that were satisfied with their family's spiritual outlook was in regard to obtaining support from their peers, namely, other pastors and spouses. Perhaps their higher satisfaction rating is due to drawing support from those with whom they have relationships and who understand the weight of their ministry call and responsibilities, as well as their needs. When they were having trouble within their church, they sought help from their denomination's leadership. But when considering support for their family journey, there was rarely the same level of support available to them.

The Value of the Unofficial Support from Family and Friends

Having observed the (official) ministry-related support structures that pastors and spouses relied on for their ministry/family journey, the (unofficial) support ministry families receive from their family and friends was also considered as a valuable resource. The importance of giving attention to developing both structured support and unstructured support systems for ministers, their spouses, and their families is vital to consider.

Over one-fourth of participants mentioned the support of their friends, and over 20 percent of participants stated they received support from family members. They also mentioned the male spouses received support from their female spouses and vice versa. A pastor whose wife is also a pastor emphasized, "My wife and I are very strong and make sure that we communicate and support each other." Although I have outlined the dangers of placing a heavy reliance on family members regarding ministry issues due to the intimacy or vulnerabilities within the family, there is certainly a place and very real need for family support. Many participants indicated their appreciation of their family regarding family support from their parents and siblings. The opportunity to have their children grow up with their grandparents, uncles, aunties, and cousins nearby was greatly treasured by those who were able to enjoy such a privilege.

The importance of good friends was a recurring theme throughout my research. As pastors and spouses made recommendations to those starting out in ministry a frequent recommendation was to have good friends in ministry. A male participant emphasized the support he can call upon from his friends: "I guess I have a lot of contacts that would call me their friends. And I don't use that term lightly—many of them call me friend. They are people who if I need their input, they will give it to me." Another male minister stated the value he placed upon the friends that have supported him throughout his ministry crises:

> I have the valued advice and friendship of close mates, which is the most important structure for me. Friendships have always been the most important thing for me, and I can't remember a major crisis or problem that I handled without having the benefit of close friends around me to help me through it.

Although this source of support is greatly valued by those pastors and spouses that participated in my research, the number of couples who indicated they received support from their family and friends or each other was still well below 50 percent. In that light, it can be concluded that over 50 percent of the ministry families who were interviewed may not have received any form of support from their family or friends. Unfortunately, the transience of many pastors often results in a distance and disconnection with their friends and family, leaving them isolated and lonely, and often in the situation of making life-determining decisions without any support or wise counsel. Unless ministers and their spouses give attention to maintaining reliable support structures with their family for their ministry/family journey, important moments and opportunities in their ministry/family lives may be jeopardized due to lack of support or counsel.

Place Some Support Structures around Your Children

As they discussed the support structures they have in place regarding their ministry/family journey, the importance of providing support structures for their children was also acknowledged. As stated earlier in this chapter, many ministers and their spouses tend to receive support from their peers and other pastors, or possibly their church denominational leaders in more serious church matters. However, building support structures for their children's ministry/family journey also needs to be addressed in an intentional way.

The evidence in my research revealed those who don't establish support structures for their children are more likely to experience an unsatisfactory outcome regarding their children's spiritual outlook. Those who were satisfied with their children's spiritual outlook emphasized they attempted to put some support structures around their children. A minister whose wife was also a minister explained:

> We certainly tried to make sure that our kids had support. There were times when there were some people that were *de facto* grandparents for our kids. And when they grew up a little bit more, if we did find a person or a couple that we believe would speak into their lives positively, and as it were, echoing our values, we would expose them to those people. That way they would hear that from other people and not just from Mum and Dad. So rather than say, 'This is what you want, Mum and Dad,' they would say, 'This is what these other people are saying.' And so, we would look for people that would have similar values as our own to speak into our kids' lives.

Another minister explained:

> I think we've tried to really put some support structures around our kids, so that as they have been growing up, we've always tried to connect them and help them form friendships that are going to be healthy. We encourage them to pursue good friendships with good families that we know, and that sort of stuff.

Giving attention to the support structures for the children is very important to having a satisfied outcome regarding the children's spiritual outlook. The children of the minister and spouse often face difficult situations they cannot necessarily handle on their own. The value of this is again evident in the data as the participants who indicated they were satisfied with their children's spiritual outlook were the only participants that commented on the value of intentionally establishing support structures for their children. A pastor's wife who was heartbroken by her children drifting away from God and church explained, "Perhaps if I had my time over again, we would cover them more in prayer, I don't think you can pray enough over your kids. Maybe we should have supported and protected them more spiritually." Perhaps for those that desire to avoid such heartache, a key ingredient is to intentionally establish some support structures around your children as soon as possible.

The purpose of this book is not to condemn or shame pastors and spouses who have experienced the heartache of seeing their children drift away from God and his church. In contrast, my desire is to see families reconciled to God and each other in a way that has both an immediate and eternal effect upon their family life. I pray the outcomes of my research will help pastors and their spouses discover what helps families play together, stay together, and pray together in the kingdom of God as they serve him in the ministry vocation. I encourage pastors and spouses to establish some strong and joyful support structures around their children that will enhance their children's well-being socially, psychologically, and of course spiritually.

Sustaining Resources

As we have discussed throughout this book, ministers experience many challenges due to the unique factors associated with the ministry vocation. Often these challenges can spill over into their everyday lives, and if not acknowledged and safeguarded, these challenges can have a negative impact upon the minister's family. In order for ministers and their families to flourish rather than falter, it is important for ministers and their families to be able to draw upon available resources that will strengthen and sustain them as they fulfill their ministry calling.

Previously in this chapter we discussed the importance of ministers and their spouses establishing stable support structures for their ministry/family journey. We will now briefly focus on the importance of having sustaining resources from which ministers and their families can draw strength and vitality. These resources were acknowledged by participants as essential in sustaining them and their families as they navigate their ministry/family journey. I have divided these resources into two categories, i.e., Spiritual Resources and Relational Resources.

Spiritual Resources

The spiritual resources discussed in the interviews were vital toward upholding a positive motivation and attitude throughout their ministry/family journey. Though the blessings that are mentioned as a spiritual resource were often experienced as material or monetary gifts, the participants recognized them as evidence of God's provision for their family and therefore described these as spiritual blessings. Their encounters with God were also spiritual resources that sustained them, as were the blessings of having a Christian upbringing, as we will observe.

God's Blessings

When discussing their ministry/family journey, many ministers and spouses commented on the blessings of being in ministry that affected the family in a positive way. An attitude of appreciation toward God for his goodness was revealed in the hearts of the participants as they reflected upon these blessings. Those who identified this attitude of gratefulness toward God would also discuss their appreciation of God's blessings due to being involved in ministry with their family. Such appreciation became contagious throughout their family and often resulted in the children being glad to have been raised in a pastor's home and many wanting to engage in some form of ministry service themselves. Focusing on the blessings of ministry had a positive effect upon the spiritual well-being of the whole family and inspired them to continue to serve God.

God Encounters

Another spiritual resource that ministers and their spouses discussed in the interviews were their moments of encountering God's presence and leading. Participants acknowledged these experiences as moments of transformation. These moments may have occurred in private times of prayer where they felt God speaking to them, or they may have occurred in public meetings through dynamic preaching or during special times of prayer at the altar. For many, due to their commitment to the local church after their conversion, the ministers and spouses encountered a divine call to ministry. During the interviews for this research, further

God encounters that inspired the participants to continue to follow the call of God as a family were discussed.

Although many of these God encounters were related to their personal encounters with God, many also commented on the joy of seeing others within their church and ministry also encountering God. A spouse of a female pastor noted the joy of their family being able to be involved in ministry alongside his minister wife and the results of seeing people encountering God, saying, "Seeing people set free and growing spiritually has been a great blessing."

Another female pastor also commented on the blessings their children have experienced by witnessing other people being transformed by God: "Being a part of and seeing the possibility of change in people, our kids have seen what God can do and I think they have all ran with that. They have all developed a big faith in the possibility of change.... They see God's presence and power is real and part of that is because of the privilege of being in a ministry family." Consequently, the spiritual resources of experiencing God encounters, both personally and in other people's lives, often sustain ministry families to continue to serve God, even in difficult times.

Christian Upbringing

The strength of a Christian upbringing was frequently mentioned amongst the participants in my research as a valuable spiritual resource to sustain the family in the ministry/family journey. This privilege of being raised in a Christian family was identified as a cherished foundation. A spouse of a pastor expressed that her ideal picture of the ministry/family journey would be to have had a Christian upbringing and a Christian legacy for her children:

> We are first-generation Christians, so everything looked rosy at the beginning but when we began in ministry it all changed of course. But I think when looking at families in the church, when they had history going back with Christianity, they seem to be more stable. We're building that, because we're first-generation Christians and our children are second-generation Christians, so we will eventually have what I really value and see in others. When my kids visited their grandparents or their aunties, uncles and cousins, there was no value of Christianity in that part of the family. So, your family history is really important, the

family values of Christianity. We pray for our family all the time, however there is nobody in our family behind us praying for us. So, I think it would make a real difference.

In reality, there are many ministers and spouses whose parents and extended family are not Christians and therefore have to create a new generational line of Christian values for the generations that follow. Many of those who were interviewed in my research expressed that having a Christian upbringing was not just an advantage, but also a valuable spiritual resource to draw upon in their ministry/family journey.

Relational Resources

As has been discussed previously in this chapter, the importance of establishing stable support structures is vital for the spiritual well-being of ministry families. The following supportive relationships were also frequently discussed as important resources to sustain ministry families throughout their ministry/family journeys. We will only briefly focus on these relational resources due to having discussed these areas in more detail previously.

Family Resources

The relational support of extended family, such as parents and siblings, was discussed as a valuable resource for participants. We must be careful in this conversation to not just consider the extended family as necessary for support, but also as being necessary as an emotional resource for the minister, spouse, and children. The emotional resource that close family members stimulate in the hearts of ministers and their spouses is very rarely replicated outside of the family circle. In many cases, where family has become distant due to geographical moves by the ministers and spouses, modern technology has helped maintain these close relationships that are such vital resources for the minister's family.

Denominational Resources

The resource of the regional, state, and national leadership in their denomination and the relationships they developed with their denominational leaders were described as having a profound influence upon their lives and ministry. One female minister explained, "I viewed myself as not necessarily having my own ministry due to being a female, even though I sensed a unique call of God on my life. However, when I went to an ACC (AOG) church, I realized that God had called me to my own unique ministry." As we have discussed the value of denominational support regarding establishing stable structures previously in this chapter, we will not delve deeper into this resource at this time, except to emphasize the spiritual and emotional value that these kinds of relationships offer to ministers and their families to sustain them in their ministry/family journey.

Mentors

The resourceful relationships that participants developed with mentors who walked alongside them was also discussed. Such mentoring relationships helped sustain participants throughout their ministry/family journey. The importance of having the support of a mentor was also discussed as a stable support structure previously in this chapter. However, mentors were not just considered as stable support structures, but also as essential for the emotional and spiritual sustainability of ministers and their spouses.

Having analyzed the comments of the participants that indicated they were satisfied with their children's spiritual outlook compared to those that said they were unsatisfied, the research indicates that drawing upon spiritual and relational resources to sustain the minister's family is more likely to result in a satisfied outcome for the spiritual well-being of their children.

Chapter Summary

This chapter has described the stable support structures and sustaining resources ministers and their spouses in my research said they rely upon. The need to have stable support structures in place, particularly in regard to establishing relationships with personal mentors and denominational leaders, as well as maintaining contact with family and friends over time, was a key focus for ministers and their spouses as they discussed their ministry/family journey.

Stable Support Structures and Sustaining Resources

If you don't feel you have any stable support structures or sustaining resources for your ministry/family journey, may I suggest you act quickly to change this situation. For the sake of your ministry and family, you can't live as an island in the great ocean of ministry and family responsibilities. Unfortunately, the devil may cause some kind of tsunami to rise up in the midst of that ocean that will crash upon your ministry and family. Without support systems and resources in place it is likely the tsunami will destroy everything you are called to do and everyone you love. Act today to ensure a flourishing family as you fulfill your call to a fruitful ministry.

Support Structures

The Value of Having a Mentor

The Value of Structured Ministry-Related Support

The Value of Support from Family and Friends

The Value of Placing Support Structures around Your Children

Resources

God's Blessings

God Encounters

Christian Upbringing

Family Resources

Denominational Resources

Mentors

Personal Reflection

Support Structures

What support structures do you rely upon?

Who are your closest friends?

Which friends and family members do you rely upon for support?

Who is your mentor?

Who in your denomination's leadership structure do you relate to for support?

Do you only pursue support for your ministry?

Who do you draw from for family-related support?

What support structures have you established for your children?

Resources

What are the major resources you draw from to sustain you in your ministry/family journey?

What key relationships sustain you in your ministry/family journey?

Is God still the major spiritual resource you rely upon?

When was the last time you had a divine encounter with your Creator and Savior?

What relational resources have you allowed to become extinct in your life?

What relationships do you need to rekindle?

Chapter 11

Recommendations

THE FINAL QUESTION POSED to the participants in my research interviews was, "What recommendations would you make to a person beginning their ministry/family journey?" The essence of their answers serves as a further resource for those seeking wisdom for their own ministry/family journey. I have categorized the answers to this question into several categories: Family-Focused Recommendations, Protection-Focused Recommendations, Ministry-Focused Recommendations, and Spiritually Focused Recommendations.

Family-Focused Recommendations

An intentional focus on the family was revealed when the participants discussed recommendations to couples beginning their ministry/family journey. These recommendations are particularly focused on the health of the minister's and spouse's relationships, as well as giving attention to their family in general. While important for all families, it is particularly true for clergy families, as they often face severe personal demands.[1] Understanding the stakes, participants in my research provided some insightful recommendations based on their own life experiences and observations. Many recommendations were given in regard to the well-being of the emerging ministry couple's family.

---

1. Rediger, *Clergy Killers*, 39.

Make Sure Your Family is Number One Priority

Their highest recommendation was to make sure the family is the number one priority. Each family member deserves equal respect and equal priority. Jack and Judith Balswick propose that, "from a biblical perspective, the ethic of family includes the mandate that each member is to be cared for, thus emphasizing the value of each family member and their entitlement for respect, consideration, sensitivity and understanding within the family relationship."[2] A minister suggested the following in giving intentional priority to the family while engaged in ministry:

> I think I would just really encourage them to have strong family values, to really have that private life right. Because I think if your private life is unhealthy it will inevitably flow out into your public ministry life. So, I would encourage them to set those boundaries of having a good solid home life where they have time as a couple together and time with their kids.

Ensure that Your Marriage Relationship is Strong

Following the more general recommendation to make sure the family is the number one priority, a more specific recommendation to ensure your marriage relationship is strong was expressed. A pastor's wife emphasized, "It's really important to stay best friends. If there's issues to work through, don't put the issues aside hoping that they'll sort themselves out. Actually, get in and deal with the marriage issues that arise." Another spouse of a female minister suggested, "I would encourage them before they even went into ministry to ensure that their marriage and their relationship with themselves as a couple was strong and can cope with the ups and downs of life that ministry can bring upon them, before they even get into it."

Further comments came from a pastor whose wife was also a minister: "I'd say that the first thing that you need to have is a great marriage. When you have a great marriage, and a great family, you can then disciple people from that strength." A spouse of a female pastor suggested, "I would probably recommend to them to recognize the fact that their marriage is a ministry on its own, and it's the most important one. You can't preach healthy marriages if you don't have one." Many more comments were made regarding the recommendation of keeping your marriage

---

2. Balswick and Balswick, *Family*, 317.

strong, however I will conclude these comments with a practical recommendation from a pastor as to how to keep their marriage strong: "I think that every pastor and spouse should have one night at least as a family night and at least one night together as husband and wife where they have personal time together."

Have Good Communication within the Family

It is very easy for pastors and spouses to get so caught up with ministry responsibilities that they can cease to communicate well with each other or their family. Sometimes they get so peopled out during the day at the church that they don't want to talk so much at home. This can be a very real danger. A pastor whose spouse was also in ministry suggested, "I would suggest that they communicate and talk with each other regularly so that they are both on the same level. . . . You really need to talk those things through." A female pastor whose spouse was also in ministry suggested she would give the following recommendations, all of which were connected to having good communication:

- Talk about things openly to each other
- Let your marriage partner know of your desires and wishes
- Tell each other daily that you love them; don't take it for granted
- Don't go to sleep angry, talk it over and pray and commit disagreements to God before turning in for sleep
- Ask your marriage partner if there are some aspects that you are not measuring up to in your relationship
- Never speak against your marriage partner to another person, praise them openly to others
- Be prepared to let them know if they did a good job
- Praise quickly and often
- Don't correct or criticize quickly, bring it up a few days later for discussion
- Hold hands (touch) when you pray together
- Meet each other's personal and sexual needs
- Be prepared to confess, "I was wrong" and "you were right."

Learn How to Balance Their Ministry/Family Priorities

The recommendations to learn how to balance ministry and family priorities flowed from their own experiences and lessons learned in that regard. One pastor suggested, "Make sure you've got the structures in place to always balance your family with your ministry responsibilities, especially when your kids are growing up, so that they never think that they missed out on things because you are a minister." A male pastor explained how he and his wife prioritized the family by postponing her ministry involvement until the children were older:

> The values for us was that family was a priority and as the kids were coming, we aimed toward those values. For my wife who had a call to ministry, and had gone to Bible college, that would mean that she wouldn't have the same expression that she saw others expressing in their ministry. She placed a priority on raising our children above her own call in ministry at that season.

Give Priority Time to Your Family

Priority can be measured in several ways. Firstly it can be measured regarding focus. Secondly, it can be measured alongside ministry expression, as mentioned above. Another measure of priority is regarding the measure of time people give priority toward something or someone. When making recommendations to those starting out in ministry the importance of prioritizing time for their family was expressed by several participants in my research. A female minister emphasized the importance of giving priority to time with the family while they are still with you: "There will always be another sermon to prepare; there will always be another needy person to visit; there will always be another meeting to run. If you don't do that today, they'll be there tomorrow. However, your kids are only here for today." Another pastor recommended, "Work hard at maintaining priority time and input to those who are going to remain for the long haul (Wife, kids, close friends)."

A pastor's spouse recommended, "Make sure that your family is a priority. Even though church is a priority, your family has to be a priority as well. A counselling session can wait another day if your children need you that day. If you can't make a meeting, that's okay, because your children are important. God values the family." Another pastor's spouse emphasized, "I would say definitely treasure their own personal family time, make sure that's a large priority in their life and navigate that to the best of their ability." Following is a practical recommendation from a pastor to protect family time: "Have your days off with your family and turn your telephone off at the meal table."

Have Great Holidays Together

Having great holidays together was recommended frequently by participants in my research. Having great holidays together was also spoken of as a blessing of being in ministry and something that has great importance for families engaged in ministry. A female pastor's spouse commented, "I would also encourage them to have memory-making times during their times together, such as great holidays, great family days together." Another pastor recommended that they, "Schedule quality time that gives priority to your children that is nonnegotiable, i.e., regular family holidays and even weekends throughout the year." Another female pastor who ministered alongside her husband recommended, "Have a yearly holiday, even if it's just a few long weekends where you are just together as a family having fun together away from the church."

Understand that Your Family is Indispensable

Many pastors and spouses minister as if they are indispensable to the church, and therefore don't maintain a measured approach to their ministry/family journey. A male minister stated he would stress the following to pastors and their spouses who are just starting out in ministry:

> Don't think that you are indispensable, but understand that your family are indispensable—you can't afford to lose them. At some time, you may leave your church, and then you ask yourself what you have left. You've either got a great relationship with your kids and with your wife, or you had a great relationship with your church and may have possibly lost your kids and your wife by living a life as if you are indispensable to the church.

As a pastor leading churches, every now and then a congregation member would come to see me and explain that they couldn't continue in their role in the church or they were transferring to another location and therefore their role would need to be filled by someone else. They would often have a sense of guilt for letting God and the church down. My approach to them was that no one is indispensable. I would encourage them and express that they would be irreplaceable as people and personalities, and we would miss them for who they are, rather than for what they do. They needed to be free to move on and understand they weren't indispensable, that God would have someone in mind to fill the role they were vacating.

This is also true of pastors and their families. If they left the church to take another ministry role or for any other reason, they would be irreplaceable in regard to their personality and in regard to who they are and what they bring to the church in that regard. However, no pastor is indispensable to their church. God will often call a new pastor to the church who will lead the church further in his purposes, and very soon the church will attach themselves to that new pastor and his family and love and follow them just as they did the previous pastor. Once a pastor understands the reality that they are not indispensable, but that their family is indispensable, they will more likely focus on the well-being of their family as well as the health of their church.

Understand the Various Seasons of Your Family

As there are natural seasons in regard to the weather, there are also seasons of life we all experience. The family also progresses through different seasons, from being newlyweds to being young parents, to being parents of toddlers, children, teenagers, young adults, and eventually being grandparents and hopefully great-grandparents. And then the cycle continues with our children and grandchildren.

In light of this, it was recommended by pastors and their spouses that those starting out in ministry also understand the various seasons of their family and respond to their family according to the season they and their children are experiencing at that particular time. A female pastor recommended that couples understand the season their family is in at any time and adjust their lives accordingly: "I would say, know what season that you are in and be present in that season." Another female pastor recommended they come to a point of agreement in how they will navigate the ministry/family journey, and reassess that in the different seasons.

A pastor's spouse explained, "There is the season when the family is very young, and they need more of your time. There is also the season when they are teenagers and you need to be more involved with their social life so you know what they are doing, where they are going, and who their friends are. God knows that and there is a season when they become adults and you are at liberty to focus more on ministry." Seasons in life are not obstacles to ministry, but rather opportunities for your family to grow together. It's important you understand what season your family is currently experiencing and live through that season with them as you also engage in your ministry responsibilities.

Include Your Family on the Journey

The recommendation from several pastors and spouses in my interviews were to include your family in your ministry journey. A female pastor recommended they include their kids in what they're doing. Another female pastor also recommended, "As much as possible, include them on the journey in terms of reminding them of the privilege that it is to be in church and to serve God and to love people and to be in a privileged position." A pastor's spouse commented,

> I'd say that as your kids get older you should try and include them in the decisions that you make. . . . We would say that we want you to be praying about this and getting them involved, so you are not just uprooting them, moving them to the other side of the country or whatever, without them feeling involved as well.

Including the family in the ministry, whether it be in regard to praying about ministry decisions or being involved in ministry roles, helps the family have some personal ownership of the ministry. This may also prepare and develop them for future leadership responsibilities, either in the church, in their employment, or within their community.

Speak Positively about One Another

Several pastors and spouses recommended ministry couples speak positively about each other. One female pastor said, "Speak generously about one another, rather than the jokey humor that puts one another down. Verbally build one another up." Another female minister made the recommendation to "Never speak against your marriage partner to another person, praise them openly to others." Building one another up by speaking positively to each other and about each other brings health, wholeness, and strength to your marriage relationship while you are engaged in ministry. This also holds true in regard to speaking to your children as well as speaking about your children to others.

Be Present in the Moment

The recommendation to be fully present with the family when you're with them arose many times in my research. A pastor explained, "I'd just be saying to make sure that when your home, your home, you are there, you're present, your mind isn't elsewhere, and your body is there. Make sure that they have got your whole self when you're at home with the kids, and let the kids see that ministry is not stealing from them, but is adding to them."

A female pastor recommended, "I would say know what season that you are in and be present in that season." Another female minister affirmed, "I learned to be present in the space. You will be more effective in your work if you rest better, so rest hard and play hard and work hard. Be in the space that your life's situations demand, especially when you are with your family."

Many ministers find it so hard to be present when they are with their family, normally having their mind in another place dealing with issues, thinking about congregation members, worrying about finances, etc. The recommendations to be present with the family came mostly from ministers and spouses who were satisfied with their children's ministry outlook, confirming one of the secrets to their success, i.e., being aware of their children's needs and paying attention to their spouse and children.

Keep Extended Family Relationships Healthy

As we have observed previously, many pastors and spouses acknowledged the value their extended families have to them in regard to the support and well-being of their immediate family. It is very easy to become so consumed with the needs within the church that your extended family receives no attention. This can result in the extended family, such as parents and siblings, drifting farther apart. This is not a healthy scenario and certainly not a great witness of the grace and goodness of God. Many pastoral families have experienced this and suffered the grief and sadness that accompanies such situations.

A female pastor's spouse emphasized, "In regard to recommendations, I would say that people should try and make those things right with their parents at the beginning of the journey and not at the end of the journey." The value of healthy relationships with extended family cannot be overemphasized, not just for your sake as a pastor and spouse, but also for their sake, and for the sake of God's kingdom.

The family-focused recommendations for couples who are just starting out in ministry should be taken seriously by all ministry couples, not just those starting out, as we can all learn and improve and give further attention to our ministry/family journey.

Protection-Focused Recommendations

As participants spoke about the recommendations that they would make to a couple beginning their ministry/family journey, they gave some further insights regarding intentionally protecting their family while fulfilling their ministry vocation. The highest recommendation regarding intentionally protecting the family was not becoming trapped by other people's expectations. Recommendations to protect at least one day off per week with your family and not to bring the church into the home were also given. Allowing the children to be children was also suggested.

Don't Become Trapped By Expectations

As stated in previous chapters, investigations regarding the effects that growing up in a minister's home has upon the religious commitment of the adult child found that the strongest negative stressor was "expectations" due to being the pastors' child.[3] Lee and Balswick explained that "although all children must learn to adapt to social expectations, the expectations placed on preacher's children may be more intensive than most."[4] They continued to state that "in addition to an expectation of great piety, clergy children are also expected to attend every church

---

3. Anderson, "Experience of Growing Up," 393.
4. Lee and Balswick, *Life in a Glasshouse*, 163.

function and to volunteer more readily than their peers."[5] In alignment with Lee and Balswick's findings, the participants in my research also found other people's expectations to be more of a hazard than a help for their family. Therefore, many ministers and their spouses recommended those starting out in ministry not allow the minister or their family to become trapped by others' expectations. A recommendation worth paying attention to.

Protect at Least One Day Off Per Week with Your Family

The recommendation to protect at least one day off per week with your family also received frequent comments from participants in my research interviews. A pastor suggested Saturday be the day off for pastors as their children are not at school on Saturday:

> Probably I would say that if they have got young children that they really need to take all of Saturday off, so that they can spend that time with their children. Because on the Monday, if they have Monday off, their children are probably at school and therefore get no time to have together. I would encourage them to get their preparation done before the weekends, so that they can have the whole of Saturday off rather than using that day as a preparation day for the Sunday.

Such a recommendation is critical for pastors, as the most frequently emphasized issue when pastors and spouses were asked what issues they wrestled with in their ministry/family journey was the issue of time with their family. This recommendation serves to help pastors and spouses starting out in ministry to have quality time that will refresh and strengthen their family well-being.

Don't Bring the Church into the Home

Another frequent comment was not bringing the church into the home. The following recommendation from a pastor explains the reasons for not bringing the negative church issues into the home:

> You can't bring the church into your home; you know the problems that go with it. You can't spend all your time at home

---

5. Lee and Balswick, *Life in a Glasshouse*, 91.

talking about it because your family hear that, and it does affect them. If someone gives you a hard time in the church, and your family hears about it from your discussions, then they get very resentful and angry and protective. Then the situation gets sorted out, but they are still left with all that anger and dislike toward those people. So, you've got to keep the church issues out of your home, and certainly not around the dining room table either.

Allow the Children to Be Children

The recommendation to allow the children to be children has great wisdom. Many pastors' children are exposed to adult issues in the church all too soon. Added to this, many pastors' children are expected by both the church congregation and many times by their parents to serve in the church before they have had the opportunity to just play with their friends at church and enjoy the whole experience.

The wife of a pastor, and the mother of a son that has turned away from the church and also his faith, lamented the mistake they made by not protecting their child enough and allowing him to grow up as a normal child while he was quite young: "Our son had some major issues in that he had people putting expectations upon him to behave like a pastor's kid and didn't allow him just to be a normal child and grow up in the church." As they grow there will be many opportunities for the minister's children to serve in the house of God. Unfortunately, many minister's children get involved in serving too soon and when they mature, they no longer see such service as a privilege and honor, but rather seek for opportunities to avoid attending church at all.

These protective recommendations have emanated from the experiences of participants and their children throughout their ministry/family journeys. Those who indicated they were unsatisfied with their children's spiritual outlook tended to be more engaged with these discussions as they had experienced difficult circumstances that have possibly contributed to the fact that their children no longer attend church or continue to pursue their faith. Their protective recommendations need to be seriously considered.

Ministry-Focused Recommendations

As participants discussed the recommendations they would make to a couple beginning their ministry/family journey, there were many recommendations made regarding their ministry focus. The main recommendations are as follows.

Don't Do Ministry Alone

Research on the nature of stress associated with the clerical profession suggests not only that clergy experience unique stressors related to their careers, such as counselling individuals and families, teaching, guiding, and carrying out administrative responsibilities, but that these stressors may exacerbate the effects of work on their personal lives.[6] The value of connecting with other pastors and having ministry/family mentors is you can break out of the lone wolf syndrome and draw from others to help see the challenges of ministry from a different perspective. Calling on others for help and support can also help carry and even lift the load off your ministry burdens.

Get Some Sort of Financial Structure Early

Another common recommendation from participants was the wisdom of getting some sort of financial structure early. Comments regarding the financial needs of pastors have appeared in several places throughout my research interviews. An ongoing challenge for most ministry families is limited finances and a battle with the budget. When commenting on the difficulty of ministry finances, Lee and Balswick state: "Quite simply, if they don't have enough money, their financial obligations become burdens and a certain source of family stress."[7] A pastor expands on his recommendation of getting some sort of financial structure early:

> I would also recommend that they get some sort of financial structure early . . . many in the ministry have struggled financially due to pioneering and pastoring small country churches, and so you need to have something in place. So, get yourself

---

6. Wells et al., "Relationship between Work-Related Stress and Boundary-Related Stress," 215.

7. Lee and Balswick, *Life in a Glasshouse*, 193.

a property, a house or an asset that will appreciate, so that no matter where your ministry is, you've got something. Because I have seen so many in the generation that has gone before, whose lives have ended with nothing, and that puts great pressure on the family.

Having financial strength was also stated as an ideal regarding ministry/family life.

Count the Cost

Several ministers and spouses recommended that those starting out in ministry should count the cost of ministry involvement well before they enter the ministry so they are prepared for the many challenges ministry bestows upon the ministry couple and their family. In a study of 14 clergypersons in the USA, Marianne Grabowski found that the minister's spiritual journey includes: self-awareness; significant positive and negative personal experiences; vocational awareness; the call to ministry; and a vocational response to the call to ministry.[8] One of the many costs is the negative personal experiences that ministers and their families encounter from time to time. A minister explained the importance of being aware of the cost of ministry involvement. "When we took on our church it was exciting, and we wanted to change the world and give it our best shot . . . but I think going into ministry, the costs take you by surprise." Jill Anne Hendron et al. state that clergy and their families are also faced with the very real dangers of secondary traumatization in the line of professional duty, which can significantly alter the life direction of a minister.[9] The dangers of secondary traumatization in the line of pastoral duty is a high price many ministers pay. A spouse of a female minister suggested, "I think it's important that if they do engage in ministry that they are realistic with what they are about to do and the time pressures that will be involved."

There are many costs involved when ministers and their families are engaged in ministry: financial costs, time costs, personal costs, stresses, etc. The recommendation for ministry couples that are starting out in ministry to count the cost has great wisdom. Jesus also recommended counting the cost in Luke 14:27–28 (NIV): "And whoever does not carry

8. Grabowski, "Holy Darkness, Blessed Night," 140.
9. Hendron et al., "Unseen Cost," 229.

their cross and follow me cannot be my disciple. Suppose one of you wants to build a tower. Won't you first sit down and estimate the cost to see if you have enough money to complete it?"

Take Charge of Your Own Life

The recommendation to take charge of their own life has emanated from ministers and spouses who have experienced the pressures that ministry imposes upon people to the point where they feel they no longer have a say in their personal and family lives. One pastor recommended, "I would also suggest that they take charge of their own life and take ownership of their future." Many pastoral couples, as well as their children, come to a place where they realize if they don't take control of their own lives, then others in the church will control their lives for them. This lack of personal control can lead to burnout, and possibly marriage and family breakdown. A pastor's spouse explained, "I've heard older pastors say at retirement age, that if they had their time over again, they would place more emphasis on living life and having fun and not letting the ministry become all consuming." These comments from retiring ministers need to be heeded now, rather than being a regretful comment at the end of your ministry/family journey. Assume control of your own life and enjoy a fruitful, fulfilled, and flourishing ministry/family journey.

Be Committed to the Wider Body of Christ

The recommendation of being committed to the wider body of Christ rather than just connecting with people in your own denomination was recommended by several participants in my research interviews. One pastor suggested the following:

> Don't be committed to your denominational oversight to the absolute exclusion of the wider body of Christ. That is not to suggest that we can dispense with appropriate accountable oversight. However, people now attach themselves to the "family of believers" rather than the denominational label that would otherwise identify us. A misguided sense of loyalty can often result in a narrow, severely restricted worldview.

Recognizing and respecting Christians and ministry couples across the denominational landscape adds to the lives of ministers and their families and expands their horizons for ministry fellowship, ministry fruitfulness, and ministry influence.

Be Patient When Building a Church

Many ministers and their spouses tend to have huge dreams and expectations for their ministry when they are first starting out. These dreams are wonderful and are often linked to their heart for God and desire to bring salvation to their world. However, building God's church also involves God building his kingdom in the minister and spouse. This doesn't always happen overnight. In a similar way, God's church is also being built from the inside out, developing a right culture, character, and composition of believers that will truly reflect his purpose for humanity. This also takes time in individual congregations. A pastor's spouse encouraged pastors and spouses that are just starting out in ministry with these words: "God doesn't expect you to achieve everything all at once. Be patient when building a church. It will take time, but it will be worth it."

Passionate impatience at its extreme can often result in ministers and spouses being driven by egotistic ambition rather than pastoral aspiration. This then results in pastors and spouses pushing people, and even their own families, to a place of exhaustion in their pursuit of growing a church for the sake of larger numbers rather than effective disciples. An earlier statement in answer to the question of what you would avoid or do differently was "I would avoid going ahead too fast." This statement was linked to impatience and premature timing issues.

Be Realistic in Your Expectations of Ministry

A further recommendation that is possibly linked to the previous recommendation is to be realistic in your expectations of ministry. Some research in the United States regarding people who attend seminaries discovered that the majority of people who go to seminary often do so from megachurches. However, most people that graduate from seminaries are usually employed in small local urban or small country churches. The gap between their expectations for their ministry appointments and the realities of such is called disappointment. Many went to college or seminary expecting to be placed on a megachurch ministry team, similar to the church they left, following their graduation. However, there are not many positions available for young graduates in megachurch ministry teams, whereas there are often many smaller country churches crying out for pastors of any age or description.

Other couples starting out in ministry have expectations of being well compensated, well cared for, and instantly successful at the commencement of their ministry. The gap between unrealistic expectations and the realities of ministry life is also described as disappointment, which can lead to discouragement and disillusionment. The recommendation to be realistic in your expectations of ministry, if heeded, can avoid disappointment, discouragement, and disillusionment. Proverbs 12:13 says, "Hope deferred makes the heart sick, but a longing fulfilled is a tree of life." A key is to have realistic expectations and celebrate the blessings ministry brings to the minister and family, no matter how large or small.

Hold the Ministry Lightly

Another ministry-focused recommendation made by several participants in my research interviews was the recommendation to hold the ministry lightly. A critical issue for many ministers is they become obsessed with the ministry and hold it so tightly that they can strangle or smother it. We need to keep reminding ourselves God has called us into ministry and he will bring it to fulfillment and fruition. Jesus said he will build his church; it is his call and his bride, and he knows best how to build it. When we hold it too tight, we make it our responsibility to grow it and therefore start to drive the congregation by obligation rather than lead them and draw them by grace. By holding the ministry lightly, we make it less about us and more about God.

Conduct a Church/Family Compatibility Assessment

Many difficulties in church life can occur when the church and the minister and/or their family are not compatible. A female pastor whose husband is also a pastor addressed the challenge of matching the church with a ministry family:

> Another thing that I would recommend to a couple just starting out is that they check out the church and the community that they are going to and ask questions about whether this would

be good for their family and good for the kids. Although this is very practical it is also very important, because I've seen city pastors go to country towns and find that the culture of the town is so different to the culture of a city. . . . There is a lot to be gained by researching the area and understanding yourself and how well you would fit into those scenarios.

A male pastor made the recommendation to conduct a church/family compatibility assessment for pastors prior to accepting a call to be the pastor at a church. This would help a pastor to decide if this is an appropriate church to lead in light of the results of this assessment. Furthermore, even if the couple still went ahead and became the pastors, such an assessment would give them an awareness of things they need to put in place to maintain health within their families while engaged in the ministry at those particular church settings.

Include a Session Regarding Ministry/Family Issues During Ministry Training Seminars

Another recommendation was regarding the training of emerging ministers. The spouse of a female minister recommended the idea of including a session regarding ministry/family issues during ministry training seminars. Many denominations have regular ministry training seminars as part of their professional development programs for their ministers and spouses. Often these professional development seminars focus on ministry-specific training sessions. The recommendation of including a session regarding ministry/family issues during these ministry training seminars would help prepare and enhance the ministry/family journeys of many.

Get Some Experience on a Church Ministry Team First

The recommendation to get some experience on a church ministry team before taking on the responsibilities of a senior pastoral role has great wisdom. In times past there were many young graduates from college that immediately accepted senior pastoral responsibilities before having gained some experience on a ministry team. As a consequence, many have struggled and then resigned, not only from their church but sadly from ministry altogether, feeling discouraged and disillusioned. The wisdom of getting some experience under a seasoned pastor for a time, as well as learning how churches function and developing some confidence, should not be ignored by pastors starting out in ministry. The development of ministry and leadership skills and being mentored by a senior pastor would build a strong foundation for a pastor's future ministry.

Don't Compare Yourself with Other Churches or Ministers

One of the great dangers that unsettles ministers and their spouses is the danger of comparing yourself or your church with those around you. A great source of discouragement for pastors and spouses is to feel as if they are not cutting it. We often fall into the trap of comparing ourselves with the exceptions rather than the rule. Many ministers compare their church and progress with megachurches, and this makes them feel inadequate in their own ministry. We can learn from other churches and other ministers that are doing ministry as we are, however when that learning becomes comparison, we place too much pressure on ourselves, our church, and ultimately our family. First Timothy 6:6 (KJV) tells us that "Godliness with contentment is great gain." To maintain contentment, don't compare, don't compete, and don't complain.

Warn Them that it is a Challenge Being a Woman in Ministry

A female pastor recommended female ministers be warned that it is a challenge being a woman in ministry. She continued, "So I would say remain steadfast in your call and that God loves you and he has chosen you, and so at first it's going to be a bit of a battle with that, so keep your confidence and keep reminding yourself that you have been called." Another female minister also commented regarding being a female in ministry:

> My thoughts regarding ministry for a female, would be to just continue to be there and persist rather than hold back. Embrace the opportunity and take the opportunity and believe in yourself and your call, so that God can continue to use you, rather than holding back and closing yourself off to ministry opportunities.

Life has been a challenge for many women for thousands of years. The apostle Paul addressed the inequality of the respect and treatment of women in the early church, and therefore gave women a new sense of dignity and purpose in Christ. The recommendations for women called by God to pursue all that God has called you to do and be in the kingdom of God has great potency and purpose for all women called to ministry. Whether you are a female minister, a female spouse of a minister, or a female child of a ministry family, the value God places on your life and ministry far outweighs the value Western culture places on women who aspire to ministry.

Understand that You Can Have it All, but You Can't Have it All at Once

One final ministry-focused recommendation comes from a female pastor who is very acquainted with the trials and triumphs of ministry life. She emphasized to ministry couples (women in particular) that they can have it all; however, they can't have it all at once. This insight emphasizes the need to be patient when building God's church and building your family. Eventually you can have it all: the relationships, well-being, growth and provision. However, you must be patient as you can't have it all at once, all at the same time. God will give you your heart's desire over the course of your life and ministry, little by little as he determines. As we wait on him expectantly in faith, he will give us all the desires of our hearts as Psalm 37:4 reminds us.

Spiritually Focused Recommendations

The concept of having an intentional spiritual focus for the family was identified as the participants spoke about the recommendations they would make to couples beginning their ministry/family journey. This spiritual intention is revealed in the recommendations they would make to those starting out in ministry. This again gives insight into the importance of having an intentional spiritual focus for their family as a ministry couple.

Prioritize God in Your Life and Family

The most comments came in regard to prioritizing God in their life and family. Research has revealed that 45 percent of pastors' wives say the greatest danger to them and their family is physical, emotional, mental, and spiritual burnout.[10] Sometimes a lack of private devotional time and the disappointments in people or ministry outcomes create a disillusionment toward God and the ministry. The recommendation to prioritize God in their life and family is certainly a key to avoiding spiritual burnout.

Make Sure You and Your Spouse Have Heard from God

The recommendation to make sure you have heard from God was the second-most common comment from participants who had indicated they were satisfied with their children's spiritual outlook. The emphasis on making sure they have heard from God was strongly stated by a pastor's spouse who remarked: "I would suggest that they make sure that they have heard from God first, and that ministry is something that they really want to do, that God has called them. Because if it's not what God has called them to do, it's not going to work out." A pastor also stated: "I would say . . . the first thing is asking them if they have really heard from God. You really need to know that this is what God has called you to. . . . Because the seasons come and the seasons go, but you've got to have something that you can lean on."

Prioritize God's House

Giving priority to God's house in both action and attitude, as well as in positive conversation within the family, was recommended by several ministers and spouses as they discussed their recommendations to those starting out in ministry. A great danger in ministry families is that the house of God is portrayed as a difficult work site, or possibly even a battle ground where the minister and spouse have been stationed. Rather than God's idea of the church being a place of love, liberty, prayer, power, purpose, and peace, many ministers' and spouses' conversations allude to negative connotations when discussing God's house. Therefore, both the ministry couple and their children can become resentful of the church rather than holding it in high regard. They then look for opportunities to get away from church, rather than being glad to go to church. Having roast pastor or roast people for lunch on Sunday after the church service certainly won't prioritize the house of God. Whereas speaking positively

---

10. Cordeiro, *Leading on Empty*, 32.

regarding God's house endears the family to God's house and inspires a desire to continue to attend church and serve God more often.

Keep Reminding Yourself that You Have Been Called By God

To many involved in full-time Christian ministry, their primary motivation to begin such a vocation has much to do with a sense of an inner call rather than pursuing a preferred career. The value of pastors reminding themselves of the time they experienced a call into ministry should not be underestimated regarding their ministry/family well-being. Research suggests that callings are associated with identity formation, leadership gifting, and self-legitimization.[11] It is argued that work takes on new meaning and transcendent significance when it is seen as a calling, a sacred duty, a service opportunity, or a way to serve God for a higher purpose.[12]

If pastors embrace the joy of being called and celebrate the fruitful results of their call, they will continue to dedicate themselves to fulfill the demands their call requires. Pastors who become disillusioned with their ministry and sense of calling often become indecisive and disheartened regarding their future, as this bedrock sense of purpose is challenged. Katherine Brookes, when describing the difference between a job, a career, and a calling, explains that, "Individuals with a calling orientation often describe their work as integral to their lives and their identity. . . They are found to be more satisfied in general with their work and their lives."[13] A regular reminder regarding their ministry calling leads to ministry/life fulfillment for both the minister, their spouse, and their family.

Stay Authentic

If one is not careful, involvement in ministry can easily slide from the passion that existed in the initial call into the ministry to a passive performance of ministry duties. The end result of such a slide is a lack of authenticity in the home. A female minister explained the importance of staying authentic regarding the ministry and home life:

---

11. Grey, "Divine Calling, Organizational Voice," 51.
12. Christopherson, "Calling and Career in Christian Ministry," 219.
13. Brooks, "Job, Career, Calling," 1.

I would also tell them to stay authentic, because the thing that I experienced over many years was the disconnect between my real self and my public self. That can lead to finding yourself in a place where you are no longer enjoying what you are doing, because you're not being your real self, and you're trying to perform rather than minister. You need to be who you are all the time, rather than having two different versions of who you are.

The value of an authentic example is a family experiencing and enjoying authentic relationships with each other and with their Creator.

When comparing the recommendations of those who indicated they were satisfied with their children's spiritual outlook with those who indicated they were not satisfied with their children's spiritual outlook, overall, satisfied participants recommended a greater intentional spiritual focus for the family than participants who were not satisfied. My research confirms the value of being intentional regarding the spiritual focus of the ministry couple and their family. Those who frequently focus on the values of being intentional regarding the spiritual focus of the ministry family will more likely result in a satisfied and fulfilled experience regarding the spiritual outlook of their family.

Chapter Summary

This chapter has considered the reflections of ministers and their spouses regarding the recommendations they have made to couples starting out in ministry. Recommendations that ministers and their spouses made to couples starting out in ministry consisted of Family-Focused, Protection-Focused, Ministry-Focused, and Spiritually Focused Recommendations. The heart of the ministers and their spouses was that those who were starting out in ministry could learn from the experiences of those who had gone before them, and perhaps not make the same mistakes as their predecessors. These recommendations were practical and still applicable to those starting out in ministry today. They are also recommendations current ministry couples could find comfort in and learn from. These recommendations are extremely important in maintaining healthy marriages and families in the midst of fulfilling their ministry responsibilities. I will conclude this chapter with recommendations from an older minister from my research interviews which are well worth following:

Put your family first before the ministry, and speak to a mentor on a regular basis, and try to keep your heart fresh, because when you begin you're all fired up, but if you're not careful that fire will die out and you will lose sight of what you began to do. Don't compare yourself with other churches or ministers but enjoy the ministry and enjoy each other.

Family-Focused Recommendations

Make Sure Your Family is Number One Priority

Ensure that Your Marriage Relationship is Strong

Have Good Communication within the Family

Learn How to Balance Your Ministry/Family Priorities

Give Priority Time to Your Family

Have Great Holidays Together

Understand that Your Family is Indispensable

Understand the Various Seasons of Your Family

Include Your Family on the Journey

Speak Positively about One Another

Be Present in the Moment

Keep Extended Family Relationships Healthy

Protection-Focused Recommendations

Don't Become Trapped By Expectations

Protect at Least One Day Off Per Week with Your Family

Don't Bring the Church into the Home

Allow the Children to Be Children

Ministry-Focused Recommendations

Don't Do Ministry Alone

Get Some Sort of Financial Structure Early

Count the Cost

Take Charge of Your Own Life

Be Committed to the Wider Body of Christ

Be Patient when Building a Church

Be Realistic in Your Expectations of Ministry

Hold the Ministry Lightly

Conduct a Church/Family Compatibility Assessment

Include a Session Regarding Ministry/Family Issues During Ministry Training Seminars

Get Some Experience on a Church MinistryTeam First

Don't Compare Yourself with Other Churches or Ministers

Warn Them that it is a Challenge Being a Woman in Ministry

Understand that You Can Have it All, but You Can't Have it All at Once

Spiritually Focused Recommendations

Prioritize God in Your Life and Family

Make Sure that You and Your Spouse Have Heard from God

Prioritize God's House

Keep Reminding Yourself that You Have Been Called By God

Stay Authentic

Personal Reflection

What recommendations resonated with your ministry and family experiences?

What recommendations did you discover that you had not considered before?

What recommendations are you going to activate in your ministry and family journey?

From your own experiences, what further recommendations would you make to couples starting out in ministry?

Conclusion

The Triple "A" Model of Ministry Function and Family Fulfillment

THIS BOOK IS BASED upon key theoretical constructs that have informed, guided, and provided the basis for the development of the new Triple "A" Model of Ministry Function and Family Fulfillment. It builds on family stress theory in light of the ongoing stressors ministry families experience as a result of the ministry vocation. A critical analysis of semistructured interviews with ministry couples from within the Australian Christian Churches (ACC) explored the keys that contribute toward the spiritual well-being of their family, while fulfilling the unique responsibilities associated with the ministry vocation. Throughout the analysis several key components became prominent in the interview data that I have termed: aspiration, awareness and attention.

Aspiration: The Aspirational Journey from Conversion to Ministry

In the analysis of the minister's journey, although most participants began with a somewhat idealistic aspiration in regard to ministry, their descriptions of their ministry journey laid a foundation for a realistic understanding of what the journey toward vocational ministry entails. The emphases on their conversion, their commitment to their local church, the recognition of the call of God to vocational ministry, and their dedication to preparation and training in Bible college paved the way for a realistic/unrealistic approach to the ministry vocation. Overall the participants highlighted their commitment to their local church and the sense of God's calling to ministry as the most significant stages of their journey toward their ministry vocation, which laid the foundations for their ministry.

Awareness of the Ongoing Advantages and Adversities of the Ministry/Family Journey

Advantages of the Ministry/Family Journey

A common theme that emanated from the analysis was the impact the participants' ministry vocation had upon the lives of the ministers' family members. An awareness of the benefits the family enjoy due to the ministry vocation, such as travel and holidays, the relationships they formed in the church and through ministry connections, becoming closer as a family, fulfillment as a couple, social skills, the provision of God, opportunities that came their way, leadership development for the family, and enjoying some of the benefits of being a pastor's kid (PK) helped the family appreciate the blessings of the ministry/family journey.

In regard to the satisfied and unsatisfied participants, group one—the satisfied—were more expressive overall regarding the benefits and blessings of their ministry upon their family when compared to participants from group two—the unsatisfied. Perhaps being aware of their blessings has more value and impact than is often realized in regard to the family's spiritual well-being.

Adversities of the Ministry/Family Journey

An awareness of the adversities of the ministry/family journey was also revealed throughout the analysis chapters. Ministry-related issues such as time constraints, unrealistic expectations, limited finances, competing priorities, the demands of ministry, and church conflict were emphasized. Added to these were family-related issues such as the difficulties of relocation, ministry/family balance, challenges with the children, bringing church issues home, lack of privacy, family intrusions, and the loneliness of the minister's spouse. The analysis revealed all participants encountered similar issues throughout their ministry/family journeys; no one was exempt from these realities as such. However, there seemed to be a greater awareness of these issues expressed by those who were satisfied with their children's spiritual outlook than those who were not satisfied. An awareness of these issues alerts the participants to respond and give attention to their families to help their families flourish while they are engaged in ministry.

Attention: An Attentive Focus for The Family

Throughout the semistructured interviews, as participants discussed their ideals for the ministry/family journey, how their spouses and children handled the ministry/family journey, what works for them, what they would do differently, and what recommendations they would make to those starting out in ministry, a theme regarding an attentive approach to the family became evident.

An Intentional Focus for Their Family

Participants expressed an intentional focus for their family as they discussed topics such as prioritizing the family, ensuring ministry/family balance, doing ministry together as a family, continuing communication with the family, having family meals together and doing things together as a family, making time for having fun, and having great holidays together. They also discussed the intentional value of keeping their marriage relationship strong, going on dates, keeping Saturday as a day to spend time with the family, understanding that the family is indispensable, understanding the various seasons of the family, being present when with the family, strengthening and encouraging each other, and speaking positively to each other.

Throughout the analysis chapters, those that were satisfied with their children's spiritual outlook emphasized a focus of being intentional regarding their family more than the other participants, again highlighting a key theme that can contribute toward safeguarding the spiritual well-being of their family while fulfilling the unique responsibilities associated with the ministry vocation.

A Spiritual Focus for Their Family

My research also revealed the importance of having a spiritual focus for the minister's family. When discussing their ideal picture regarding ministry/family life, the participants highlighted a clear desire for the spiritual health of their family. Throughout the discussion of the blessings ministry involvement has for the family, topics such as helping to grow the kingdom as a family, doing ministry together with the whole family, the authentic modelling of the God-life lived in the home, seeing the family developing a deeper faith, seeing the reality of God at work, the blessing of people praying for the family, positive role models in the church, and the opportunity to hear amazing speakers were highlighted.

As participants discussed the things that work for them in their ministry/family journey, again a spiritual focus for their family surfaced. Concepts such as maintaining spiritual health in the family, making church a very special thing, involvement in ministry together, modelling appropriate behaviors, and being content and satisfied with your circumstances were discussed. As participants made recommendations for those starting out in ministry, there was again a clear spiritual focus. Recommendations like prioritizing God in their life and family, making sure they have heard from God, prioritizing God's house, reminding themselves continuously that they have been called by God, and staying authentic were suggested. Ministry parents also discussed how their children handled the ministry/family journey. Throughout this discussion a concept defined as an inspiring spiritual focus was identified. Comments that they have made good personal spiritual life choices, draw on their parents' experience and values, support their being in ministry, have gone through Bible college, and have developed godly character were expressed.

The responses of the participants also demonstrated a distinct difference of emphasis, with those that indicated that they were satisfied with their children's spiritual outlook being clearly more positive in the emphases of their spiritual focus for their family than the other participants within their analytical perspectives. This spiritual focus would naturally have an overflow into the spiritual outlook of their children, which those who indicated they were satisfied with their children's spiritual outlook would have apprehended.

A Protective Focus for Their Family

Another aspect that comes under the theme of an attentive focus for the family while engaged in ministry is the protective focus of ministers and spouses for their families. Participants discussed the importance of protecting their families from the issues that can be imposed due to the ministry vocation. Issues such as unrealistic expectations, church crises, criticism from church members, the politics of church life, intrusions into the home by church members, lack of privacy, and many other issues were spoken about by participants as they discussed their ministry/family journeys.

The ideal picture of the ministry/family journey was discussed, with participants emphasizing protective ideals such as protecting the family from negative church issues, living in a sustainable model, having less burden on the pastor's wife, and having no expectations on the children. While covering things that work for them in their ministry/family lives, participants spoke about protecting their family from the negative issues of ministry while they were serving God. They did not allow other people to put expectations on the family and they protected the family from unhealthy church issues. They also kept their home as the family home, rather than an extension of the church office or church auditorium. In other words, they developed the skill of saying "no" and they protected Saturdays for time with the family. In regard to what participants would do differently if they had their time over again, another protective concept was revealed. Statements like "I would protect my family from church issues," "I would learn to say 'no' more," "I would avoid the expectation scenarios," and "I would manage people's demands better," were stressed.

As participants spoke about the recommendations they would make to a couple beginning their ministry/family journey, they gave some further insights in regard to intentionally protecting their family while fulfilling their ministry vocation. Proposed recommendations included: don't become trapped by other people's expectations; protect at least one day off per week with your family; don't bring the church into the home; allow the children to be children; and set some boundaries before you go into ministry. As spouses discussed how their spouse handled the ministry/family journey, the male participants stated their female spouses were protective of the family during church conflict. The female spouses stated their male spouses were protective of their family from church leadership issues. As ministry parents discussed how their children handled the ministry/family journey, the ministry parents declared a resolution to shield their children from ministry burdens.

Overall a resolute protective focus for the family was evident in the data, as families discussed their ideals and experiences. Those that were satisfied with the spiritual wellbeing of their family were, overall, more expressive regarding a protective focus for their family than those that weren't satisfied with their children's spiritual outlook This protective focus for the family while engaged in ministry is another attentive focus for their families that contributes toward a flourishing family as ministers and their spouses fulfill their ministry responsibilities.

Sustaining Resources for Their Family

In order for ministers and their families to flourish rather than falter, it is important that ministers and their families have available resources to draw upon that will strengthen and sustain them as they fulfill the call of God for their lives. Another attentive focus that contributes toward a flourishing family is the concept of sustaining resources that was identified as the participants discussed their ministry/family journey.

Sustaining resources such as the blessings that were bestowed upon the family as a result of serving God in ministry, and the God encounters that inspired the participants to continue to pursue the call of God as a family were discussed. The value of their Christian upbringing was also acknowledged as a sustaining resource in their lives. Added to these sustaining resources were the significant and supportive relationships that ministers and their families enjoyed. Relationships developed through their Christian upbringing, their extended family, and their movement and mentors were affirmed by participants as essential in sustaining them and their families as they continue their ministry/family journey.

The main emphases regarding these sustaining resources emanated from those that were satisfied with their children's spiritual outlook—these participants recognized the value of such resources to sustain their families as they sought to fulfill their ministerial responsibilities.

Established Support Structures for Their Family

Having appropriate support structures in place is a very important component for ministers and their families as they continue on their journey.

As participants reflected upon the support structures for their ministry/family journeys, an analysis of the data revealed over one-half of the participants from those that were not satisfied with their children's spiritual outlook revealed they had no real structured support in place for their ministry/family journey. When discussing informal support structures, the participants revealed they received support from their family members, friends, and each other. The satisfied participants indicated they received more informal support than those that were unsatisfied with their children's spiritual outlook.

Participants also indicated a small degree of ministry-related support. Sources of ministry-related support were pastoral peers; other pastors and their spouses; attending conferences for ministry support; the ministers' church eldership and board; the state executive members; regional leaders; and ministry networks.

Relationships with ministry mentors was also discussed by participants. The satisfied participants emphasized this mode of support more than those that were unsatisfied with their children's spiritual outlook. This approach to support takes more initiative and is at times less convenient for those who engage in mentor relationships.

The value of effective support structures for both ministry support and family support are imperative for ministers and their families to utilize. Such support is an invaluable ingredient of this component of an attentive focus for the family while engaged in ministry. This final ingredient of having established support structures for the family adds to the other attentive ingredients such as having an intentional focus for the family; having a spiritual focus for the family; having a protective focus for the family; and drawing upon sustaining resources for the family.

In summary, there are three major components that contribute to a flourishing family life while engaged in a fulfilling ministry life. The first component is in regard to a measured ministry aspiration—those who develop a realistic and progressive aspiration from their conversion to their credentialed ministry begin their ministry and family life on a solid foundation. The second component is awareness—those who have a sound awareness of both the advantages and the ongoing adversities of the ministry/family journey continue their ministry/family journey along a steady path. The third component is attention—those who give attention to their family while engaged in ministry via an intentional focus on their family, give a spiritual focus to their family, and implement a protective focus for their family, all while drawing on sustaining resources and establishing solid support structures, will more likely experience a flourishing family life while engaged in a fulfilling ministry vocation.

The Triple "A" Model of Ministry Function and Family Fulfillment

Ministers and their spouses who enter the ministry with a measured aspiration; have a continual awareness of the advantages and adversities associated with the ministry/family journey; and give attention to their family by responding intentionally, spiritually, and protectively, while drawing upon sustaining resources and establishing reliable support structures, will more likely experience satisfaction in regard to the spiritual well-being of their family as they function in their ministry calling. The following model for the Triple "A" Model of Ministry Function and Family Fulfillment was developed from the data:

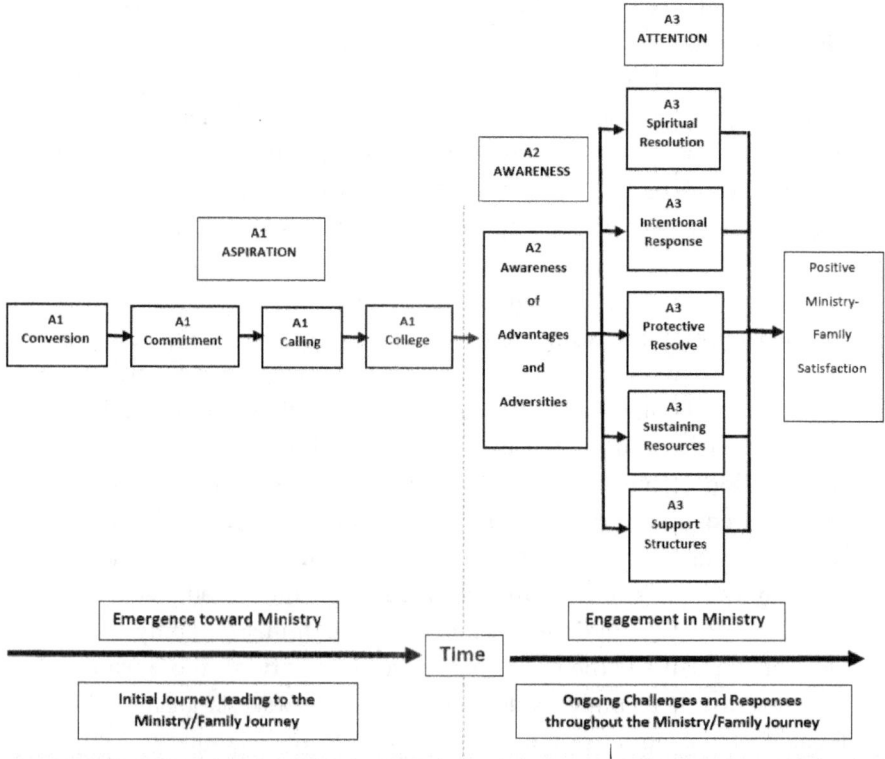

Figure 10:2 The Triple "A" Model of Ministry Function and Family Fulfillment

Recommendations

There are several stakeholders to which this research and book have relevance, such as those starting out in ministry, current ministers, families of ministers, congregations of ministers, and the leadership of Christian denominations. The recommendations for those starting out in ministry, as suggested by the participants of this research, are worth considering. Recommendations such as prioritizing God in one's personal life and family; making sure there is a clear divine calling; prioritizing God's house; and many other recommendations as mentioned in this research are valuable in order to assist those starting out to do so on secure footing.

Understandably many current ministers have already travelled their aspirational journey from conversion to credentialed ministry. Whether such a journey was affected by an idealistic distortion or advanced with a realistic aspiration, the journey is now where it is. However, the awareness and the attention components of the Triple "A" Model still have relevance for those currently functioning in a ministry vocation. Having an awareness of the advantages and adversities that are experienced by a family whose spouse/parent(s) are in ministry lays the groundwork to give the appropriate attention to family to mitigate these challenges and assist them in flourishing as a family, collectively and as individual family members. When discussing what the minister and spouse would do differently if they had their time over again, many stated they would communicate with their family better. Communication is not just a one-way conversation; it takes more than one person to have good communication. Open and honest communication between the minister and spouse, as well as between the parents and children, can create a pathway to resolve the imposed difficulties and celebrate the blessings.

Recommendations for congregational members include: encouraging their pastors and the pastors' families; respecting their pastors' time with their family; being careful not to place unrealistic expectations upon the noncredentialed family members of the pastor's family; being willing to help ease the load of the pastor; and finally, praying for the pastor and their family as they are in the frontline of ministry.

Some final recommendations are to the leadership of denominations. Establishing some formal support structures for ministers and their families would be a significant service for pastors. Another recommendation is the ministry/family journey be included in the training days to prepare ministers and their spouses for success in this vital focus.

A further recommendation is to conduct ministry/marriage retreats for couples, whether they are new to ministry or have been in ministry for some time. Furthermore a "Church/Family Compatibility Assessment" could be developed for pastors when they consider taking on a new church to pastor. This would help eliminate mismatches of pastors' families and churches. In light of this assessment, developing a manual entitled "Guidelines for Pastors and Churches When Appointing a New Pastor" would be helpful.

The three main components of the Triple "A" Model for Ministry Function and Family Fulfillment are essential ingredients to consider for those who are employed in the ministry vocation or related to a minister that is thus employed. Having a realistic aspiration, being aware of the advantages and adversities the family encounter, and giving attention to the family while engaged in ministry will assist those in ministry to conduct their ministry in a way that will help their family flourish and strengthen the spiritual well-being of each family member.

Personal Reflection

Aspirations:

What are your aspirations for the spiritual well-being of your family?

Do your ministry aspirations align with or detract from your spiritual aspirations for your family?

Awareness:

What advantages (blessings) are you aware of that your family enjoy due to your ministry role?

What challenges are you aware of that your family endure due to your ministry role?

Attention:

What attention do you need to give to help your family flourish in the midst of fulfilling your ministry calling?

Bibliography

Anderson, Carolle Brousson. "The Experience of Growing Up in a Minister's Home and the Religious Commitment of the Adult Child of a Minister." *Pastoral Psychology* 46.6 (1998) 393–411.

Anderson, Ray S., and Dennis B. Guernsey. *On Being Family: A Social Theology of the Family.* Grand Rapids: Eerdmans, 1985.

Balswick, Jack O., and Judith K. Balswick. *The Family: A Christian Perspective on the Contemporary Home.* Grand Rapids: Baker, 2007.

Barna, George. *Today's Pastors.* Ventura, CA: Regal, 1993.

Barton, Stephen, *The Family in Theological Perspective.* Edinburgh: T. & T. Clark, 1996.

———. *Life Together: Family, Sexuality and Community in the New Testament and Today.* New York: T. & T. Clark, 2001.

Bayer, A. E., et al. "Children of Clergyman: Do They Fit the Stereotype?" *Christian Century* 89 (June 1978) 708–13.

Beckett, Cynthia. "Family Theory as a Framework for Assessment." Unpublished manuscript, 2000. Microsoft Word file.

Bickerton, Grant R. *Spiritual Resources as Antecedents of Work Engagement among Australian Religious Workers.* PhD diss., University of Western Sydney, 2013.

Blaikie, Norman W. H. *The Plight of the Australian Clergy.* Brisbane: University of Queensland Press, 1979.

Boquist, Douglas W. *Pastoring First Church: A Resource to Equip Pastors in the Spiritual Formation of Their Children.* DMin diss., Ashland Theological Seminary, 2011.

Brooks, Katharine. "Job, Career, Calling: Key to Happiness and Meaning at Work." *Psychology Today* (June 2012). www.psychologytoday.com/us/blog/career-transitions/201206/job-career-calling-key-happiness-and-meaning-work.

Christopherson, Richard W. "Calling and Career in Christian Ministry." *Review of Religious Research* 35.3 (March 1994) 219–37.

Clinton, J. Robert. *The Making of a Leader.* Colorado Springs: NavPress, 1992.

Cody-Rydzewski, Susan. "Married Clergy Women: How They Maintain Traditional Marriage Even as They Claim New Authority." *Review of Religious Research* 48.3 (2007) 273–89.

Cordeiro, Wayne. *Leading on Empty.* Bloomington, MN: Bethany House, 2009.

Darling, Carol Anderson, et al. "The Paradox of Children in Clergy Families." *Journal of Family Issues* 27 (2006) 439–63.

———. "Understanding Stress and Quality of Life for Clergy and Clergy Spouses." *Stress and Health* 20.5 (2004) 261–77.

Davidson, James C. and David P. Caddell. "Religion and the Meaning of Work." *Journal for the Scientific Study of Religion* 33.2 (1994) 135–47.

Deddo, Gary W. *Karl Barth's Theology of Relations: Trinitarian, Christological, and Human: Towards an Ethic of the Family, Volume 2*. 2 vols. Eugene, OR: Wipf & Stock, 2015.

Doctrinal Basis of the Australian Christian Churches (Assemblies of God in Australia). https://www.acc.org.au/about-us/doctrinal-basis/.

Doolittle, Benjamin R. "The Impact of Behaviours among Parish–Based Clergy." *Journal of Religion and Health* 49 (2010) 88–95.

Feddes, David J. "Caring for God's Household: A Leadership Paradigm among New Testament Christians and its Relevance for Church and Mission Today." *Calvin Theological Journal* 43 (2008) 274–99.

Frame, Marsha Wiggins. "Relocation and Well-Being in United Methodist Clergy and Their Spouses: What Pastoral Counselors Need to Know." *Pastoral Psychology* 46.6 (1998) 415–30.

Frame, Marsha Wiggins, and Constance L. Shehan. "The Relationship between Work and Well-Being in Clergywomen: Implications for Career Counselling." *Journal of Employment Counselling* 42.1 (2005) 10–19.

———. "Work and Well-Being in the Two-Person Career: Relocation Stress and Coping among Clergy Husbands and Wives." *Family Relations* 43.2 (April 1994) 196–205.

George, Viji, ed. *Reweaving the Fabric: The Family in Context*. New York: The Good Shepherd Centre, 1999.

Goetz, David. "Is the Pastor's Family Safe at Home?" *Leadership* 13 (Fall 1992) 38–44.

Grabowski, Marianne Sickles. "Holy Darkness, Blessed Night: A Phenomenological Study of Spiritual Journey in the Lived Experience of Protestant Clergy." DMin diss., Lancaster Theological Seminary, 2014.

Greeff, Abraham P., and Kerry-Jan Van Der Walt. "Resilience in Families with an Autistic Child." *Education and Training in Autism and Developmental Disabilities* 45.3 (September 2010) 347–55.

Grenz, Stanley J. *The Social God and the Relational Self: A Trinitarian Theology of the Imago Dei*. Louisville: Westminster John Knox, 2001.

Grey, Jacqueline. "Torn Stockings and Enculturation: Women Pastors in the Australian Assemblies of God." *Australasian Pentecostal Studies* 5.6 (2001) 48–73.

Grey Matter Research. "Pastors and the Health of their Family and the Pressures Associated with Being the Family of a Minister." https://greymatterresearch.com/pastors/family

Grey, Terry. "Divine Calling, Organizational Voice." *Journal of Adult Theological Education* 9.1 (2012) 44–60.

Grice, Vivian. "Pastor's Kids: A Study of the Impact upon the Spiritual Belief Systems and Practice of Young Adults aged 18–35, as a Result of being the Child of Parents Involved in Pastoral Ministry with Baptist Churches in NSW/ACT." DMin diss., Australian College of Theology, 2008.

Grosch, William N., and David C. Olsen. "Clergy Burnout: An Integrative Approach." *Journal of Clinical Psychology/In Session* 56 (2000) 619–32.

Hagerman, Ronald Wayne. "Occupational Stress and Clergy Support within the United Baptist Convention." DMin diss., Acadia University, 2000.

Hendron, Jill Anne, et al. "The Unseen Cost: A Discussion of the Secondary Traumatization Experience of the Clergy." *Pastoral Psychology* 61 (2012) 221–31.

Hetzendorfer, Ruth. "Assessing the Positive Attributes of Preachers' Kids." *Enrichment Journal* (Fall 2000) 1–2.

Hileman, Linda. "The Unique Needs of Protestant Clergy Families: Implications for Marriage and Family Counselling." *Journal of Spirituality in Mental Health* 10.2 (2008) 119–44.

Hill, E. Wayne, et al. "Understanding Boundary-Related Stress in Clergy Families." *Marriage and Family Review* 35.1–2 (2003) 147–66.

Hill, Reuben. *Families Under Stress: Adjustment to the Crisis of War Separation and Reunion*. New York: Harper & Row, 1949.

Hulme, William E. *Managing Stress in Ministry*. San Francisco: Harper & Row, 1985.

Inzer, Lonnie D. and Chris B. Crawford. "A Review of Formal and Informal Mentoring: Processes, Problems and Design." *Journal of leadership Education* 4.1 (Summer 2005) 31–50.

Jones, Brian Llewelyn. "Exploring the Impact of Parental Church-Based Ministry on the Lives of Clergy Children: A Critical Reflection." PhD diss., University of Manchester, 2016.

Kerrick, Sarah Pierson. "Positive Coping Practices among Wives of Male Christian Clergy: Translating Qualitative Findings for a Lay Audience." PhD diss., Wheaton College, 2010.

Kim, Kirsteen, ed. *Reconciling Mission: The Ministry of Healing and Reconciliation in the Church Worldwide*, New Delhi: ISPCK/UCA, 2005.

Kinnison, Quenton P. *Transforming Pastoral Leadership: Reimaging Congregational Relationships for Changing Contexts*. Eugene, OR: Pickwick, 2016.

Ledermann, Thomas, et al. "Stress, Communication, and Marital Quality in Couples," *Family Relations* 59.2 (April 2010) 195–206.

Lee, Allen A. *Ministry Longevity, Family Contentment, and the Male Clergy Family: A Phenomenological Study of the Experience of Ministry*. PhD diss., Liberty University, 2017.

Lee, Cameron. "Patterns of Stress and Support among Adventist Clergy: Do Pastors and Their Spouses Differ?" *Pastoral Psychology* 55.6 (2007) 761–71.

———. "Specifying Intrusive Demands and Their Outcomes in Congregational Ministry: A Report on the Ministry Demands Inventory." *Journal for the Scientific Study of Religion* 38.4 (December 1999) 477–89.

Lee, Cameron, and Jack Balswick. *Life in a Glasshouse*. Grand Rapids: Zondervan, 1989.

Lee, Cameron, and Judith Iverson-Gilbert. "Demand, Support and Perception in Family-Related Stress among Protestant Clergy." *Family Relations* 52.3 (2003) 249–57.

London, H. B., Jr., and Neil B. Wiseman. *Pastors at Greater Risk*. Ventura, CA: Regal, 2003.

Mace, David, and Vera Mace. *What's Happening to Clergy Marriages?* Nashville: Abingdon, 1983.

McCubbin, Hamilton I., et al. *Social Stress and the Family: Advances and Developments in Family Stress Theory and Research*. New York: Haworth, 1983.

McCubbin, Marilyn A., and S. T. Tina Huang. "Family Strengths in the Care of Handicapped Children: Targets for Intervention." *Family Relations* 38.4 (October 1989) 436–43.

McMinn, Mark R., et al. "Care for Pastors: Learning from Clergy and Their Spouses." *Pastoral Psychology* 53 (2005) 563–581.
Meek, Katheryn R., et. al. "Maintaining Personal Resiliency: Lessons Learned from Evangelical Protestant Clergy." *Journal of Psychology and Theology* 31 (2003) 339–47.
Morris, Michael Lane, and Priscilla White Blanton. "The Availability and Importance of Denominational Support Services as Perceived by Clergy Husbands and Wives." *Pastoral Psychology* 44.1 (1995) 29–44.
———. "Denominational Perceptions of Stress and the Provision of Support Services for Clergy Families." *Pastoral Psychology* 42.5 (1994) 345–64.
———. "The Influence of Work-Related Stressors on Clergy Husbands and Their Wives." *National Council on Family Relations* 43.2 (1994) 189–95.
———. "Predictors of Family Functioning among Clergy and Their Spouses: Influences of Social Context and Perceptions of Work-Related Stressors." *Journal of Child and Family Studies* 7.1 (1998) 27–41.
———. "Work-Related Predictors of Physical Symptomology and Emotional Well-Being among Clergy and Their Spouses." *Review of Religious Research* 40.4 (1999) 331–48.
National Church Life Leaders Survey 1996. www.ncls.org.au/.
Nesbit, Paula D. "Marriage, Parenthood, and the Ministry: Differential Effects of Marriage and Family on Male and Female Clergy Careers." *Sociology of Religion* 56.4 (1995) 397–415.
Niebuhr, H. Richard. *The Purpose of the Church and its Ministry*. New York: Harper & Row, 1956.
O'Connor, Thomas P., et al. "The Relative Influence of Youth and Adult Experiences on Personal Spirituality and Church Involvement." *Journal for the Scientific Study of Religion* 41.4 (December 2002) 723–32.
Orthner, Dennis K., et al. "The Resilience and Strengths of Low-Income Families." *Family Relations* 53.2 (March 2004) 159–67.
Oswald, Roy. *Clergy Self-Care: Finding a Balance for Effective Ministry*. Washington, DC: The Alban Institute, 1991.
Papanek, Hanna. "Men, Women, and Work: Reflections on the Two-Person Career." *American Journal of Sociology* 78.4 (Jan. 1973) 852–72. https://doi.org/10.1086/225406
Pappas, Anthony G. *Pastoral Stress*. New York: The Alban Institute, 1995.
Patterson, Joan. "Families Experiencing Stress: The Family Adjustment and Adaptation Response Model." *Family Systems Medicine* 5.2 (1988) 202–37.
———. "Understanding Family Resilience." *Journal of Clinical Psychology* 58.3 (March 2002) 233–46.
Praskova, Anna, et al. "The Development and Initial Validation of a Career Calling Scale for Emerging Adults." *Journal of Career Assessment* 23 (2015) 91–106.
Rediger, G. Lloyd. *Clergy Killers: Guidance for Pastors and Congregations Under Attack*. Louisville: Westminster John Knox, 1997.
Rickner, R. G., and Siang-Yang Tan. "Psychopathology, Guilt, Perfectionism, and Family of Origin Functioning among Protestant Clergy." *Journal of Psychology and Theology* 22 (1994) 29–38.
Ruether, Rosemary Radford. *Christianity and the Making of the Modern Family*. Boston: Beacon, 2000.

Shehan, Constance L., et al. "Feeding the Flock and the Family: Work and Family Challenges Facing Female Clergy Women." *Sociological Focus* 32.3 (1999) 247–63.

"Slain Pastor's Wife Convicted of Voluntary Manslaughter: Attention Focused on Pressures on Ministers' Wives." *Christian Century* 4.10 (2007) 14. https://www.christiancentury.org/article/2007-05/slain-pastors-wife-convicted-voluntary-manslaughter-0.

Stamper, Scottie Jane. "Clergy Spouse Well-Being." EdD diss., University of North Carolina, 2016.

Strange, Kimberley Sparrow, and Lori A. Sheppard. "Evaluations of Clergy Children Versus Non-Clergy Children: Does a Negative Stereotype Exist?" *Pastoral Psychology* 50.1 (2001) 53–60.

Straus, Anselm, and Juliet Corbin. *Basics of Qualitative Research: Techniques and Procedures for Developing Grounded Theory*, 2nd Ed. London: SAGE, 1998.

Taylor, Mary G. and Shirley F. Hartley. "The Two-Person Career: A Classic Example." *Sociology of Work and Occupation* 2 (1975) 354–72.

Thatcher, Adrian. "Theology and Children: Towards a Theology of Childhood." *Transformation* 23.4 (2006) 194–99.

———. *Theology and Families*. Oxford: Blackwell, 2007.

Trihub, Bobby L., et. al. "Denominational Support for Clergy Mental Health." *Journal of Psychology and Theology* 38.2 (June 2010) 101–10.

Walsh, Froma. "A Family Resilience Framework: Innovative Practice Applications." *Family Relations* 51 (April 2002) 130–37.

Weaver, A. J., et. al. "Mental Health Issues among Clergy and Other Religious Professionals: A Review of Research." *The Journal of Pastoral Care and Counselling* 56 (2002) 393–403.

———. "What Do Psychologists Know about Working with the Clergy?: An Analysis of Eight APA Journals: 1991–1994." *Professional Psychology: Research and Practice* 28 (1998) 471–74.

Weber, Janice G. *Individual and Family Stress and Crisis*. Thousand Oaks, CA: Sage, 2011.

Wells, Carl R., et al., "The Relationship between Work-Related Stress and Boundary-Related Stress within the Clerical Profession." *Journal of Religion and Health* 51.1 (2012) 215–30.

Willimon, William H. *Clergy and Laity Burnout*. Nashville: Abingdon, 1989.

Wilson, Cynthia B., and Carol A. Darling. "Understanding Stress and Life Satisfaction for Children of Clergy: A Retrospective Study." *Pastoral Psychology* 66 (2017) 129–42.

Wolf, Arnold Jacob. "Toward a Theology of Family." *Journal of Religion and Health* 6.4 (1967) 280–89.

www.ingramcontent.com/pod-product-compliance
Lightning Source LLC
Chambersburg PA
CBHW062019220426
43662CB00010B/1391